THE POLITICS
OF
RACIAL INEQUALITY

THE POLITICS
OF
RACIAL INEQUALITY

*A Systematic Comparative Macro-Analysis
from the Colonial Period to 1970*

J. OWENS SMITH

Contributions in Ethnic Studies, Number 22

GREENWOOD PRESS
New York • Westport, Connecticut • London

Library of Congress Cataloging-in-Publication Data

Smith, J. Owens.
   The politics of racial inequality.

   (Contributions in ethnic studies, ISSN 0196-7088 ;
no. 22)
   Bibliography: p.
   Includes index.
   1. Immigrants—United States—Economic conditions.
2. Afro-Americans—Economic conditions.   3. United
States—Race relations.   I. Title.   H. Series.
E184.A1S66   1987   305.8'00973   87-225
ISBN 0-313-25731-0 (lib. bdg. : alk. paper)

British Library Cataloguing in Publication Data is available.

Library of Congress Catalog Card Number: 87-225
ISBN: 0-313-25731-0
ISSN: 0196-7088

First published in 1987

Greenwood Press, Inc.
88 Post Road West, Westport, Connecticut 06881

Printed in the United States of America

The paper used in this book complies with the
Permanent Paper Standard issued by the National
Information Standards Organization (Z39.48-1984).

10   9   8   7   6   5   4   3   2   1

To My Parents

Contents

Tables

Series Foreword

The Contributions in Ethnic Studies series focuses on the problems that arise when people with different cultures and goals come together and interact productively or tragically. The modes of adjustment and conflict are various, but usually one group dominates or attempts to dominate the other. Eventually some accommodation is reached: the process is likely to be long and, for the weaker group, painful. No one scholarly discipline monopolizes the research necessary to comprehend these intergroup relations. The emerging analysis, consequently, is of interest to historians, social scientists, psychologists, psychiatrists, and scholars in communication studies.

The author of this volume challenges himself and his readers with two questions concerning the waves of ethnic and racial groups that have migrated to the United States: "Why were Blacks unable to escape the slums as the European immigrants did?" and "How did the European immigrants escape the slums?" A most unpolemic reply to the questions requires, first of all, a wide-ranging analysis of the conditions in which the groups had been living in their home countries before emigrating, of their resulting frustrations and dreams there, and of the intellectual equipment and skills they did or did not carry with them. Detailed attention must next be concentrated upon the restrictions and opportunities confronting them when they arrived and tried to settle down in their adopted country. The historical context during more than two centuries is thus relevantly depicted. The author employs judiciously but not too frequently a summarizing metaphor that refers to the boots of the immigrants and the bootstraps they have or have not been offered by society and especially by government in the United States.

No simplistic explanation, therefore, is proposed to account for the plight and continuing struggle of Blacks, who are the author's main concern. He insists that we cannot fully comprehend the plight and continuing struggle of Blacks unless we also have insight into the initial qualifications and reception of the other groups. Critical, as the title of the book suggests, are the operating edicts and practices that affected and still affect the status and mobility of all newcomers. Present-day tolerance or prejudice reflect past events, the repercussions of which continue in some form and, it almost appears, may ever do so.

In order to offer this broad interdisciplinary perspective, the author criticizes commonsense views and scholarly theories that have been derived from examining a single ethnic or racial group. He avoids these errors by employing a similar approach to twelve other groups besides the Blacks: Anglo-Saxons, British West Indians, Dutch, French, Germans, Irish, Italians, Japanese, Russian Jews, Puerto Ricans, Scandinavians, and Scots-Irish. Whenever possible, quantitative data are offered in order to avoid glib intuition or theories of limited scope. These easily intelligible statistics enlighten the "macro-analytic," not micro-analytic, thesis without encumbering it.

The compelling upshot of this multivariate approach and its implied moral implications is incisively and conveniently expressed as a climax to a concluding section.

Leonard W. Doob

Preface

This is not just another book about race and ethnic relations. It summarizes the results of an eight-year study in which I sought a scientific explanation as to why Blacks have been unable to escape the slums as did the European immigrants. The term "scientific explanation" is to be understood here as a systematic interpretation of the cause of the growth and development of race and ethnic groups in America.

Ever since this question was raised by the Kerner Commission in 1968, there have been countless articles and books written on the subject. A survey of the literature reveals one common denominator: there is not a paucity of data collected on the subject but a lack of systematic interpretations of the existing data.

One of the major problems with current approaches to the study of the cause of racial inequality is that they lack a conceptual framework that is capable of explaining the cause of racial inequality with empirical accuracy. These approaches consist of writers starting their mode of analysis by constructing speculative theories and making various assumptions that allegedly explain the cause of group success, and then, turn their attention on the failure of Blacks, where they proceed to victimize them for their lack of success.

What is consistently absent from the traditional approaches to the study of the cause of racial inequality is the lack of a systematic analysis between public policies and theories of group upward mobility. For example, many writers identify groups' cultural values as the cause of their success without attempting to show a correlation between values, public policy, and the theory of socialization. It is fruitless, as it seems, to discuss groups' cultural values without examining the role that the agents of socialization played in developing and shaping these values.

Because of a lack of systematic analysis in the literature, I was trapped, like other students, in the realm of speculative research concerning the primary reason why Blacks have been unable to escape the slums as did the European groups. Because such an approach was not systematic, I was committed to a never-ending task of defending my theories and arguments.

It was not until I started searching for empirical evidence to support the theories that purport to explain why white ethnic groups were able to elevate themselves to the middle class plateau that I was able to grasp a handle of the inherent problems in studying the cause of racial inequality. To my surprise, I found that the evidence to support the most widely used arguments was often too flimsy to fit into a scientific argument and that the theories themselves were, at best, speculative.

Conspicuously absent from the literature is a systematic analysis of the role that the government played in the economic success of white ethnic groups. The historical data overwhelmingly supports the theory that white ethnic groups have been able to escape the slums because the government has consistently offered them a system of protection that safeguarded their civil rights to acquire property and to pursue a wide range of employment and economic opportunities, and it failed to do the same for Blacks. This unequal application of the laws has led to, and sustained, racial inequality.

To avoid the pitfalls of the traditional approaches to the study of racial inequality, I conducted a systematic comparative macro-analysis of the historical experience and immigration/migration of thirteen race and ethnic groups. I began my mode of analysis by examining the economic and political linkages that groups fashioned between themselves and the American polity from the colonial period to 1970. I purposely limited my analysis to 1970 because the effect of the civil rights laws is reflected in the data after this period. Briefly, these laws offered Blacks a system of protection that safeguarded their civil rights to acquire property and to pursue a wide range of economic and employment opportunities that were previously closed to them.

The Southeast Asian groups and the Hispanic—except the Puerto Ricans, Japanese, and Chinese—will be excluded because these groups immigrated in large numbers after the implementation of affirmative action policy, which constitutes a system of protection.

In the Introduction chapter, I develop a conceptual framework for group analysis. Chapter 2 consists of an analysis of those ethnic groups that immigrated during the colonial period. Chapter 3 consists of an examination of the first and second wave of immigrants who immigrated during the early and mid-part of the nineteenth century; that is, the Irish, the Germans, and the Scandinavians. This chapter focuses on the differences and similarities in those economic and political linkages that these groups fashioned with the American polity and the ones they had maintained in their homeland.

Chapter 4 addresses the experience of the late-nineteenth-century immigrants; that is, the Italians and the Jews. I advance the argument in this chapter that the human capital that these groups brought with them had a determinative impact upon their rates of adjustment.

In Chapter 5, I examine the experiences of three racial groups: the British West Indians, the Japanese, and the Puerto Ricans. Here, I demonstrate that both the acquisition of human capital and a system of protection are the best variables that can explain group success.

In Chapter 6, I examine the chief cause of the lack of economic success among Blacks. My basic units of analysis were those laws that foreclosed the freedom of Blacks to elevate themselves onto the middle-class plateau from the end of the Civil War to the 1970s.

Chapter 7 consists of an assessment of group adjustments and the economic and political linkages that groups have fashioned with the American polity in their early stages of contact.

Chapter 8 examines the role that the government played in assisting European groups to elevate themselves from up off the beaches of the culture of poverty onto the middle-class plateau.

THE POLITICS
OF
RACIAL INEQUALITY

1

Introduction

There is, perhaps, no other single current issue so widely discussed and heavily charged emotionally as the explanations given for the cause of economic inequality found among racial and ethnic groups in America (hereafter, racial inequality). This issue is nothing new. It has frequently been referred to as "the race problem" or "the Negro problem."[1] W.E.B. Du Bois dedicated his entire career to studying the cause of this problem. Gunnar Myrdal's classic study *An American Dilemma* (1944) identified the Black problem as a "problem in the heart of the American. It is there that the decisive struggle goes on."[2] He further observed that at the core of the problem "is the moral dilemma of the American—the conflict between his moral valuations on various levels of consciousness and generality." He correctly predicted that American society was moving toward two societies: one Black and one white. In 1968, the Kerner Commission on Civil Disorders documented this prediction.[3]

After the publication of the Kerner Commission report, modern students began raising the following questions: Why have Blacks not escaped the slums as did the European immigrants?[4] Why are Blacks not being incorporated into mainstream America? What is the cause of the income difference between Blacks and whites?[5] These questions have left social scientists baffled because they have been unable to isolate and identify the independent variable(s) that can best explain the cause of racial inequality with conceptual clarity and empirical accuracy. Because racial inequality has policy implications, the debate over its cause has spilled over into the 1980s.

In an attempt to analyze the cause of racial and ethnic group inequality, scientists have too often selected the plight of Blacks (dependent variable) as their basic unit of analysis. For example, Daniel P. Moynihan, who pioneered in this area of inquiry in 1965, advanced the argument that the pattern of broken families found among Blacks and the pathology of their community were the primary causes for the deterioration of the Black community.[6] Edward C. Banfield has gone so far as to suggest that such pathology may be related to their "biologically inherited intelligence." He argues that "strong correlations have been shown to exist between IQ score and socioeconomic status, and some investigators have claimed that these correlations are attributed to genetic factors."[7] Arthur Jensen went a step further in arguing the inferiority status of Blacks. His study implies that because of the genetic inferiority of Blacks, there is nothing that society could possibly do to improve their socioeconomic status because such improvement presupposes an improvement in their IQ.[8] These reports served as the backbone for the victimization arguments that preceded the Kerner Commission Report on Civil Disorders.

Before the Kerner Commission issued its report, Black scientists had become infuriated with the victimization theories, and started offering alternative explanations as to why Blacks have been unable to escape the slums. Stokely Carmichael and Charles Hamilton, for example, drew an analogy between the Black community and a colony and argued that the primary reason why the Black community was in a state of stagnation, or deterioration, was because it was controlled politically and exploited economically by outsiders. As a solution to the problem they suggested that Blacks needed to develop an ideology of self-determination.[9] These arguments and counterarguments continued to dominate the literature on racial inequality from the 1960s to the present day.

During the 1960s, many studies were conducted, and programs were proposed to solve the race problem. Based on these studies and proposals, President Lyndon B. Johnson declared a war on poverty and adopted many of these proposals as a part of his Great Society programs. The thrust of these programs was to employ the government in taking affirmative steps to incorporate Blacks, and other minority groups, into the mainstream of American society. Because of the civil rights movement and social unrest at the time, policy-makers and commentators supported many of the Great Society programs at face value; the programs were seen as a panacea for resolving the social unrest plaguing society at the time.

Of all the arguments and theories advanced at the time, the concept of self-determination attracted the most attention from policy-makers.[10] The Republicans, in particular, found the concept appealing because it was consistent with their ideology that social problems can best be solved through the private sector. They argued that many of the Great Society programs consisted of a "band-aid" approach to Black problems because they consisted of establishing programs to train Blacks for jobs that did not exist.[11]

The Republicans also viewed many of the Great Society programs as being antagonistic to the free enterprise system. To resolve this dilemma, they unsuccessfully attempted to give the self-determination concept the full blessing of the federal government by introducing the Self-Determination Act of 1968.[12] On the heels of their defeat, the Nixon administration established several programs through executive orders that were designed to promote self-sufficiency among non-white groups. These programs consisted mostly of minority small businesses, A-8 Set Aside, minority contract programs, and so on.

Before these programs could emerge from their infancy, various critics started attacking them. The critics' objectives were multifarious. First, their attacks were directed toward casting doubt on the basic premise on which these programs rested. Their purpose was to convince policy-makers that the Black problem should be taken off the public and official agenda.[13] Second, they attempted to argue that social programs contribute to racial inequality instead of eliminating it. Finally, they argued that the cause of racial inequality can be attributed to factors other than anything that white society has done to Blacks.[14]

The leading advocate against civil rights programs is economist Thomas Sowell, who suggests that racial inequality is not caused by discrimination but by such variables as age, geographical distribution, and fertility rates.[15] He summarily dismisses the role that government plays in group mobility. He argues:

What determines how rapidly a group moves ahead is not discrimination but the fit between elements of its culture and the requirements of the economy. To get ahead, you have to have some ability to work, some ability at entrepreneurship or something else that society values.[16]

Sowell's argument adds impetus to the movement to take civil rights off the public and official agenda. This movement will have broad political implications for the protection of non-white civil and human rights. Therefore, there is a dire need for scientists to offer a scientific explanation for the cause of racial inequality.

The controlling purpose of this book is twofold: first, to develop a conceptual framework within which to analyze group behavior with conceptual clarity and empirical accuracy; second, to offer a scientific explanation for the cause of racial inequality.

The thesis of this book is that in order for a group to make it to the middle-class plateau collectively it needs more than cultural values and the subscription to the Protestant work ethic. Instead, it needs both a pair of "boots" and a set of "bootstraps." A pair of boots consists of human capital. A set of bootstraps consists of a system of protection that (1) safeguards the property and liberty interest rights of groups (hereafter civil rights) to acquire property and to pursue a wide range of economic and employment opportunities, and (2) guarantees them access to the mainstream of society's income redistribution system.

Human capital, to hypothesize, is something that a group or individual can acquire by its own initiative by delaying present gratifications for future ones, as Edward C. Banfield has maintained.[17] But a set of bootstraps must be government issued. No group has made it to the middle-class plateau without the government first issuing it a set of bootstraps.

Before continuing, a set of definitions is in order.

The term *income redistribution system* consists of mercantilism (trade and commerce) and real estate. It is the mother lode of society's system of wealth (hereafter the mother lode of society's income redistribution system). To have access to this system is a fundamental right. In fact, the framers of the Constitution took special care to devise a system of laws to safeguard the individual's right to acquire property. They relied heavily, it must be noted, on the philosophy of John Locke, who maintains that the right to acquire property is inalienable. Therefore, the major function of the government is to provide a political framework by which the right to acquire property is safeguarded.[18]

Embedded within the income redistribution system are various sources of income: (1) income from labor, (2) income from property, and (3) supplementary income payments.[19] As we shall see in Chapter 8, four-fifths of all income produced in the United States goes to those who provide labor services.[20] Supplementary income payment adds an additonal 20 to 30 percent to an individual's income.[21] The size of supplementary income varies with companies. For example, union workers receive a higher percent of supplementary income than non-union workers.

The term "system of protection" will be used throughout this book as meaning a set of rules, *de facto* and *de jure*,[22] that safeguards groups' liberty and property interest rights (1) to interact in a human capital environment, (2) to pursue those economic and employment opportunities that are considered common to life, and (3) to participate in society's income redistribution system. Hereafter, the term "liberty" and "property" interest rights (see definitions below) will be used interchangeably throughout this book with the term "civil rights to employment opportunities." These rights, according to the Declaration of Independence, are inalienable, and therefore, cannot be taken away from citizens without due process of law.

The term *human capital* is to be understood here in the same sense as it was defined by economist Gary Becker. It consists of (1) on-the-job training, (2) acquiring skills, (3) education, and (4) knowledge of how the economic and political systems work.[23]

This system of protection is politically significant in three ways in relation to group mobility. First, it takes groups' civil rights to employment off the goodwill of management and places it on a principle of law. Next, it enables groups to secure economic benefits that are not available to others. Finally, it encompasses the "Madisonian" theory of democracy.

In his *Federalist* No. 47, James Madison argued that there will be a "severe deprivation" of natural rights when the accumulation of all powers (that is, the legislative, executive, and judiciary) is concentrated in the same hands, regardless of whether it is in the hands of the minority or majority. Robert Dahl, a contemporary political scientist, restructured Madison's theory in the following propositions, which are applicable to the understanding of the basic cause of racial inequality.

If unrestrained by external checks, a minority of individuals can be expected to tyrannize over a majority of individuals. . . . If unrestrained by external checks, a majority of individuals will tyrannize over a minority of individuals.[24]

It follows then that in the sphere of employment, management will tyrannize over the liberty and property interest rights of employees unless there are external checks and balances placed over its powers. There always exists an adversary relationship between the employers and employees. The employers, first of all, operate within the Lockean liberal theory, which subscribes to the principle of self-interest and self-preservation. Locke argues that the inalienable rights of the individual are preserved by his acquiring and accumulating property; and that, he is constantly working in his own self-interest to acquire more property. Therefore, it is within the self-interest of management to maximize its profits, and one means of doing so is to reduce the cost of labor. This, in turn, reduces the civil rights of workers to acquire property (because of reduced wages and fringe benefits).

If we apply both the Madisonian theory of democracy and Lockean liberal theory to explain groups' economic success, we can expect a severe deprivation of workers' civil rights to economic upward mobility. For there can be no group job upward mobility if all of the decisions concerning hiring, wage, promotion, and layoff are concentrated within the domain of managerial prerogatives. For employers will have absolute authority over the civil rights of employees to climb the economic ladder. As we shall see in later chapters, the nineteenth-century immigrants were not able to elevate themselves to the middle-class plateau until external checks and balances were installed to safeguard their civil rights to employment and economic opportunities; that is, these rights were placed on a principle of law. However, the primary reason why Blacks and Puerto Ricans have not elevated themselves to the middle-class plateau is because they never had a permanent system of checks and balances to safeguard their civil rights to pursue employment opportunities and to acquire property. Their rights have historically rested on the goodwill of their adversaries (employers) and competition (European immigrants). Such construction is inconsistent with the basic principle of American democracy, that is, we have a government of laws and not of men.

Liberty interest rights consist of those rights that qualify for protection under the Fourteenth Amendment. For example, the United States Supreme Court has defined liberty interest rights as denoting

not mere freedom from bodily restraint but also the right of the individual to contract, to engage in any of the common occupations of life, to acquire useful knowledge, to marry, to establish a home and bring up children, to worship God according to dictates of their own conscience, and generally to enjoy those privileges long recognized . . . as essential to the orderly pursuit of happiness by free men.[25]

The Court has defined *property interest rights* as "existing rules or understanding that stem from an independent source as state law . . . that secure certain benefits and support claims of entitlement to those benefits."[26] These benefits, it must be noted, cannot be denied without procedural due process.

Analyzing the system of protection that government provides to safeguard groups' access to the *income redistribution system* is the key to understanding the chief cause of racial inequality. For this system is the mother lode of America's system of wealth. America's society is built on a system of mercantilism. It follows then that any measure that government undertakes to safeguard groups' access to this system and fails to similarly undertake for other groups that are similarly situated will foster group inequality. And when this group is a racial group, it will foster racial inequality.

THE POLITICS OF INEQUALITY

The primary reason, to hypothesize, why scientists have been unable to offer an adequate scientific explanation for the cause of racial inequality has been because they have overlooked the politics of inequality. These politics can be found by critically examining the structural conditions in both groups' homeland and their places of immigration/migration (hereafter, migration will be used to refer to both terms), and the political and economic linkages that groups fashioned with the American polity in their early and initial stages of contact. Embedded in these structural conditions are several systems of protection that safeguarded groups' civil rights to employment opportunities and guaranteed them access to society's income redistribution system.

The failure of social scientists to isolate and identify the independent variables that promote racial inequality can be attributed to their narrow conceptual frameworks. For example, up to the 1970s, scientists have basically used a micro-analysis to explain racial inequality.[27] In the mid-1970s, this author conducted a systematic comparative macro-analysis of the historical experience of thirteen racial and ethnic groups in America. This analysis was part of his doctoral dissertation and an extension of Ira Katznelson's comparative analysis of Black migrant groups.[28] A comparative macro-analysis, this author found, allows scholars to examine all those variables that could possibly influence group behavior, thus avoiding the pitfalls of speculative assertions that characterize a micro-analysis. A critique of the current thought patterns will shed some light on the inherent shortcomings of a micro-analysis.

A CRITIQUE OF THE CURRENT THOUGHT PATTERNS

The following list summarizes the arguments that scientists have used to explain the cause of racial inequality: (1) time factors, (2) Protestant work ethic, (3) racism, and (4) the family structure. These arguments have been advanced through a micro-analysis. This approach has prevented scientists from fully examining many of the possible variables that could influence group behavior. Conspicuously absent from micro-analyses is a discussion of the politics of racial inequality; for example, the role that the government played in assisting European and other immigrant groups to escape the slums, but failed to do the same for racial groups.

The inherent problem with a micro-analysis is that it forces scientists to narrow their focus at the outset. To validate their research, they have too often drawn from a micro-data base[29] in which they have established axioms and made assumptions about group behavior, which may or may not be true. Such methods of research have been partially responsible for the current debate over the cause of racial inequality. A critique of each of the above arguments will lend credence to this contention.

Time Factor

It has often been argued that the time factor can account for the lack of Blacks' and Puerto Ricans' economic success. This argument has two components. First, some writers have argued that the primary reason for these groups' lack of economic success is that they have not had enough time to get adjusted to American urban life.[30] As soon as they make the adjustment, the argument goes, they will adopt the middle-class value system and achieve economic success as have other immigrants. Second, this argument holds that these groups are the newcomers and when they migrated to the cities all of the skilled jobs were taken.[31]

The social time theory has several major flaws. First, it is too narrow in scope to explain the magnitude of the problems involved in racial inequality, and the evidence to support it is flimsy. Second, this argument does not account for the technological changes that took place in America since the New Deal. For instance, from that period to the present, the American economy has been transformed from smokestack industries to modern technology.[32] Numerous skilled jobs were created that were not remnants of the previous jobs of the smokestack industries. As we shall see in Chapter 8, groups acquired skills after the government established the national apprenticeship program during the 1930s; Blacks were systematically excluded because of race.

Third, the lack of a pattern of achievement among certain white ethnic groups further weakens the time factor argument. For example, the Jewish immigrants of the late nineteenth century have achieved economic success at a much faster rate than the Irish, who preceded them by approximately two generations. Furthermore, if the social time factor were the independent variable involved in group economic success, the majority of the Irish-Catholics should be clustering at the top of the middle-class stratum of society. Except for the Anglo-Saxon Protestants and the other colonial immigrants, the Irish have been in American cities longer than any other ethnic group. Their slow upward mobility is evidence that the time factor plays a minor role in group mobility. Although the Irish started emigrating to America in the 1840s and 1850s, they only started to climb the economic ladder after the 1930s. As will be demonstrated, the primary reason why they were able to climb out of the slums was because the government provided workers with a system of protection that safeguarded their civil rights to acquire property and to pursue employment opportunities; and to enter society's income redistribution system.

Fourth, the "social time" theory overlooks economic conditions at the time of a group's migration. If the condition of the economy were an independent variable, then both Blacks and Puerto Ricans should have achieved economic success at a faster rate than some of the European immigrants. For example, Blacks migrated to the northern cities during the prosperous years of World Wars I and II. In fact, the war economy was one of the underlying causes promoting their migration north. Unlike the Irish and other poor immigrants who rambled over the country from city to city seeking employment, Blacks had jobs waiting for them when they arrived in the northern cities during the two wars. However, conditions were different during peacetime, as will be demonstrated in Chapter 6.

The Bootstrap Theory

Social scientists and commentators alike have often asked why Blacks do not pull themselves up by their own bootstraps as did the European immigrants. This question is predicated on the false assumption that all European immigrants came over poor and poverty stricken. They accepted dirty and low-paying jobs, the argument goes, worked hard, and subsequently pulled themselves up by their own "bootstraps."[33] This argument is little more than partisan exaggeration. It has too often clouded the interrelationship between boots, bootstraps, and the economic success of groups. To clarify this issue, it is necessary to analyze the functions of the bootstraps separate from the boots.

In order to obtain a clearer understanding of the above relationship, it is scientifically fruitful to formulate some hypotheses about (1) groups' status in their homelands before emigration, (2) the factors that precipitated their migration, and (3) their relative status in relation to dominant groups in their new place of settlement.

The most common factor precipitating emigration for most groups was the downward mobility they experienced in their homeland. There they were being pushed off the middle-class plateau onto the beaches of the culture of poverty.[34] To avoid falling victim to the culture of poverty, they emigrated to America. However, when they arrived, they did not settle on the middle-class plateau but, unfortunately, on the beaches of the culture of poverty in the new land. They remained there until the government issued them a set of bootstraps.

Within the above framework, a pair of "boots" can be viewed as the value of an education, job training, and other related social credentials and academic degrees. These values can be acquired on an individual basis through hard work and adhering to the spirit and letter of the Protestant work ethic. But in order for a group to pull itself up off the beaches of the culture of poverty and onto the middle-class plateau, it must not only possess a pair of boots but also a set of bootstraps. These bootstraps, it will be demonstrated, are government issued.

It follows then that a pair of boots without straps may prove useless in helping groups acquire economic security and success. The straps are what fasten boots around a runner's feet so that he can run the race with ease. Once securely fastened to his feet, the runner can concentrate on winning the race and not having to worry about losing his boots during the race. In terms of a group's economic success, bootstraps serve as a system of protection that locks groups into the economic system and provides them with a sense of job security. With such security, groups are able, according to the Weberian theory of social upward mobility, to plan for the future with calculation.[35] Groups that are not granted such security, to hypothesize, will develop the culture of poverty, which has the propensity for self-perpetuation.

Hence, it takes more than hard work and the acceptance of dirty and low-paying jobs to escape the slums. From the end of slavery to the present day, Blacks have been forced to work hard at such jobs. However, they have not been able to escape the slums because the government has historically failed to provide them with a system of protection to safeguard their civil rights to acquire property and to pursue a wide range of employment opportunities. Despite such failure, many Blacks worked hard, saved their money, and managed to acquire a pair of boots (that is, education, skills, and other related social credentials), but were unable to escape the slums because the government has consistently refused to issue them a set of bootstraps on the same scale as those issued to European immigrants. Consequently, Blacks found themselves acquiring college degrees but being forced to work at non-skilled jobs, such as in the Post Office, where the prerequisite for employment was the possession of a high school diploma. Or they acquired skills in the craft and artisan categories and found their freedom to interact in such environments foreclosed by the unions—actions sanctioned by the federal government.

The Protestant Work Ethic

Scientists have too often assumed that one of the reasons why Blacks have been unable to escape the slums as the European immigrants did was because they rejected the Protestant work ethic. The rejection of these values seems to be a central theme that scientists use to justify Black oppression. For example, Stanley Lieberson noted that some scholars "have argued that personality, orientation to work, and expectations about work all affect a group's chances. In turn, it is claimed that blacks on the aggregate have less favorable characteristics than did some of the European groups."[36]

Edward C. Banfield has argued that, in order to get ahead, it requires the "ability to discipline oneself to sacrifice present for future satisfaction."[37] Both writers' arguments do not take into account the inducements that the government provides some groups to subscribe to the Protestant work ethic in the form of a set of bootstraps; that is, free land, collective bargaining laws, fringe benefits, and subsidized home mortgages. Thus it is that the possibility of acquiring a set of government issued bootstraps encourages individuals or groups to delay present for future gratification, and not their freedom to accept or reject particular values.

Racism and Racial Prejudice

"White racism is essentially responsible for the explosive mixture which has been accumulating in our cities since the end of World War II," states the Kerner Commission Report on Civil Disorder.[38] The inherent problem with this argument in explaining Blacks' lack of economic success is that it has (1) the tendency to explain everything and nothing at the same time, (2) an extraordinary propensity to cloud government actions that operated to deprive Blacks of their civil rights to acquire property and to pursue a wide range of economic opportunities, and (3) a tendency to reduce scientists' analyses from macro to micro.

In our systematic comparative macro-analysis, the term "racism" needs a more precise definition than the one given in current literature. For example, Stokely Carmichael and Charles Hamilton constructed a schema in which the term racism could be viewed as *covert* (institutional) and *overt* (racial prejudice) actions.[39] Before Carmichael and Hamilton's study, racism was thought of as an attitudinal phenomenon. Consequently, the critics' argument against anti-racist legislation was that attitudes could not be legislated. This argument overlooks the fact that racial attitudes are short-lived unless they are sanctioned by government actions.

The current definition of racism is too loose to fit into a systematic comparative macro-analysis. It allows European ethnic groups to claim falsely that they too have been victims of past discrimination; and that they have overcome this adversity through hard work and strong family values. The corollary to this argument is that "We have made it and Blacks can do the same if they would only straighten out their sexual mores, live in a nuclear family, and internalize the Protestant work ethic."[40] Hence, this line of argument diverts social scientists' attention from government actions and focuses it on self-victimization analyses.

Within our schema, the term "racism" is broken down to make a distinction between attitudinal phenomena, which are protected by the First Amendment (freedom of expression), and public policies, which operate to deny groups their civil rights to acquire property and pursue economic opportunities.

Under the United States Constitution, a citizen has a constitutionally protected right to express his opinion on any subject. However, there are certain constraints placed on this freedom for the purpose of regulating public safety and safeguarding the individual's property interest rights to his reputation. As will be demonstrated in this book, it was not simply racial attitudes that were responsible for the lack of economic success among Blacks, but also those public policies that operated to deny them their civil rights to economic and educational opportunities.

It is scientifically unfruitful to argue that a group has become the victim of past discrimination unless government actions are selected as the basic units of analysis. The evidence to support such a contention would at best be flimsy. It follows then that in order to validate an argument of past discrimination, social scientists must identify laws, regulations, statutes, and rules of understanding, stemming from government action, which grant some groups rights to acquire property but deprived the same right from other groups that were similarly situated.[41] And such denial must not be related to any proper government objective.[42]

In the present-day affirmative-action policy, the courts use statistics to determine whether an agency is discriminating against a particular group. These statistics may prove useful to determine whether companies are in compliance with government regulations, but they are inadequate for scientists to use in an attempt to validate a public policy of past discrimination. Instead, these scientists must search for evidence of government action that (1) operated to deprive groups of their liberty and property interest rights to pursue those occupations common to life, and (2) imposed upon such groups a stigma, or other disabilities, so as to foreclose their freedom to take advantage of a wide range of job opportunities that were common to life and encompassed a system of fringe benefits.

Within this schema, we can find sufficiently strong evidence to support the claim that Blacks and Puerto Ricans have been the victims of past racial discrimination in the area of employment and educational opportunities. But evidence to support the argument that European groups have been victims of past discrimination is flimsy at best. What European immigrants have been calling past discrimination has consisted mostly of overt attacks on certain groups and an offensive propaganda campaign against them. These acts, in many cases, were short-lived and did not consist of government action. But when the term past discrimination is used in this study, it is to be understood as government action, either *de jure* or *de facto*, which operated to deprive an entire group of their liberty and property interest rights to employment and educational opportunities.

The Family Structure Argument

The pattern of female-headed households found among Blacks was identified by Daniel P. Moynihan as the chief cause of their lack of economic success in urban America.[43] At the heart of this argument were the assumptions that (1) the family is an independent variable in groups' success, and (2) the institution of slavery destroyed the structure of Black families and, consequently, affected their capacity to function in American society after emancipation. Moynihan attempted to validate his argument by comparing the economic success of the European ethnic groups and their apparently strong family structures with those of Blacks.

Andrew Billingsley and Herbert Gutman offered counterevidence to Moynihan's conclusion. Basically, they argued that the Black family was not particularly disorganized either during slavery or in the early period of Black migration.[44] Briefly, there are many arguments and counterarguments concerning the role that the family plays in economic success.[45] However, there is little advantage in recapitulating them here.

A scientific analysis of the family unit and the role it plays in group success is too complex to address in this study. It is a subject that warrants discussion by itself. Scientists have too often overlooked the essential theories and variables in their attempt to assess the role that family plays in group mobility. For example, it is fruitless to select family structure as a basic unit of analysis without viewing it within the framework of the process of socialization and evaluating the impact of discrimination in education policies and resource allocation based on race. A review of the literature will reveal that the most famous landmark decisions handed down by the United States Supreme Court have centered around discrimination in education.[46]

It follows then that the processes of socialization and discrimination in education policies are key variables in evaluating groups' cultural values, family values, orientation to work, and expectation about work. As we shall see in Chapter 8, these variables are institutionally prescribed.

In short, the micro-analyses that have been conducted to explain the cause of racial inequality are too narrow to encompass all of the essential variables that influence group behavior. A macro-analysis is needed.

A FRAMEWORK FOR ANALYZING GROUP BEHAVIOR: A MACRO-ANALYSIS

In developing a conceptual framework for analyzing group behavior, it is imperative, for the reason of conceptual clarity, that social scientists take care to ensure that their theories are not only "valid and internally consistent but sufficiently encompassing as well."[47] That is, the theories must be broad enough to examine all of the independent variables that could possibly influence the dependent variables (group behavior) that the students are trying to understand. Theories, it must be noted, could be empirically valid and internally consistent, but if they do not cover the subject area that students are trying to understand, they may be, as Amitai Etzioni has perceptively noted, "manifestly irrelevant."[48]

The Advantages of a Macro-Analysis

To avoid the pitfalls of micro-analyses, and at the same time add conceptual clarity and empirical accuracy to this area of inquiry, this study will consist of a systematic comparative macro-analysis of the behavior and interaction of thirteen racial and ethnic groups in America. We will begin our mode of analysis not with the American polity, as is the case with the micro-analyses, but with (1) the structural conditions of groups' homelands, (2) the structural time period in which groups emigrated, (3) the structural conditions in America during the time of migration, and (4) the linkages that groups fashioned between themselves and the American polity in their early stages of contact. Our basic unit of analysis will be to determine to what extent these conditions provided groups with a system of protection to interact freely in a human capital environment and to enter society's income redistribution system.

This approach will allow us to systematically "abstract from the whole social system those variables which seem to cohere more closely with others"[49] and that can better explain the politics of racial inequality. Furthermore, it will enable us to avoid falling into the intellectual habit of selecting variables that do not hold true under systematic scrutiny. In his book *Black Men, White Cities,*[50] Katznelson warned social scientists about using groups' behavior patterns as the starting point of their analyses. He argued that social scientists should begin examining the "linkages fashioned between racial groups and the American polity in their early, fluid period of interracial contact" because these linkages have a "determinative impact on subsequent patterns of racial group behaviour."[51]

CLASSIFYING UNITS OF ANALYSIS

One of the major problems with the current models of analysis is that they do not allow us to classify group behavior according to differences and similarities. Examining the structural time periods during which groups immigrated/migrated and the structural conditions both in the groups' homelands and in America will allow us to overcome this dilemma. It is worth noting, however, that the structural time period contemplated here is not synonymous with the "social time factor." The latter addresses the length of time that groups have been in America, while the former leans toward an examination of the structural conditions limiting immigration to certain social classes within these time periods. For example, the Immigration Act of 1917 restricted immigration to the professional, the educated, and the skilled immigrants. This condition has what is known as the "siphoning effect"; that is, it draws the cream of the crop of immigrants/migrants and excludes the lower- and under-classes.[52]

Social scientists too often fall into the trap of comparing biological characteristics of groups instead of comparing groups' interactions with their environment. This method prevents writers from comparing groups' behavior on a one-to-one basis. Instead, Social scientists tend to compare Blacks' behavior with that of an aggregate of all-white ethnic groups. Writers' reference to the "melting pot" concept is evidence that they assume all whites behave the same socially and economically because of race.

Our greatest data-gathering institution, the United States Bureau of the Census, has helped perpetuate this assumption by collecting data in terms of Blacks, whites, and others. First, this method of data collecting induces researchers to assume that groups' behavioral patterns are derived from their biological make-up instead of historical interaction with the economic, political, and social institutions in society. Second, lumping all white ethnic groups together obscures the fact that each racial and ethnic group in America constitutes a functioning subsystem, that is, a political or social unit, within the whole social system that is "distinct from the rest of the population."[53] It must be noted here that each group has a set of distinct behavioral patterns that they developed over periods of time through interaction with the economic, political, and social institutions in their homeland. These institutions limited and defined groups' freedom to pursue certain occupations over generations.

The concept of the race relations cycle lends further credence to the argument that racial and ethnic groups constitute subsystems within the whole social system. Stanley Lieberson has argued that racial groups attempt to establish the social order that approximates the one of their homeland in their early and initial stages of contact.[54] The groups with a superordinate social order superimpose their social order upon those racial and ethnic groups whose social order is subordinate to theirs. The latter groups do not totally abandon their social order but maintain a certain degree of autonomy within the framework of the superordinate social order.

In classifying these groups, it will be scientifically fruitful to make a distinction between the three types of subsystems that can be relatively identified as units of analysis within the whole social system; namely: formal, substantive, and normative subsystems. A formal subsystem is a membership system that functions as a distinct economic, political, or social unit within the whole social system and operates on a set of formal rules; that is, the court system, the school system, etc.

A substantive subsystem is a group of persons that can be distinguished from other groups in the whole social system by their "memories of colonization and migration." This subsystem has an internal mechanism for self-containment, which fights against the radical intrusion of foreign membership in their workplace and neighborhoods. In American society, such a subsystem is usually found clustered around certain organizations of work and has established an economic base in the workplace.

A normative subsystem is also a group of persons that can be distinguished from a substantive subsystem on the basis of its religious characteristics. Unlike the latter subsystem, a normative subsystem is held together because of its denominational belief. What distinguishes a normative subsystem from a substantive one is its economic base. For example, a normative subsystem can be used to explain the religious behavior of all denominational groups such as the Jews, the Catholics, the Protestants, etc., in America; but it cannot be used to explain the economic, political, and social behavior of these groups. A denominational group (normative subsystem) is scattered throughout the country in various geographic areas and occupational categories. It is not all-inclusive of persons who can be distinguished from other groups by their memories of colonization and migration. It does not have an economic base by which we can find patterns of economic, political, and social behavior.

The definitions of normative and substantive subsystems often overlap when describing religious groups, but differ when used to describe ethnic groups. For example, the term "Jews" is used to describe both a religious group and an ethnic group. But because of the Jews' historic experience, they are highly concentrated in certain occupational categories and geographic areas. Therefore, we can find patterns of economic and social behavior among them while the same cannot be found among Protestants. Hence, for analytic purposes, we will classify all racial and ethnic groups as subsystems based on their memories of colonization and migration.

In short, a comparative macro-analysis will allow us to systematically examine those variables that influence group behavior without being forced to make various assumptions that may not hold true under close scrutiny.

NOTES

1. W.E.B. Du Bois, *The Souls of Black Folk* (Greenwich, Conn.: Fawcett Publications, 1961), pp. 291-292.

2. Gunnar Myrdal, *An American Dilemma* (New York: Harper & Row, 1962), p. lxxi.

3. The Kerner Commission, *Report of the National Advisory Commission on Civil Disorder* (Washington, D.C.: Government Printing Office, 1969), p. 279.

4. See, for example, John J. Appel, "American Negro and Immigrant Experience: Similarities and Differences," *The Alien,* ed. Leonard Dinnerstein and Frederic Cope Jaher (New York: Appleton-Century-Crofts, 1970), pp. 339-347; Philip M. Hauser, "Educational Stratification in the United States," *Sociological Inquiry* 40 (1970): 102-129; Irving Kristol, "The Negro Today Is Like the Immigrant Yesterday," *New York Times Magazine* 11 (1966): 50-51, 124-142; Thomas Sowell, *Race and Economics* (New York: David McKay, 1975), pp. 100-102.

5. Christopher Jencks, *Inequality: A Reassessment of the Effect of Family and Schooling in America* (New York: Harper & Row, 1972), chapter 7.

6. Daniel P. Moynihan, *The Negro Family* (Washington, D.C.: The United States Department of Labor Policy Planning and Research, 1965), p. 5.

7. Edward C. Banfield, *The Unheavenly City* (Boston: Little, Brown and Company, 1968), p. 48.

8. Arthur R. Jensen, "How Can We Boost IQ and Scholastic Achievement?" *Harvard Educational Review* 39 (Winter 1969): 1-123. Jensen based his argument on a study conducted by C. Burt, "Intelligence and Social Mobility," *British Journal of Statistical Psychology* 14 (1961): 3-24. It was later discovered that Burt's research was manufactured.

9. Stokely Carmichael and Charles Hamilton, *Black Power* (New York: Vintage Books, 1967), p. 48.

10. William Tabb, *The Political Economy of the Black Ghetto* (New York: W. W. Norton, 1970), chapter 3.

11. See U.S. Congress, Senate, *Hearings on A. 3876,* 90th Congress, 2d session, July 24, 1968, p. S9284.

12. Ibid.

13. See the *Manhattan Report: Special Edition,* Manhattan Institute for Policy Research, Vol. 1, No. 8 (Winter 1982): 1-11.

14. For a discussion of how scientists are trying to shift the blame for racism to factors other than government actions, see Louis L. Knowles and Kenneth Prewitt, *Institutional Racism in America* (Englewood Cliffs, N.J.: Prentice-Hall, 1969), p. 10.

15. Thomas Sowell, *Market and Minorities* (Boston: Basic Books, 1981), p. 18.

16. "Culture—Not Discrimination—Decides Who Gets Ahead," *U.S. News & World Report* 91 (October 12, 1981): 74-75.

17. Banfield, *The Unheavenly City*, p. 47.

18. John Locke, "Of Property," Second Treatise of Government in *Two Treatises of Government*, ed. Peter Laslett (New York: Mentor, 1960), pp. 327-344.

19. See Lloyd G. Reynolds, *Labor Economics and Labor Relations* (Englewood Cliffs, N.J.: Prentice-Hall, 1970), chapter 10.

20. Ibid., p. 261.

21. Ibid., p. 632.

22. David Easton, *A Framework for Political Analysis* (Englewood Cliffs, N.J.: Prentice-Hall, 1965), p. 7.

23. See Gary S. Becker, "Investment in Human Capital: A Theoretical Analysis," *The Journal of Political Economy* 70 (October 1962), pp. 9-49.

24. Robert A. Dahl, *A Preface to Democratic Theory* (Chicago: The University of Chicago Press, 1956), p. 6.

25. In *Meyer v. Nebraska*, 262 U.S. 390, 388, the United States Supreme Court held that the freedom to engage in those occupations that are common to life are rights guaranteed by the Constitution. In *Korematsu v. United States*, the Court also held that these rights cannot be abridged without proper government objective, 320 U.S. 216 (1944).

26. In *Board of Regents of State College v. Roth*, The United States Supreme Court defined "property" interest rights, 403 U.S. 365, 374 (1971).

27. Ira Katznelson, *Black Men, White Cities* (London: Oxford University Press, 1973), chapter 1.

28. See Jesse Owens Smith, "Race and Ethnic Groups in America: A Systematic Comparative Macro-Analysis," unpublished Ph.D. diss., University of Chicago, 1976.

29. Herbert G. Gutman, "The World Two Cliometricians Made," *Journal of Negro Education* 60 (1):98.

30. Oscar Handlin, *Newcomers* (Cambridge: Harvard University Press, 1959).

31. For a discussion on this topic, see Michael Novak, "Further Thoughts on Ethnicity." *Christian Century* 10 (1973): 40-43; Bayard Rustin, "From Protest to Politics." *Negro Protest Thought in the Twentieth Century*, ed. Francis L. Broderick and August Meier (Indianapolis: Bobbs-Merrill, 1965), pp. 409-411; Sidney Wilhelm, *Who Needs the Negro?* (Cambridge, Mass.: Schenkman, 1970), p. 17.

32. John Kenneth Galbraith, *The Affluent Society* (New York: Mentor, 1969).

33. See Stanley Lieberson, *A Piece of the Pie: Black and White Immigrants Since 1880* (Berkeley: University of California Press, 1980), p. 3.

34. For a discussion of the theory of the culture of poverty, see Oscar Lewis, *La Vida* (New York: Random House, 1965), p. xliv.

35. For a discussion of the Protestant work ethnic, see Max Weber, *The Protestant Ethic and the Rise of the Spirit of Capitalism* (New York: Charles Scribner's Sons, 1958).

36. Lieberson, *A Piece of the Pie*, p. 14.

37. Banfield, *The Unheavenly City*, p. 48.

38. Kerner Commission, *Report of the National Advisory Commission*, p. 279.

39. Carmichael and Hamilton, *Black Power,* pp. 4-6.

40. Gutman, "The World Two Cliometricians Made," p. 226.

41. See the *Board of Regents of State College v. Roth,* p. 577.

42. See *Bolling v. Sharpe,* 347 U.S. 499-500 (1954).

43. Moynihan, *The Negro Family,* p. 5.

44. Andrew Billingsley, *The Black Family in America* (Englewood Cliffs, N.J.: Prentice-Hall, 1968); Herbert G. Gutman, *The Black Family in Slavery and Freedom, 1750-1925* (New York: Pantheon, 1976).

45. Lieberson, *A Piece of the Pie,* p. 8.

46. For a discussion of racism in the field of education, see *Legislative History of the Equal Employment Opportunity Act of 1972,* H.R. 1746 Senate, Subcommittee on Labor of the Senate Labor Committee on Labor and Public Welfare (H.R. 174, P.L. 92-261), Amending Title VII of the Civil Rights Act of 1964, pp. 416-420.

47. Amitai Etzioni, "Social Guidance: A Key to Macro-Sociology," *Acta Sociologica* 4, Fasc. 4 (1968): 198-99.

48. Ibid., p. 199.

49. David Easton, *Political System* (New York: Alfred A. Knopf, 1953), p. 97.

50. Katznelson, *Black Men, White Cities,* p. 18.

51. Ibid., p. 24.

52. This concept is discussed extensively in Chapter 5 of this work.

53. Lieberson, "A Societal Theory of Race and Ethnic Relations," *American Sociological Review* 26 (December 1961), p. 902.

54. Lieberson, *A Piece of the Pie,* chapter 1.

2

The Colonial Immigrants, 1600–1776: Anglo-Saxons, Dutch, French, and Scots-Irish

This chapter consists of an examination of the economic, social, and political linkages that the colonial immigrants fashioned between themselves and the American polity. The thesis of this chapter is that the vast majority of the colonial immigrants were not poor and poverty-stricken, as is widely discussed in the literature.[1] They were largely middle-class, primarily an emerging class of manufacturers who were "moderately prosperous and not the hopeless indigent."[2] Trailing this class were the uprooted yeomen, farmers, craftsmen, and merchants who were "skilled in industry, often independent in resources, and well trained in the intellectual controversies of religion and politics."[3]

The colonists emigrated to the colonies not so much to seek religious freedom—although religion was a factor—as to escape their predicament. The Industrial Revolution had transformed European societies from a feudal system to an industrial one; in the process, it uprooted farmers, artisans, craftsmen, and merchants. With a diminishing need for their service, this group found itself being pushed off the middle-class plateau onto the beaches of the culture of poverty. To avoid this, these groups emigrated to the colonies. If they had remained on the beaches for more than a generation, the culture of poverty itself would have developed among them. Once developed, it has an extraordinary propensity for self-perpetuation. To avoid this predicament, they emigrated to the colonies.

When they arrived in the colonies, they did not settle on the middle-class plateau but on the beaches of the culture of poverty. They remained there until the government (that is, their respective government) issued them a set of bootstraps in the form of free land.[4] This free land connected them to the mother lode of America's income redistribution system. Thus, these bootstraps prevented even the penniless immigrants from falling victim to the culture of poverty.

An analysis of the adjustment of the colonial immigrants would not be complete if we overlooked the role Protestantism played in shaping and forming the basic ideals and institutions of America.

THE ORIGIN OF AMERICAN BASIC
IDEALS AND INSTITUTIONS

Although the colonial immigrants came from different countries, the majority of them were imbued with the doctrines of Protestantism. These doctrines provided the foundation on which American basic ideals and institutions were built. Again, the origin of these doctrines can be traced more to the Protestant Reformation rather than to Anglo-Saxon traditions.[5] From their extreme manifestations, these doctrines prepared the hearts and minds of the Protestants for the concept of a free government based on constitutional principles such as trial by jury, separation of power, freedom of religion and press, equality of economic opportunities, and the ownership of private property.

The Protestant Reformation movement was based on the doctrine that man had an inherited right to approach God directly without the intercession of any priest, sacrament, or institution.[6] Again, this doctrine in its totality provided the basis for individualism, freedom of thought, and ideals that are important components of modern democracy. It is equally important to note that John Calvin, one of the Protestant reformers, "demonstrated in his development of the Presbyterial type of church government" that "democratic principles function effectively through representative agencies."[7] Hence, these principles helped to politicize the Puritans for the concept of freedom and self-government. This was, perhaps, the underlying impetus prompting the Puritans to seize the reins of government in England from the royalty in 1640, returning them "in 1660 under conditions which established for all times the supremacy of Parliament."[8]

The concept of a free government based on constitutional principles was nurtured by Renaissance learning, which "encouraged successive genera-tions of Englishmen to seek the restoration of primitive Christianity,"[9] thereby drawing them closer to the doctrines of Protestantism than to Anglo-Saxon institutions and ideals. These doctrines became the frame-work on which democratic institutions and ideals both in England and in America were established. They were also the magnet that drew the colonial immigrants together toward one common belief, and subsequently facili-tated their adjustment to American life.

Protestantism received its strongest support from the manufacturers, merchants, and lesser gentry class in Europe, particularly in England,

France, Germany, and the Scandinavian countries.[10] These classes of people—except the Scandinavians—constituted the majority of the religious refugees during America's colonial period.

THE CHANGING ECONOMIC CONDITIONS IN EUROPE

At the beginning of the sixteenth century, England witnessed an increase in population growth after a century and a half of decline precipitated by the conditions of the Dark Ages.[11] In an attempt to sustain the effect of this new growth, economic conditions in Europe were structured so that every person was a part of an economic unit. The peasants and artisans were bound together by the organization of the agricultural life of the village. Neither one could move without the village officer telling them which strip of land was to be cultivated and which artisans could set themselves up in trade.[12]

The economic system during this period for all practical purposes was a closed system. The farm tenants' capacity to improve their lot by learning a trade was constrained by the apprenticeship program. The Statute of Apprenticeship of 1563 prohibited those below the rank of yeoman (a class of landowners below the gentry who cultivated their own land) from withdrawing from agricultural pursuits to become apprentices in trade.[13] Even in the trade itself, only the master craftsmen made a decent living. Journeymen, apprentices, and day laborers made just enough for bare necessities.[14]

The inevitable consequence of the above constraints was restricted population growth. As early as the thirteenth century, marriage was contingent upon the male's ability to obtain land in order to support a family.[15] As the population continued to increase, and land became more and more scarce, the European countries established the primogeniture system, the custom of passing the land down undivided to the oldest son. This practice of primogeniture profoundly affected the age of marriage until the domestic woolen industry was introduced; it offered the male an alternative economic means by which he could support a family.[16]

The woolen industry was introduced into the English economy sometime during the last quarter of the sixteenth century. From this period onward, the economic conditions in Europe began to break the bonds that had kept the peasants and artisans inextricably tied to an agricultural life. The woolen industry increased the demands for the manufacture of clothing, thereby discouraging agricultural production. These developments encouraged the fencing in of open farmland for the raising of sheep. As demands for woolen material continued to increase, the landowners started a protracted process of enclosure, which had the inevitable effect of forcing numerous farm tenants off the farms.[17] The process of enclosure promoted the practice of large-scale farming in which comparatively less labor was needed.[18] This process then created, for the first time, a labor surplus in Europe.[19]

As the population began to shift from rural to urban areas, a class of merchants and manufacturers began to emerge among the craftsmen, artisans, and yeomen.[20] For a long period of time, the upper classes consisted of noblemen who earned their living by renting out their large plots of land to farm tenants. But with these economic changes, wealth was being redistributed to include manufacturers, merchants and traders, and other townspeople who were involved in foreign trade.[21] These changes began to restructure the social order of northern European countries. At the top of the social structure, there were the landowning aristocrats, who were followed by the rich merchants and yeomen, the poor farm tenants and husbandmen, the artisans and craftsmen, and the common laborers.[22] The new classes below the aristocracy were predominantly Protestants, more or less, who had bitter memories of the royalty's favoritism toward the aristocracy in renting the land under the feudal system.

The class of merchants and traders began to augment the English economy, which in turn created new and increasing demands for raw materials, which England herself could not produce. Consequently, England began seeking raw materials from abroad. Long before this class began to constitute a potent economic and political force in England, the Tudor kings of England, in the period between 1485 and 1603, began to express a desire to make England a powerful and wealthy nation through the enlargement of her trade opportunities in competition with the rest of the world. England, however, found the trade market somewhat dominated by other countries. In order to expand economically, she had to find new lands and territories from which raw materials could be obtained; consequently, she turned her attention to the New World.

As the emerging middle- and upper-class merchants and traders continued to grow, they created a need for overseas expansion. The groups who responded to the expansion were southern planters, followed by the Puritans in the New England colonies.

THE SOUTHERN COLONIES

The establishment of the southern colonies was but one ploy within England's mercantile system at the time. During the seventeenth century, England established colonies around the globe for the purpose of strengthening its empire through the mercantile system.

The English Empire was the most complete embodiment of the ideal. The factories in the Spice Islands and on the coasts of India supplied the products of the Orient, not to be obtained elsewhere. Africa provided the negroes, upon whose labor was based the production of sugar in the West Indies, which formed one of the mainstays of the Empire's commerce. St. Helena and Bermuda were strategic points on the Indian and American trade-routes. Virginia and Maryland were wholly devoted to the staple crop of tobacco, which was another of the important elements in British trade. The fisheries of New Foundland provided England with an article to exchange with the Catholic countries of southern Europe for the wine, salt, and other products imported from them.[23]

Although the mercantile system promoted the establishment of the southern colonies, the structural conditions there restricted immigration primarily to the aristocrats, a few indentured servants, and Black slaves.

The first prominent English settlement in the New World was established in Jamestown, Virginia, in 1607 by a group of planters who were an extension of the upper class of England that showed loyalty to the King and the Anglican Church.[24] They consisted of "sons of noble families, others from lesser nobility, and still others from the English middle class."[25] The chief occupation of these early settlers was farming. They settled primarily in the colonies of Virginia, the Carolinas, and later Georgia, where the soil was fertile and the long hot summers were conducive to farming.[26]

The aristocratic class attempted to establish the same economic and social order that approximated the one in their homeland: namely, large-scale farming and the plantation system.[27] The plantation system within itself placed constraints upon social mobility. The southern social system, structured in the Anglo-Saxon tradition, was based on the principle that a wealthy minority should control the government and hold this power by restricting the political activity of the majority. Larger estates were indispensable for agricultural production based on cheap labor; this labor was first supplied by white indentured servants and later by Black slaves.

The structural conditions during this period necessitated the importation of numerous white indentured servants. Most of these servants cannot be considered to be synonymous with poverty-stricken individuals. They were the displaced artisans, craftsmen, yeomen, and farmers who had been reduced to the status of wage-earners or who, for some reason, found themselves in debt. The indentured system was a way by which individuals could extricate themselves from the humiliation of poverty. They could either rot in prison for their debts or they could indenture themselves and immigrate to the colonies. Many took the latter alternatives.

The nature of the southern colonies was such that it discouraged the influx of poverty-stricken individuals and attracted skilled and industrious ones. First of all, the attempt to establish a colony in the New World was so precarious that the venture was too big for any individual or group to undertake alone. Therefore, in order to minimize the risk involved, the English adopted the concept of a joint-stock company from the Dutch. In essence, this company provided for three or more persons to invest in an adventure so that the loss, if any, would be shared. The company membership consisted of two types of people: adventurers and planters. The adventurers were the ones who invested capital but remained in England, while the planters settled in the colonies.[28]

For a period of ten years, the rate of return for these shareholders' investment was very meager. As a result, the planters had a hard time recruiting people to populate the colony despite the fact that there was a surplus of labor in England, which was precipitated by the Industrial Revolution.[29] Laborers were reluctant to emigrate to the colonies because they were uncertain about whether a far-off land could offer them better opportunities than those existing in their homeland.

The settlement of the colonial immigrants was not made possible solely by private means. Government action was also required. The Charter of 1609 was designed both to raise capital for the voyage across the sea and to give the planters incentives (bootstraps) to settle in the New World. The charter stipulated that any person above the age of ten would be provided food, clothing, shelter, and one hundred acres of land for himself and for each member of his family after serving the company for a period of seven years.[30]

The colony was not attractive to the mass of the people in England partly because it had not established a solid economic base. It was not until Thomas Dale began to administer the colony in 1712 that the cultivation of tobacco in Virginia began to offer the planters a stable economy.[31]

After an economic base had been achieved, the planters established the "headright" system, which was designed to increase the population in the colony. This system promised each man 150 acres of land and 150 more for every able male servant that he brought with him, and 100 acres more for every woman and male servant under the age of sixteen.[32]

The headright system had both political and social motives. Politically, England was afraid that Spain would extend her colonies northward along the Atlantic coast as she had done on the Pacific. In order to provide a check upon this expansion, England created the headright system as an incentive to populate the New World.[33] The population of the colonies attracted those displaced farmers, artisans, and craftsmen who were able to survive in a distant land. This demand, therefore, drew heavily from the yeomen and farm tenants who were being reduced to common laborers in England. It seems logical—after an economic base had been established—that the colony would have been appealing to those farmers who could thus make their families economically secure and spare themselves the humiliation of being reduced to common laborers in England.[34]

Socially, the headright system was designed to draw a skilled class of people to the colony. After the planters established the plantation system as their economic base, there was a need for additional labor to do the maintenance work, which required artisans and craftsmen. Much of this labor was supplied by the employment of the whole family in the early stage of settlement. And, in many cases, heavy work was done through communal work service.[35] But there was an additional need for artisans and craftsmen who were not attracted to the New World by the desire to become independent farmers.[36]

Because the artisans and craftsmen were being reduced in socioeconomic status in England, many did not have enough money to pay for their passage to the New World. Their interest was not so much in obtaining land but in pursuing their learned trades. Therefore, in order to increase this stock the planters established the indentured servant system, which provided for persons to indenture themselves for a certain length of time in return for free passage to the colony.[37] They indentured themselves to the ships' captains, who, in turn, transported them to the colony and sold their bounties to the planters for a fee commensurate with the cost of the passage. Hence, the indentured system, as will be demonstrated in the later part of this chapter, was a vehicle for social upward mobility.

The economic conditions in the southern colonies provided such a high propensity for upward mobility for artisans and craftsmen that the planters were confronted with a pattern of runaway servants. The manufacturing industry in the colony required such small initial capital that the average enterprising craftsman or artisan could save enough money in a year or so to set himself up in an independent business.[38] Again, because of the opportunities for economic advancement, the planters had to turn to Black slaves in order to obtain a more permanent source of labor.[39]

The introduction of slaves had an immediate economic and political effect upon the southern colonies. Economically, the slaves began to provide a stable source of labor, which enabled the planters to plan their economic growth through calculation.[40] This source of labor precluded the possibility of an emerging middle class. This phenomenon is in conformity with historical developments in plantation system.

After the slaves were introduced, there was still a need for white servants to provide a buffer between the planters and the slaves. White servants were used as overseers and provided a defense for the planters against the Indians.[41] The demand for this type of labor called for a different breed of person than that called for by the headright system. The persons who responded to this labor demand usually came from the rank of disbanded soldiers, defeated rebels, orphans, convicts, and poor Protestants.[42] However, during most of the eighteenth century, the data indicate that this class of people never constituted a significantly large percentage of the population in the southern colonies. Although the data for the southern colonies on slaves and servants are not accurate, the figures that are available lend credence to the argument that the structural conditions limited immigration to the skilled and the well-to-do. The figures in Table 1 given some indication of the ratio of slaves to whites.

Table 1
Population of the Southern Colonies, 1755

Colony	White	Black
Maryland[a]	107,209	42,764
Virginia[b]	173,316	120,156
North Carolina[b]	50,000	30,000
South Carolina[b]	25,000	50,000

SOURCE: Abbot Emerson Smith, Colonists in Bondage (Chapel Hill: University of North Carolina Press, 1947), p. 332.

[a]These figures are based on Maryland census for the year 1755.

[b]The figures for Virginia and the Carolinas are based on estimations made by colonial officials of that time.

In 1755, the Maryland census indicated that there were "98,357 free whites; 6,871 servants; 1,981 convicts; 3,591 mulattoes; and 42,764 Negroes."[43] Therefore, since Virginia and the Carolinas were a part of the plantation system, these figures suggest that the numbers of white servants in these colonies were somewhat similar to those in Maryland.

THE NEW ENGLAND IMMIGRANTS: THE PROTESTANTS

The New England immigrants were from a different breed of Englishmen than the southern immigrants. The former group came from a lesser noble class than the latter group. They were predominantly Protestants who were uprooted from England by the changing economic and political conditions, which occurred during the seventeenth century. Although they were not so wealthy as their southern counterparts, the structural conditions in the colonies defined the range of choice possibilities for them in a way that created an environment conducive to their early economic success.

The doctrine of Protestantism had already politicized the New Englanders for the establishment of a free government based on constitutional principles. Many European countries—except for the Netherlands, which had a tradition of religious tolerance—considered the Protestant Reformation a threat to the status quo. This view, subsequently, set in motion a series of religious persecutions and political exiles. The victims of these persecutions were left with only the New World as an outlet.[44]

The first religious refugee group to make contact with America was the Pilgrims who landed at Plymouth Rock in 1620. It can be said without much exaggeration that the Pilgrims were the first ones to establish a form of modern democracy in America. This claim is manifested in the "Mayflower Compact," which was signed in 1620 by forty-one men, who agreed to make just and equal laws and offer obedience to the same. The political significance of the Mayflower Compact is not only that it was the first form of democracy in America, but that it preceded democracy in England by some twenty years. It was not until 1640 that the Puritans seized the reins of government in England.[45]

It is with this religious group that our conceptual framework has meaning. The linkages they created in their initial stage of contact determined the subsequent behavioral patterns of the succeeding immigrants during this period. Their settling in the New World—free of English rule—served as a magnet to draw other nonconformists after them.

The concept of contact brings into consideration the broader question of superordinate and subordinate social order and the concept of race cycle, which consists of "competition, conflict, accommodation, and assimilation."[46] The theory of race cycle and contact holds that when one or more distinct ethnic group migrate to a new area, each group has a propensity to maintain a social and political order approximating the one in their native land. Whenever such a situation occurs, the migrant groups not only differ but often conflict with each other. As we shall see, the Protestants, although they were from different countries and constituted different and distinct ethnic groups, did not differ significantly in the type of political order that they preferred; that is, a government based on constitutional principles. This group had a universal institution (Protestantism), which prescribed universal behavior patterns toward democracy.

What the Pilgrims and other Protestant groups had in common was that both groups were committed to the high ideals of Protestantism. It was their devotion to these high ideals and their heroic effort to establish a colony in the New World that made an impact upon American colonial history.[47] Although the Pilgrims constituted a self-contained social unit, they did not dominate the New England colonies because they were unable to propagate themselves sufficiently, and they did not have a constituency in England from which to draw additional immigrants. Therefore, by the turn of the seventeenth century, they were assimilated into their neighboring Puritan colonies of Connecticut and Massachusetts Bay.[48]

The Puritans, the second wave of Protestants, began to settle in New England in the 1620s. They settled in Massachusetts Bay, where a fishing post had already been established in 1623 by a group of Puritan merchants. The Puritan emigration was encouraged and financed by Puritan adventurers who wanted to establish colonies in New England along the

Massachusetts Bay to promote fisheries in this region, thereby establishing commercial and trade linkages between England and the colonies.

Trade and commerce, nevertheless, offered the Puritans means by which they could become self-sufficient in their early stages of contact; therefore, they did not have to undergo the same hardships as the southern planters and the Pilgrims.

The majority who emigrated during this period came from the southeastern counties of England where the biggest industry was cloth making.[49] During the period between 1530 and 1625, the economic conditions in this area began to decline. As discussed earlier, people of all classes became disturbed by the decline in their social status, which was accompanied by the antagonism of Bishop William Laud, who attempted to make the situation very uncomfortable for nonconformists. Economically, these conditions had begun to push them off the middle-class plateau onto the beaches of the culture of poverty. The mere fear of such deprivation gave them great incentive to emigrate to the new colonies, where land could be obtained free and where they could continue to practice Protestantism without interference.

The structural conditions of the colonies forced the Puritans to become industrious and self-sufficient in their early stages of contact. First, the geographic area in New England was not conducive to large-scale farming; therefore, it was economically advantageous for the Puritan farmers to concentrate on small intensive farming rather than extensive holdings as was typical of the southern colonies. Furthermore, the New England farmers often had sideline occupations such as manufacturing, fishing, and lumbering. The typical New England farmer was not solely dependent upon farming but on his ability to produce goods for trade as well.

Second, the New England colonies, unlike their southern counterparts, did not have any great single commodity that they could trade with England. They were forced to produce many of the necessities that the southern colonies were able to buy from England through trade. Hence, these economic conditions, buttressed by the Protestant work ethic, provided the basis for the subsequent emergence of a class of merchants and manufacturers in the colonies.[50] Out of basic necessity, the Puritans created an on-the-job training process overlapping trade, commerce, artisans and craftsmen, that is, a human capital environment.

As time progressed, the Puritans started producing a surplus of domestic provisions for intercolonial trade. Massachusetts Bay became the trade center for the colonies and remained so until the construction of the Erie Canal in the nineteenth century.

With the exception of Pennsylvania, the differentiation in the economic and social structure of the Protestant colonies was not significant enough to merit an extensive elaboration here. Pennsylvania, however, differed from the other Protestant colonies in its immigration policies, and these policies had a profound effect upon the development of its economy. The New England colonies were structured to discourage the settling of non-Protestants.[51] Despite the fact that these colonies were founded on the basis of religious freedom, they entertained a degree of religious ethnocentrism, which provided the basis, perhaps, for subsequent class and race passion in America.

Unlike Pennsylvania, the New England colonies did not extend a welcoming hand to any religious group or sect that did not share the same religious values.[52] These differences in religious practices existed separate from the Protestant doctrines of self-government. The Pilgrims, Puritans, Quakers, and others seemed to prefer isolation for religious purposes, but they were united in their political beliefs.[53]

Pennsylvania was somewhat unique because it was a haven for many religious sects. In part, this situation was responsible for its large and rapid population growth. When the King of England granted William Penn the colony of Pennsylvania in 1681—in consideration of a debt that the Crown owed his father and him—Penn decided to try out his ideals of Quakerism on a broader scale to ensure that his followers would be free from religious persecution.[54] He created the first heterogeneous colony by welcoming all religious sects. His action was due, in part, to the religious ethnocentrism that was practiced by the New England colonies—which excluded Quakers, Presbyterians, and Catholics by law.[55]

Penn was a firm believer in the doctrines of Protestantism, that is, a representative government and trial by jury, which he developed to its maximal significance in his colony. Because of his liberalism and his recruitment effort all over Europe, especially in Germany and France, the Pennsylvania colony grew faster than any other colony during the colonial period. His recruitment effort

led to an influx not only of people of religion but also of persons not socially and economically adjusted in Europe; criminals and paupers. The coming of these social variants was responsible for the opposition to free admission of aliens on a social basis; that is to the exclusion of criminals and to a method of control of those who were likely to become a burden to the colonies.[56]

Thus, Penn's liberal policies on immigration can be traced to the doctrines of Quakerism, which tended to "reduce all ranks of society to a spiritual level—spiritual democracy."[57] The doctrine has been translated in today's social science literature as social equality, equal opportunity, and social upward mobility. Again, Penn's liberal policies on immigration led the rest of the Protestant colonies to construct structural barriers (Alien Laws) to keep out those they thought undesirable.

As stated earlier, Penn went to Europe to recruit inhabitants to populate his colony. In the process of recruiting, Penn accepted all classes of people who were willing to settle in the new land. Many of the people who wanted to emigrate to the New World were poor, but skilled. The redemption system was created in order to make it possible for these people to emigrate. This system differed significantly from the white servitude system in that the former system required the emigration of the whole family while the latter provided for individuals. The redemption system appealed to the Germans, who were driven from the Palatinate regions by the wars of Louis VII.[58] The Germans who came from this area were "disciplined in the habits of industry, frugality, and patience, and were particularly fitted for the laborious occupation of felling timber, clearing land, and farming."[59]

Many Germans who were fleeing from the Rhine arrived at Rothenburg to discover that they did not have enough money to emigrate to the colonies.[60] Merchants took whatever money they had, placing themselves and their goods on a ship and contracting to pay for the balance of their passage. Whenever they could not locate their friends, in the New World, the ships' captains sold them into indentured servitude. Some German families came with the expectation of paying for their passage by indenturing their children. Since there was a shortage of labor in the colonies, many of the indentured children became apprentices to craftsmen and artisans,[61] thus emigrating into a human capital environment.

The redemption system in Pennsylvania had a positive social effect; it created a condition by which many young boys could learn a trade and thereby make themselves self-sufficient. The Pennsylvania German Society's *Proceedings*[62] indicate that the majority of the Germans who were in servitude were either apprentices, craftsmen, or artisans. Therefore, because of Pennsylvania's liberal policies on immigration and the redemption system, that colony acquired a class of craftsmen and artisans trained on a higher level than the rest of the colonies. Around the middle of the eighteenth century, "Pennsylvania held a leading place in the production of textiles, and she owed this position largely to the Germans who had settled in this province."[63] Pennsylvania led the rest of the colonies in establishing mills and factories. It was not until the end of the colonial period that the New England colonies began to establish their factories.[64]

Briefly, the policies of Pennsylvania toward immigration created a social and economic magnet that drew largely skilled people into its boundaries. These immigrants might have been without money upon their disembarkation, but the redemption and the apprenticeship system proved to be a set of bootstraps that enabled these individuals to elevate themselves up off the beaches of the culture of poverty onto the middle-class plateau. As mentioned before, the manufacturing industries required so little capital that any enterprising laborer who had the technical know-how could easily set himself up as an independent merchant or artisan. Thus, human capital proved to be the independent variable that can best explain these groups' success.

The New England colonies discouraged the influx of white servitude and redemption servants partly because they did not have a need for them. By doing so, they deprived themselves of many intellectual and industrious people. It can be said without much exaggeration that it was Penn's early insistence upon social equality, freedom of the press, and equal justice that was responsible for Pennsylvania becoming the center for political agitation during the colonial period. Economically, Pennsylvania (New York also had a policy of religious tolerance) had an advantage over the rest of the colonies in developing its industry after the colonies emerged from under the yoke of the English mercantile system.[65]

The structural economic and political conditions in Europe prevented other European countries—with the exception of Spain—from gaining an economic foothold in North America. Germany and other countries suffered from a population decline due to the effect of the Thirteen Year War. Italy, however, suffered an era of economic retardation because of the decline in commerce in the Mediterranean and the deadly effect that malaria had upon its coastal plains.[66] Therefore, these structural conditions restricted emigration during the colonial period in almost all of the European countries save England and the Netherlands (see Table 2). Before the end of the seventeenth century, the Dutch and French interests in the New World were limited to the establishment of trade posts. The structural

Table 2
Percent Distribution of the White Population According to
Nationality as Indicated by Names of Heads of Families, 1790

Nationality as Indicated by Name	Percent
English	83.5
Scottish	6.9
Irish	1.6
Dutch	2.0
French	0.5
German	5.6
Hebrew[a]	–
All others	0.1

SOURCE: Quoted in Maurice Davie, World Immigration (New York: Macmillan, 1936), p. 54, quoted from the 1908 U.S. Bureau of the Census, A Century of Population Growth.

[a] Less than one-twentieth of 1 percent.

conditions in their homelands did not lend themselves to the creation of colonies in the New World. Their institutions and ideals, therefore, had little impact upon the formulation of American basic ideals and institutions. The Scots-Irish, however, constituted a large percentage of the colonial immigrants, but their ideals and institutions were shaped and formed by Protestantism in their homeland.

THE DUTCH COLONY

When the Dutch settled in New York in 1624, they were primarily interested in expanding their commerce and trade. The Dutch had taken the lead in the commercial world, perhaps because of their pioneer efforts in abolishing all restrictions on commercial activities in the sixteenth century.[67] Unlike those in the other European countries, the Dutch people were no longer tied to their villages and farms. They were free to farm and trade wherever and however their economic capacities allowed them.

The Dutch East India Company was chartered in 1602 with the powers of conquest, colonization, and government. It became a model for rival companies founded by the French and English. During the first half of the seventeenth century, the Dutch moved rapidly in forming a monopoly in commerce and trade on the shores of the Baltics, and in most of "the cities and states of Germany."[68] They also controlled commerce in Scotland, Ireland, and other British colonies—which was one of the reasons the British were powerless to stop them.

The Dutch perhaps could have established the dominant social, political, and economic institutions in America had they had the "pushing" forces typical of other countries. The Protestant Reformation, which was one of the dominant pushing forces in Europe, did not affect social conditions in the Netherlands, because the Netherlands had very liberal policies toward religion.[69] While religious persecution was a common practice for many of the northern and western European countries, the Netherlands welcomed all religious sects. Therefore, before the English conquest of the Dutch colony in 1664, the pushing force behind Dutch emigration to the New World was commerce and trade. The Dutch had little interest in the New World other than for this purpose.

After the English conquered New Netherland, New York became a haven for immigrants who were excluded from other colonies that practiced religious ethnocentrism. Thus, the Dutch colonists became Anglicized, for reasons we shall discuss later. Their population in America consisted of traders, artisans, farmers, and a few indentured servants who were, in most cases, skilled workers.[70]

THE FRENCH

France's first contact with America was initiated by her government in

1607. Her purpose was to explore the possibility of setting up trade posts.[71] The explorers pushed inland along the Great Lakes and rivers and established trading posts along the banks of both the rivers and lakes. The right to set up trading posts was granted to those merchants who were favorites of the King. Unlike the English, the French establishment of a colony in the New World was not a private enterprise venture.

The French colonial system was designed to discourage the development of agriculture and to prevent the growth of a large population. Its purpose was to strengthen its commercial system, which had been retarded by the country's frequent involvement in wars. The French did not have the manpower to establish an agricultural industry in the New World, so they adopted a policy of coexistence with the Indians.[72] They saw no serious problems in fraternizing and intermarrying with the Indians. This practice, in part, distinguished them from the English, who assumed a posture of superiority over the Native Americans.

Some consideration, however, was given to agriculture by the signeuries along the St. Lawrence River, but a shortage of manpower resulting from the wars forced France to place tight restrictions on emigration. The manpower shortage is explained in the following passage:

Far different was the situation of France. One Army after another was called up from the villages, sent off to the front, and annihilated on the fields of battle. The peasantry was bled white, and in the last campaign of Napoleon sixteen-year-old boys filled the places left vacant by their fathers. From this drain upon her manpower France did not recover.[73]

The restriction on emigration was applicable to all citizens except the French Huguenots and French Catholic religious refugees. The Huguenots were a selected "class of people, manufacturers and merchants, perhaps the most intelligent and enterprising."[74] They were driven out of France in 1685 when France ended its toleration for non-conformists (the revocation of the Edict of Nantes).[75]

The French Catholics, totalling 15,000,[76] settled in New York and Pennsylvania. The rest of the colonies were very hostile to the Catholics. Anti-Catholicism found its expression in legislative measures in 1674, when Massachusetts made it impossible for Catholics to become citizens.[77]

The French emigration to America before the American Revolutionary War never included large numbers of peasants and wage earners; it was limited to adventurers and the educated.[78] The structural conditions of France, as mentioned above, restricted emigration to the French Huguenots, who happened to be predominantly middle class, educated, and merchants. In fact, the English government was instrumental in helping the French emigrate to America. Its purpose was to aid the French in establishing Navy stores along the banks of the Great Lakes.[79]

By the end of the Revolutionary War, the French had become assimilated with the planters and professional classes. They had become "English in language and Protestant in religion, British in sentiment and policies. The fulcrum by which it [the assimilation] was accomplished was economic necessity, the lever was political preferment."[80] This assimilation was facilitated by the fact that the French felt no ties to their mother country, which was intolerant of their religious belief. The French Protestant ideals and institutions did not differ significantly from those of the English. This is precisely why the French ideals and institutions had little or no influence in shaping American institutions. French colonization ended when England passed a series of navigation acts designed to monopolize trading enterprises in North America.

THE SCOTS-IRISH

The Scots-Irish were the third largest ethnic groups to emigrate to the colonies to stay. They were called "Scots because they lived in Scotia and they are called Irish because they migrated to Ireland."[81] They were uprooted from Ireland by a combination of economic, political, and religious factors.

Economically, the Scots-Irish had become successful manufacturers and merchants. The latter class was influential in getting Parliament to pass an act in 1698 forbidding the Scots-Irish from exporting any goods to any country save England. This act was one of a series of acts passed by Parliament to achieve maximum use of its commercial system known as mercantilism, a system used by many nations in the seventeenth and eighteenth centuries, designed to make the colonies dependent on their mother countries.

The mercantilism system strangulated the Scots-Irish economy. Their ships were excluded from colonial trade and their woolen manufacturers, who had developed a prosperous industry in Ireland, could no longer export their goods freely in the commercial system.[82] The industrial center of Ireland at the time was Ulster. When Parliament applied the principle of mercantilism to Ireland, it nearly destroyed Ulster's industry.[83]

Socially, the Church of England implemented a plan to make the Scots-Irish, who were Presbyterians, conform to its religious beliefs. To remain in Ireland meant that the Scots-Irish had to undergo radical changes in their religious and political behavior patterns as well as experience economic retardation. To avoid this political, social and cultural repression, the Scots-Irish decided to emigrate to America.

The Scots-Irish began emigrating to America at the beginning of the eighteenth century. By 1718, it was estimated that over 4,200 Scots-Irish had settled in America. In their initial stage of contact with America, they occupied peculiar positions in the New World, a phenomenon due partly to their experience in Ireland and the structural conditions in America:

At the time of their arrival in America the lands along the Atlantic coast were already well occupied. Thus, due to the religious exclusiveness of Massachusetts and the well-settled character of the country, as well as due to a more or less general feeling of hostility of the English colonists towards certain types of immigrants, they chose as their destination New Hampshire, Vermont, Western Massachusetts, and Maine, and, most of all, Pennsylvania, and the foothill regions of Virginia and the Carolinas. By nature typical pioneers, they pushed into Western Pennsylvania, Ohio, Kentucky, and Tennessee.[84]

The Scots-Irish did not want to settle in Massachusetts because that meant conforming to the state's church in order to be admitted to citizenship. This was one of the main reasons they had left Ireland. The Puritans of New England preferred that they settle on the frontier to serve as a buffer between the Indians and them. New York, however, was open to them because of the long-standing policy of the Dutch, even after the English conquest, of religious tolerance.

The majority of the Scots-Irish, nevertheless, settled on the frontier, not because they were forced to do so, but primarily because they felt at home there. As frontiersmen, they had developed productive farms from the marshlands of Ireland. They were familiar with clearing forests for farm land.

In short, when the Scots-Irish emigrated to America, their hearts and minds were set on developing a free and self-governing society. Their ideals and institutions did not differ significantly from those of England. They had experienced a degree of autonomy in Ireland before England fully implemented its mercantile system. Hence, they encountered very few problems, if any, in adjusting to the American frontier.

INDENTURED SERVANTS AND THEIR BOOTSTRAPS

The culture of poverty did not develop among the indentured servants during the colonial period because the structural conditions provided them with a system of protection that safeguarded their civil rights to acquire property and to pursue employment and economic opportunities. In fact, this system plugged a cork into the hole of the barrel from which the stream of poverty flows.

The culture of poverty usually develops among the second generation of migrant groups when they are prevented from participating in the major institutions of society.[85] Many of the indentured servants, who were penniless when they made contact with the colonies, were prevented from falling victim to the culture of poverty, because the structural conditions of the colonies took their civil rights to pursue employment opportunities away from the goodwill of their masters and placed them on a principle of law. For example, the immigrants' rights were protected by a set of legal codes, which "required that masters should feed and clothe their servants and provide them with medical care, shelter, and certain 'freedom dues' prescribed in their contracts."[86]

The servant codes provided stiff penalties upon those masters who violated the servant rights. These codes gave the servant the legal right to "sue his master for breach of contract, in which case a local magistrate might free the servant, reduce the time of servitude, or order that compensation be given to him by his master at the end of his term."[87]

Once the servant completed his time of servitude, for example in the southern colonies, the law required that he be given "freedom dues" (bootstraps). These dues consisted of "fifty acres of land," which was granted "either by the master or the colony; in New England they consisted of tools, clothing, and livestock, or in lieu of these, many payments varying from" two to five pounds.[88]

Any poor or penniless family that might have been standing on the threshold of the culture of poverty upon its disembarkation was prevented from falling victim to it because of the system of protection that the colonies provided for poor people to pull themselves up by their bootstraps. For example, if a poor man, for any reason, felt it necessary to place himself and his family into servitude, he might find such an endeavor to be a blessing in disguise, for he could indenture himself and his wife into servitude through which they could pay off their debts and look forward to "freedom dues" at the completion of their service. In the meantime, if they had any children, the boys had the great opportunity to be assigned to an apprenticeship. For such "apprenticeship was more than a form of labor: it was also a method of educating the poor and of implanting good morals."[89] After a boy came of age, he was prepared to walk into a labor market, where great demands for his skills awaited him.

In short, the indentured servant, the headright, and redemption systems were systems of protection that extricated the poor from the jaws of the culture of poverty and catapulted them on to the middle-class plateau.

To summarize, this chapter examined the economic linkages that the colonial groups fashioned with the American polity. These linkages were similar to those that they had fashioned with the polity in their homelands before they were uprooted. Because of the system of protection offered these groups by the structural conditions in the colonies, or the government of their homelands, they did not fall victim to the culture of poverty. Both the uprooted peasants and the indentured servants were issued a set of bootstraps, which enabled them to elevate themselves to the middle-class plateau.

The next chapter will examine the political and economic linkages that the second wave of immigrants fashioned with the American polity.

NOTES

1. See Thomas Sowell, *Race and Economics* (New York: David McKay

Company, 1975); Stanley Lieberson, *A Piece of the Pie: Black and White Immigrants Since 1880* (Berkeley: University of California Press, 1980); and Nathan Glazer, *Affirmative Discrimination* (New York: Basic Books, 1975).

2. Abbot Emerson Smith, *Colonists in Bondage* (Chapel Hill: University of North Carolina Press, 1947), pp. 45-46.

3. John R. Commons, *Races and Immigrants in America* (New York: Macmillan, 1913), p. 25.

4. See Chapter 1 for a discussion of the "bootstraps" concept.

5. Around the end of the nineteenth century, many historians argued that American basic ideals and institutions derived in essence from Anglo-Saxon sources. Social scientists have not yet questioned the validity of this thought pattern. For example, see Edward N. Saveth, *American Historians and European Immigrants: 1865-1952* (New York: Columbia University Press, 1948), chapter 5.

6. J. Minton Batten, *Protestant Background in History* (New York and Nashville: Abingdon-Cokesbury Press, 1946), p. 83.

7. Ibid., pp. 90-91.

8. Madison Grant, *The Conquest of a Continent* (New York: Charles Scribner's Sons, 1933), p. 66.

9. Batten, *Protestant Background,* p. 97.

10. Ibid.

11. Grant, *The Conquest of a Continent,* p. 66.

12. Oscar Handlin, *The Uprooted* (Boston: Little, Brown and Company, 1951), chapter 1.

13. Ibid.

14. Jonathon D. Chambers, "Enclosures and the Rural Population: A Revision," in *The Industrial Revolution in Britain,* ed. A. M. Taylor (Boston:. D.C. Heath and Company, 1958), pp. 64-73.

15. See Phyllis Dean, *The First Industrial Revolution* (Cambridge: Harvard University Press, 1940).

16. Marcus Lee Hansen, *The Atlantic Migration 1607-1860* (Cambridge: Harvard University Press, 1940), p. 17.

17. Paul Mantoux, "The Destruction of the Peasant Village," in *The Industrial Revolution in Britain,* ed. A. M. Taylor (Boston: D. C. Heath and Company, 1958), p. 68.

18. For a discussion of enclosure see Chambers and Mantoux in *The Industrial Revolution in Britain,* pp. 64-150.

19. Clarkson, *The Pre-Industrial Economy in England 1500-1700* (New York: Schocken Books, 1972), p. 31.

20. Mantoux, *The Industrial Revolution in Britain,* p. 72.

21. See Maurice Dobb, *Studies in the Development of Capitalism* (New York: International Publishers, 1963), chapter 3.

22. Marcus W. Jernegan, *The American Colonies: 1492-1750* (New York: Longmans, Green and Company, 1956), pp. 21-22.

23. James Truslow Adams, *The March of Democracy* (New York: Charles Scribner's Sons, 1932), p. 185.

24. Charles M. Andrew, *The Colonial Period of American History* (New Haven: Yale University Press, 1938), p. 34.

25. Jernegan, *The American Colonies: 1492-1750,* p. 96.

26. Philip Bruce, *Economic History of Virginia in the Seventeenth Century,* 2

vols. (New York: Macmillan Company, 1896; reprint ed., New York: Johnson Reprint Corp., 19XX), Vol. 1, chapter 1.

27. Ibid.

28. Oliver P. Chitwood, *A History of Colonial America* (New York: Harper and Brothers, 1931), p. 63.

29. Mantoux, *The Industrial Revolution in Britain,* p. 69.

30. F. N. Thorpe, *The Federal and State Constitutions, Colonial Charter* (Wilmington, Del.: Scholarly Press, 1968), pp. 383-389.

31. L. G. Tyler, *Narratives of Early Virginia* (New York: Charles Scribner's Sons, 1907), pp. 239-44.

32. Warren B. Smith, *White Servitude in South Carolina* (Columbia: University of South Carolina Press, 1961), p. 19.

33. Bruce, *Economic History of Virginia,* chapter 1.

34. Clarkson, *The Pre-Industrial Economy in England 1500-1700,* p. 246.

35. Chitwood, *A History of Colonial America,* p. 72.

36. Abbot Emerson Smith, *Colonists in Bondage,* chapter 2.

37. Ibid., p. 27.

38. Chitwood, *A History of Colonial America,* p. 211.

39. For a discussion of slavery in Virginia, see James C. Ballagh, *A History of Slavery in Virginia* (Baltimore: The Johns Hopkins University Press, 19XX; reprint ed., New York: Johnson Reprint Corp., 1968).

40. For a discussion of labor and white servitude in Virginia, see Marcus W. Jernegan, *Laboring and Dependent Classes in Colonial America: 1607-1783* (Chicago: University of Chicago Press, 1931); Theo D. Jervey, *Genealogical Magazine* 12 (1911): 163-178.

41. Warren B. Smith, *White Servitude,* p. 141.

42. Ibid., p. 38.

43. Ibid., p. 324.

44. John T. Adams, *The Founding of New England* (New York: Atlantic Monthly, 1963), p. 74.

45. Grant, *The Conquest of a Continent,* p. 66.

46. Stanley Lieberson, "A Societal Theory of Race and Ethnic Relations," *American Sociological Review* 26 (December 1961): 902.

47. See Charles Banks, *The English Ancestry and Homes of the Pilgrim Fathers* (Baltimore: Genealogical Publishing Co., 1971).

48. See Alexandra Young, *Chronicles of the First Planters of the Colony of Massachusetts* (New York: Da Capo, 1971).

49. See tables 5 and 6 in Margaret G. Davies, *The Enforcement of English Apprenticeship* (Cambridge: Harvard University Press, 1956), p. 115.

50. See Edmund Morgan, *The Puritan Dilemma: The Story of John Winthrop* (Boston: Little, Brown and Company, 1958).

51. See V. L. Parrington, *The Colonial Mind 1620-1800* (New York: Macmillan Company, 1920), pp. 42-43.

52. For a discussion of religious intolerance see Sanford H. Cobb, *The Rise of Religious Liberty in America* (New York: Research Service, 1970).

53. Hansen, *The Atlantic Migration,* pp. 5-6.

54. Lawrence Guy Brown, *Immigration* (New York: Longmans, Green and Company, 1933), p. 44.

55. Jernegan, *The American Colonies: 1492-1750,* p. 209.

56. Ibid., p. 209.

57. Karl Frederick Geiser, *Redemptioners and Indentured Servants in the Colony and Commonwealth* (New Haven: Tuttle, Marchouse and Company, 1901), p. 27.

58. Ibid.

59. Ibid., pp. 110-11.

60. Abbot E. Smith, *Colonists in Bondage,* p. 20.

61. Warren B. Smith, *White Servitude,* p. 49.

62. The Pennsylvania German Society, *Proceedings* 44 (October 1907): 10.

63. Chitwood, *A History of Colonial America,* p. 446.

64. Ibid.

65. See Victor S. Clark, *History of Manufacturers in the United States: 1607-1860* (New York: McGraw-Hill Book Co., 1929).

66. Robert F. Foerster, *The Italian Emigration of Our Times* (New York: Russell and Russell, 1968), pp. 59-63.

67. Hansen, *The Atlantic Migration,* p. 7.

68. Andrew, *The Colonial Period,* pp. 22-23.

69. Carl Wittke, *We Who Built America* (Cleveland: Case Western University Press, 1964), p. 14.

70. Ibid.

71. Jernegan, *The American Colonies: 1492-1750,* p. 41.

72. See Thomas F. Gossett, *Race: The History of an Idea in America* (Dallas: SMU Press, 1963), p. 18.

73. Hansen, *The Atlantic Migration,* p. 24.

74. Commons, *Race and Immigrants,* p. 14.

75. Wittke, *We Who Built America,* p. 4.

76. Ibid., p. 23.

77. Brown, *Immigration,* p. 52.

78. Commons, *Race and Immigrants,* p. 25.

79. Wittke, *We Who Built America,* p. 5.

80. Arthur H. Hirsch, *The Huguenots of Colonial South Carolina* (Durham: Duke University Press, 1928), p. 90.

81. Commons, *Race and Immigrants,* p. 35.

82. Wittke, *We Who Built America,* p. 36.

83. Commons, *Race and Immigrants,* p. 35.

84. Roy L. Garis, *Immigration Restriction* (New York: Macmillan Company, 1927), pp. 6-7.

85. See Oscar Lewis, *La Vida* (New York: Random House, 1965), p. xliv.

86. Curtis P. Nettels, *Roots of American Civilization* (New York: Appleton-Century-Crofts, 1938), p. 320.

87. Ibid., p. 321.

88. Ibid.

89. Charles Andrews, *Colonial Folkways* (New Haven: Yale University Press, 1919), p. 189.

3

The Second Wave of Immigrants, 1820–1870: Irish, Germans, and Scandinavians

As the previous chapter demonstrates, the structural conditions both in Europe and the colonies restricted immigration to America largely to those groups that had acquired the necessary human capital to compete successfully in a competitive society. This was the pattern of immigration up to the American Revolutionary War. This chapter consists of an examination of the political and economic linkages that the first and second wave immigrants fashioned with the American polity after the American Revolutionary War. Our units of analysis will be to critique (1) the structural conditions that uprooted these groups in their homelands, (2) the systems of protection that granted them the freedom to interact in a human capital environment, and (3) the economic inducements (bootstraps) that the government offered them to fashion linkages with the mother lode of America's income redistribution system.

During the whole of the eighteenth century, the majority of the peasants in Europe were either tied to the land by the feudal system or restrained from emigrating by various wars. After the first quarter of the nineteenth century, a combination of peace and the aftereffects of the Industrial Revolution began to loosen the bonds that had kept the peasants tied to their villages. With this new birth of freedom, the peasants began wandering about their homelands seeking employment. Around the first quarter of the nineteenth century, the economic conditions precipitated their emigration to America in waves in the 1830s, 1840s and 1850s.[1]

The Germans and Irish began emigrating to America during the 1830s and 1850s, but the Scandinavians began their emigration after the Civil War. The Scandinavians are being compared with the Irish and Germans, who emigrated some twenty years earlier, to demonstrate that the "social time factor" plays a very minor role, if any, in the rate of group adjustment to American life.

The uprooting of the Germans and Irish during the first half of the nineteenth century was a manifestation of the eighteenth-century Industrial Revolution.[2] This revolution set in motion a chain reaction that had a ripple effect on a vast number of economic and social phenomena both in Europe and America. Economically, the revolution created, in Europe, new tools by which farmers could cultivate their farms which in turn increased agricultural productivity and economic growth. This growth created a surplus of goods for the first time since the Dark Ages.[3]

Socially, the economic growth precipitated an increase in the population, which in turn had a profound effect upon the primogeniture practice, which was common in Europe, particularly in Germany and the Scandinavian countries.[4] This practice made provision, to repeat, for the eldest son to inherit the family land. He was obligated to provide for his sisters and brothers, mother and retired father. He must by all means keep the family on the same social and economic plateau as his father had done before him, or suffer the humiliation of allowing his family to lose the social status they inherited.

Land in Germany and the Scandinavian countries was more highly valued than money. It was the sacred value that gave the peasant his social prestige in the eyes of his neighbors. If a man lived on his wife's land, he lost his dignity and was usually looked down upon by his peers.[5] Thus, it was the fear of losing their social status and the possibility of being reduced to common laborers that prompted these groups, except for the Irish-Catholics, to emigrate to America.

THE AMERICAN MAGNET

Although the precipitating forces that uprooted the Germans, Irish, and Scandinavians were different during this period, the pulling forces in America were somewhat the same; that is, promises of improvement in their social and economic status. The conditions of life in both homelands, however, caused each group to be drawn by what we shall call different magnets:[6] an urban magnet, to which the majority of the Irish responded, and the agrarian magnet, to which the majority of the Germans and Scandinavians responded.

For over two generations the structural factors both in Europe and America created a tradition where merchants, traders, craftsmen, and artisans settled in the cities and the farmers moved into the interior and settled on the frontier. This tradition had a determinative impact in prescribing the classes of people populating American cities. There was very little opportunity in the city for the unskilled laborers. Before the federal government intervened, many states had passed laws designed to exclude those immigrants who seemed to be causing social problems such as pauperism, criminality, insanity, and so on.[7]

Economic conditions in America played an important role in the character of immigrants. The construction of the Erie Canal earmarked America's first large public works project. After the canal's completion, New York became commercially important to America by opening a direct line of transportation from the Atlantic Ocean to the interior by way of the Great Lakes. New York began to grow after the completion of the canal, and thereby created a great demand for construction workers. In addition, the majority of the eastern cities had fallen behind in their construction of warehouses, docks, stores, and offices because of the effect that the War of 1812 had upon the economy.[8]

Now in a state of recovery, contractors needed masons, stonecutters, carpenters, woodworkers, and a variety of other craft types.[9] They sent agents abroad to recruit cheap labor. News of opportunities for advancement in the building of canals, turnpikes, and, later, railroads, was passed on. The recruitment of cheap labor abroad for construction of public works projects became a tradition, which lasted until the beginning of World War I. The people who usually responded to this calling were the uprooted peasants and displaced artisans who normally constituted the bulk of the surplus labor.

A critique of the conditions of life in each group's homeland will shed some light on the subsequent adjustment and economic growth in America.

THE UPROOTED GERMANS

Beginning at the close of the eighteenth century and continuing to about halfway into the nineteenth, the German traditional primogeniture system crumbled as the population increased. In each generation the land was divided to the extent that it could no longer support a family without the man engaging in day labor. "Thus, if a man with fifty morgen [acres] of land had six children, an equal division upon his death would give less than ten morgen."[10] Such a division would reduce their children to laborers, which in turn reduced their social status.

The social class system in Germany was tenaciously tied to the ownership of, and surviving on, the land. The emergence of a new middle class of merchants and traders did not occur in Germany as it had in England a century earlier. The merchants and traders were the despised, but necessary, occupations, which the Germans relegated to the Jews. The Germans' social structure and value system had the following bearing during the whole of the eighteenth century:

After the ruling prince, it was the officer who enjoyed the greatest respect, after him, or on an equal footing with him, the great landowner, after him the civil servant, then the industrialist, the artisan, the peasant, the worker. Lower than all these in social esteem stood the trading class as a whole—apart from exceptional cases and individual judgments as to its social value—and within this class again, during the whole of the eighteenth and nineteenth centuries, the merchant who dealt in money instead of real goods: the banker, the bank director, the stockbroker.[11]

As the Industrial Revolution began to spread over Europe, it called for a reorganization of Germany's rural economy; the expansion of the urban market for "foodstuffs" forced changes in the system of cultivation of land in which the application of new agricultural techniques for large-scale farming was a necessity.[12] In order to meet these new demands, peasants mortgaged their farms (after 1815) so that they could modernize them.[13] But the Germans were unable to negotiate this shift successfully because of a series of crop failures, accompanied by a diversion of credit from the agricultural industry to railroad building. This too was a product of the Industrial Revolution.

The stroke that really gave the peasants their final blow was the passage of the emancipation laws, which were intended to improve their status, but which in fact added to their economic difficulties by requiring annual cash payment in lieu of the former feudal obligation. Increasingly, mortgages were being foreclosed and numerous peasants were being pushed off their land. Fearing that they would lose their land and self-respect (being reduced to common laborers), many German peasants sold their land at any price and took their families to America.

However, many peasants and day laborers first drifted about the countryside seeking employment. Unlike those in other European countries, German factories had not developed to the stage where they could absorb the increasing surplus labor. As a result, thousands of peasants, artisans, and craftsmen were pushed out of the labor market and on to the beaches of the culture of poverty.[14] The only feasible alternative left open to them—that is, to save their dignity and self-respect and, again, to avoid falling victim to the culture of poverty—was to emigrate to America.

THE EARLY GERMAN PEASANTS

An analysis of the German peasants of the 1830s, 1840s, and 1850s would be incomplete if we restricted our mode of analysis solely to this period. The status of the Germans who emigrated during the period between 1780 and 1829 has to be considered. This group had established political and economic linkages with the American polity that had a profound effect upon the subsequent behavior patterns of the German emigrants.

The Germans who emigrated during the period between 1780 and 1829 settled on the frontier. The frontier could be divided into two components; North Central and South Central. The 1900 U.S. Census indicates that over 1,461,603 Germans settled in the North Central area, which covers states such as Ohio, Indiana, Illinois, Michigan, Wisconsin, Minnesota, Iowa, Missouri, North and South Dakota, Nebraska, and Kansas.[15] In the South Central area, they settled in states such as Virginia, the Carolinas, Kentucky, Tennessee, Mississippi, Louisiana, and Texas.[16]

The literature indicates that the Germans began settling in these areas when it was considered to be frontier land. They were lured to these areas by economic inducements offered to them by the government; that is, free land. Before the big migration of the 1830s, the early settlers sent news back to relatives in Germany informing them of how they could obtain society's most sacred value, that is, a home and a farm, "without money and without price."[17] A detailed analysis of the German emigrants before the 1830s is not the object of this study. Their settlement is only germane to the extent that it provides a panoramic view of the possible economic and political linkages the emigrants of the 1830s fashioned with the American polity in the initial stage of contact. These Germans served as forerunners for the newcomers. They provided them with assistance and information concerning frontier life and taught them how they could use the American political and economic systems to help them obtain a better life.

In addition to seeking a better life, the early German settlers were also interested in establishing a German state in America. They established a recruitment committee to encourage more farmers in Germany to emigrate to America. Many cities in the Midwest were named after cities in Germany, such as Berlin in Wisconsin, as a means to encourage farmers to emigrate to this area.[18]

One of the political significances of the earlier settlers' recruitment efforts was that they had already established economic and political linkages by which the emigrants of the 1830s could move from the seashores of the East Coast directly to the frontier with ease.

GERMAN PEASANTS OF THE 1830s, 1840s, AND 1850s

The Germans who emigrated to America before 1848 were from a different class than those mentioned above. They were political refugees and intellectuals who resisted the "reform ideas of the French Revolution."[19] Their resistance prompted the Baden government to enforce "strict censorship of the press, of public meetings and on the schools and universities."[20] Their resistance was unorganized, but it posed a threat to the political stability of the country. Consequently, government authorities became increasingly alarmed.

It was too expensive to incarcerate the thousands of political prisoners, but the authorities could ill afford to let them remain free to continue their political agitation. As a way out of this political dilemma, the government offered to pay free passage to America for the rank and file of this group. Hence, the political unrest during this period created what we referred to in

Chapter 1 as the "siphoning effect," that is, conditions where only the intellectuals, middle and upper classes (the cream of the crop) emigrated.

The majority of the uprooted German peasants of the 1830s and 1840s settled in the North Central states and Midwest states, such as Wisconsin, Minnesota, Illinois, Ohio, Indiana, and Iowa.[21] Some settled in the South Central states, as stated above. They settled at a time when this country's most sacred value was the ownership of a family farm. In fact, the family farm was considered "the backbone of democracy."[22] This is evidenced by the number of land-grant laws passed by Congress over the years.

The Land Act of 1820 offered inducements to farmers by reducing the price of land from $2 to $1.25 per acre. Furthermore, it allowed the average farmer to secure 80 virgin acres of land on credit. This land give-away, coupled with the notion that the "accumulation of wealth was everywhere recognized as a badge of success and symbol of power,"[23] provided the emigrants between 1830 and 1850 a set of bootstraps on a silver platter by the govenment.

The average family that had lost its farm in Germany could emigrate to the western frontier penniless and purchase a parcel of virgin land on credit; after a few "years of honest toil," he could meet all of his financial obligations.[24]

The Germans' adjustment on the frontier was similar, in many respects, to the Scots-Irish, who had emigrated some 100 years earlier (see Chapter 2). The climate and soil closely resembled what they "had left at home. The products of the soil were the same as they had raised in Germany for generations—wheat, rye, oats, and garden vegetables."[25] This was true whether the emigrants settled in Wisconsin, Minnesota, or Texas.

Shortly after the Germans settled on the frontier, they automatically constituted a potentially powerful political bloc. This bloc became increasingly significant to the emerging "New Democracy." This was an era in which the "common man" politics came into vogue. The influx of immigrants added to the already emerging significance of the "New Democracy." The German immigrants who settled on the southwest frontier in the period between 1800 and 1825 helped provide Andrew Jackson with the political leverage to wrest the gauntlet of power away from the elite-Eastern establishment in the election of 1829.

The newcomers did not hesitate to use the instrumentalities of government to protect their civil rights to acquire and to pursue economic employment opportunities. They walked off the boat right onto a political battlefield, where the contest being fought was over the preservation of the common man's liberty and property interest rights to the pursuit of happiness. This was the period when the common man was imprisoned for his debts and "mothers were torn from their infants for owing a few dollars."[26] As we shall see below, through political participation, these emigrants were able to secure various forms of release.

In short, the Germans emigrated from one agrarian background to another without having to make radical changes in occupational pursuits. The concept of being an independent farmer, or the ownership of property, was valued both in America and Germany. It was precisely the fear of losing their land and subsequently their social status that pushed Germans to leave Germany. Their ability to settle on a large piece of land in America served to enhance their social status instead of demeaning it.

THE SETTLEMENT OF THE INTELLECTUALS, ARTISANS, AND CRAFTSMEN

The majority of the artisans, craftsmen, and intellectuals did not follow the peasants out west to the prairie, but settled in the cities.[27] The German intellectuals sought to improve the social status of the German paupers through organized labor.[28] It is worth noting that the German political refugees came from a different region than did the artisans, craftsmen, and peasants. The former group came from the Baden area while the latter group came from regions where political agitation had been less pronounced and "where business was poor and the future of trade and agriculture was unpromising."[29]

The skilled workers and the intellectuals settled on the Atlantic Coast, where their skills were in great demand. As soon as they made contact with American polity, they began forming unions in their respective trades, in an attempt to wrest their property rights to employment away from the goodwill of management and place it on a set of principles (i.e., a *de facto* system of protection). Assisting them in this area were the intellectuals who had been driven out of the Baden region for their political agitation.[30]

The economic conditions in America for artisans and craftsmen were lucrative during the period between 1790 and the 1830s and 1840s. Therefore, the primary concern of tradesmen was to establish a system of protection to safeguard their civil rights to pursue employment opportunities within their trade. They were trying to protect their wage rates (property rights) and the right to form a monopoly over the apprenticeship programs in order to "prevent employers from replacing journeymen with learners, runaway apprentices, and women at wages below union scale."[31]

In New York, for example, employers were arbitrarily and capriciously trying to diminish the property rights of craftsmen and artisans through the process of competitive wage cutting, that is, "the workers in a local union in one city often found wages limited by wages received by similar workers in other cities."[32] To prevent this practice, the craftsmen began combining into national craft unions. The first national, The National Trades Union, was formed in New York in 1834.[33]

There were no bargainings that the German unions could engage in collectively, but their power both to control the number of persons entering the trade and to strike were sufficient to take their property rights to employment from the goodwill of employers and to place them on a set of principles. This system served as a "safety net" to prevent the artisans and craftsmen from falling victim to the culture of poverty. The system guaranteed them the freedom to select their sons and relatives for the apprenticeship programs, thereby ensuring them the opportunity to learn a trade while remaining on the middle-class plateau on which they were born.

Obtaining better working conditions was not the only benefit the unions offered workers during this period. The 1820s through the 1840s marked the Jacksonian period and the emergence of "common man" political parties, which had as their primary aim improving the lot of the working man. Through political participation, the workingmen were able to translate their personal preferences into public policies. For example, their most notable success during this period was in "bringing free public education, banking reform, mechanics' lien laws, the elimination of imprisonment for debts, and the political franchise for those who did not own property."[34] The election of Andrew Jackson provided them with a means of release. Through various laws and policies, the German farmers were able to take their civil rights to pursue economic opportunities from the goodwill of their adversaries and place them on a principle of law.[35]

THE UPROOTED IRISH

The conditions uprooting the Irish-Catholics of the nineteenth century were similar to the structural conditions that uprooted the Scots-Irish during the first quarter of the eighteenth century—the restrictive English commercial policies.[36] These policies had long-term political, social, and economic repercussions upon the social status of the Irish.

Politically, as mentioned in Chapter 2, the English Parliament passed a law in 1698 that destroyed the manufacturing industry the Scots-Irish had developed. The Scots-Irish emigrated from Ireland between 1714 and 1720. From this period to the 1830s, Ireland had a predominantly agricultural economy. Underlying this agrarian economy were factors constraining the development of middle-class behavior patterns among the Irish-Catholics.

After the Cromwellian invasion of Ireland in 1650, England passed anti-Catholic penal laws, which in effect made the Irish poorer and kept them socially prostrated.[37] There were changes in land laws that destroyed the Irish security of land tenure and created a landlord class of foreign Protestants. The Irish could no longer own land and were forced to become farm tenants, renting their land. The inevitable consequences of such practices created a spiral rent system in which the land was rented to the highest bidder. The conditions progressed to the point where farming was no longer profitable. Each year the number of farms decreased at a relatively high rate.[38]

Below the status of farm tenants were the cottiers who, by the end of the seventeenth century, constituted the largest percentage of the population, embracing perhaps four-fifths of all Irish families.

The process by which the land was rented in Ireland discouraged the farm tenant from improving his rented land. There was no system of protection that safeguarded his property interest rights to rent the land the following year. Any improvement farm tenants made to increase the productivity of their farm usually benefited the landlord; no farm tenant had preference to the expired lease; it went to the highest bidder.[39] This practice deprived tenants of their inalienable rights to improve their lot in society. The self-interest of the landlords contradicted property interest rights of the tenants to improve their lot. The former simply maximized their profits dividing their land into small plots to increase the number of plots to rent to tenants. By 1841, the landlords had divided the land into so many tiny plots that it reduced the majority of the population of Ireland to mere subsistence.

When the Industrial Revolution swept Europe, the landlords began to consider ways to adjust Ireland's agricultural system to maximize their profits. The landlords' efforts were somewhat complicated by the fact that a large number of farm tenants had numerous tiny plots of land. The landlords could not turn their land into pasture unless they pushed the farm tenants off their land. When the Corn Law, which protected Ireland's grain in the English market, was repealed in 1846, it destroyed Ireland's grain market and gave the landlords a free hand in modernizing their land by turning numerous tiny plots into pastures.[40] This process sent hundreds of cottiers wandering across the Irish Sea to seek employment in England and Scotland. This migration was stimulated by demands for cheap labor in these countries, especially in England, where there was a great labor demand for the construction of the spreading chain of railroads.[41]

From 1820 to 1841, the Irish had developed a pattern of migrating from Ireland to England in the summer, seeking employment as common laborers, and returning home for harvesting in the fall. When the potato famine struck Ireland between 1845 and 1848, this pattern had developed into a tradition. This phenomenon is significant here because it will support, as we shall see, our hypothesis that ethnic groups do not deviate significantly from the linkages that they create with a country's polity in their initial stage of contact.

During the potato famine, thousands of Irishmen wandered from town to town, begging; many died of starvation.[42] Aid was sent to the starving Irish by both Englishmen and Americans; however, this aid was not enough to relieve the grave situation—which worsened when the British ceased sending aid because of their policy of *laissez-faire* economics;[43] that is, government was to keep its hands off private enterprise because such interference, they concluded, would destroy any local incentive to solve their own problems. The only aid, thereafter, that the Irish received from England was from the landlords. They subsidized masses of hopeless peasants to board emigrant ships in order (1) to speed up the removal of the peasants from their land and (2) to expedite the process of turning farmland into pastures. While the Irish were being pushed off their land, they were simultaneously excluded from the European labor market because of surplus labor in certain countries. They were then confronted with two alternatives: die of starvation or emigrate to America. This they did in waves in the 1830s and continued until the end of the 1850s.

LINKAGES THE IRISH FASHIONED WITH AMERICA

The magnet attracting the Irish-Catholics and the skills they brought with them had the determinative impact on the economic linkages that they established in their initial stage of contact. The linkages they fashioned were with the unskilled portion of industry, unionization, and municipal employment.

The Irish broke the traditional pattern of adjustment and settlement of immigrants. For over two generations the structural factors both in Europe and America had created a tradition in which merchants, traders, craftsmen, and artisans settled in the cities and the farmers moved into the interior and settled on the frontier.

The reason the Irish broke the tradition for settlement was because they were predominantly unskilled workers. They were the only unskilled workers, except the Germans, who were allowed to emigrate from Europe in the 1830s and 1840s. In England, for example, British officials attempted to restrict the emigration of England's skilled workers by invoking its half-forgotten statute of 1803, which required all British ships "to carry one passenger for every two tons of registry but limited foreign vessels to one passenger for every five tons."[44] The statute did not apply to the Irish, who were a burden to Britain. The British government wanted to rid itself of the unskilled Irish population but, until the economic vacuum was created in America, the poor Irish were not welcome in many places.[45] This new economic development in America promised the Irish a better future than "rack" renting of small plots of potato patches, a practice that reduced them to the "morgen of subsistence in Ireland."[46]

It is commonly thought that the reason why the Irish refused to move to the interior was because they were poor and destitute peasants; consequently, they were forced to accept immediate employment upon disembarkation.[47] If the independent variable was physical poverty, the Irish could have saved enough money from their earnings to purchase the necessary apparatus for farming. As we shall see, this is precisely what the poor Scandinavians did. The Irish had developed the culture of poverty when they emigrated to America. Instead of moving into the interior, they developed a pattern of following various construction-work projects. As these projects terminated, they returned to the city with no intention of establishing themselves as independent farmers, a value which the American society cherished at the time.[48]

The Irish did not pursue farming as an occupation because they did not have the human capital for farming. As we have seen, the English government removed the system of protection that allowed the Irish to interact in an environment where they could acquire the skills for large-scale farming; consequently, they were restricted to the cultivation of small potato patches. Land used for growing the latter could support three times as many people as the same plot of land sowed with wheat. The landlords could raise more capital from their land renting small plots to numerous peasants than they could renting to farm tenants to grow wheat or corn.

The significant difference between the Irish-Catholics and the Scots-Irish was that the latter group had a tradition for large-scale farming (human capital) when they emigrated to America some one hundred years earlier. They also had developed skills for clearing marshland. These skills in part facilitated their settling on the colonial frontier. But when the Irish-Catholics emigrated to America, they had lost these skills. Special efforts were made by private organizations to lure them out to the frontier.[49] But the Irish kept returning to the cities precisely because they did not have the skills for large-scale farming, which were indispensable for survival on the American frontier.

IRISH POLITICS: POWER AND JOB SECURITY

Shortly after their arrival in America, the Irish entered politics for political power and job security. Prior to emigrating in the 1830s, they had witnessed for approximately a century how the Anglo-Saxon government had made a mockery of laws and how officials had used power to their advantage. The inequality of people under the law was engendered into the consciousness of the Irish concept of power. Everywhere they turned,they were under the influence of power; the power of the Catholic church, and "the power of the landlords and the Anglo-Saxon government authority."[50] Hence, the Irish came to view power as an instrument to be used in the interest of those who possessed it. When they entered the political arena, there was no uncertainty as to their purpose. They entered politics to gain power. More plainly, for the first time in their lives, they saw the gauntlet of power, which had held them socially prostrate for over a century, lying in the ditch; they bent over, picked it up, and used it to place their civil rights to economic opportunities on a principle of law.

The Irish quickly identified themselves with the Democratic party because of (1) their apparent lower-class status, and (2) the religious ethnocentrism practiced by the Protestants. Like the Germans, the Irish entered politics during the Jacksonian era.[51] It was the political ethos of the Jacksonian era that helped mold their attitudes and practices in politics. During this era the Irish learned that they could trade votes for tangible benefits such as jobs.

The Jacksonian politics that laid the foundation for the emergence of political machines marked the first time that the Irish had a system of protection to pursue economic security. Being the most illiterate immigrants during the period between 1830 and 1850, the Irish sought jobs in the municipal government because these jobs (police, public works, and fire department) required only rudimentary knowledge. Employment in the city bureaucracies offered the Irish a chance to leave the squalor of the slums and to obtain a small measure of economic security and personal respect. Again, this employment offered them a chance to transform from a sedentary peasant economy to one that offered them jobs in the form of social security as well as a chance to sink their culture's roots into the urban community.[52]

The significant aspect of the Irish entering politics during the Jacksonian era was that municipal jobs were low-paying and were looked down upon by the Protestants. As mentioned before, most urban dwellers were tradesmen, artisans, or craftsmen, and there was very little room for such unskilled laborers as the Irish before the Jacksonian era. Municipal jobs offered the Irish the same type of security as craftsmanship and artisanship did for other groups. In the last quarter of the nineteenth century, the Irish had full control of the municipal jobs within the great urban triangle formed by St. Louis, Washington, and Boston, when the immigrants of the 1880s appeared on American shores.[53]

The political linkages that were fashioned between the Irish-Catholics and the American polity were made through the Catholic church and the Irish saloons. The internal power structure of the church crystallized the attitudes and goals of the Irish toward the means and ends of government and gave them a base for their political organization. The dominant influence of the church in the Irish experience cannot be overemphasized. The parish and the church were closely associated with ward politics. The priests not only recruited parishioners for politics, but they also obtained patronage jobs for them. Securing jobs for the parishioners was both an organizational and a humanitarian concern for the priests. The greater the number of parishioners recruited, the greater the sum of money that could be raised for the church through donations. Therefore, every intercession that the priest made in behalf of his parishioners "strengthened the ties of politics, parish, religion, and the bonds of Irish solidarity and identity."[54]

Although the vast majority of the Irish who settled in the cities were contract laborers, there was a class of artisans and craftsmen among them. These skilled workers formed unions to protect their property interest rights to employment.

The Irish arrived in America when the labor movement was in its infancy. As we shall see in Chapter 8, the labor movement was slow in getting off the ground because companies employed a tactic called "combination of restraint in trade" to reduce unions' effectiveness.[55] The labor movement began crawling from its cradle in the 1840s and 1850s; after the Civil War, it picked up momentum to the extent that unions served as a system of protection to safeguard the Irish property interest rights to employment. But even before the Civil War, the Irish had developed a propensity for organized labor. For example, in the 1850s they "constituted three-fourths of the foreign-born masons, plasterers, and bricklayers in the city, one-half of the carpenters, and one-third of the painters."[56]

Since the Irish outnumbered the German skilled workers, they began to dominate the labor movement in the early 1850s. Around the middle of the decade, they began also to dominate the rank and file of the New York Tailors Trade Association and other unions that were on the rise as a result of America's growing economy.[57]

After the Civil War, the Irish began to organize the first mixed national body of labor (Noble Order of the Knights of Labor). As we have seen earlier, the German craftsmen formed a national union to encompass their own respective trades. But the Irish attempted to form a mixed national, on the assumption that all workers had "common interests and should join forces in improving working standards."[58]

The political significance of the Knights of Labor is that the union bound unskilled and skilled workers together by its oaths and rituals. These bonds enabled the Irish to form a monopoly in certain areas and established the framework for the organization of work that determined the relationship between union workers and employers. The unions had the power to determine who, and how many, could be allowed to enter certain occupations. Naturally, the Irish used this power to protect the liberty and property interest rights to employment for their families, relatives, and kinships in both skilled and unskilled jobs. With such a structure, the Irish-dominated unions began to grow rapidly in size "in the 1870s and reached the peak of about 800,000 members in 1886."[59] In fact, their domination of the unions led the German miners, in 1902, to protest that the "Irish monopolized the union offices, favored their own people in the distribution of strike funds, and exploited their positions in the union for personal gains."[60]

As we shall see in Chapter 8, although the Irish were able to establish a *de facto* system of protection to safeguard their rights to employment, they were not able to elevate themselves to the middle-class plateau as a group until the passage of the National Labor Relations Act of 1937. That act provided them with a set of bootstraps.

In short, although the Irish did enter other segments of the work force, their major occupation was public employment. Their political activity was expanded by their ability (1) to absorb politics into their everyday lives, and (2) make politics as desirable an occupation for themselves as a non-political career was for other ethnic groups. Therefore, the Irish political career was cast into the social structure of the old peasantry system, which they inherited from the European experience—that of the elder son pursuing the same occupation and political office as his father; that is, mentoring methodology. The Irish still follow this pattern to a large extent into the 1980s.

A COMPARATIVE ANALYSIS OF IRISH AND GERMAN ECONOMIC LINKAGES

The political and economic linkages that the Germans and Irish fashioned with the American polity in their early stages of contact reflect the amount of human capital that they brought with them. The Germans settled both in the cities and on the farm according to their chosen occupation. As we shall see in Chapter 7, they remained predominantly on the farm up until the 1950s and 1960s. Then they began to shift their occupational pursuits in accordance with changes in technological development.

The Irish, however, did not pursue farming as an occupation, because they had lost their skills for farming and had developed a pattern of seeking employment as common laborers. The Irish immigrants outnumbered the Germans two-to-one, yet the Germans constituted the largest percentage of independent farmers during this period. For example, in 1850 and 1860, the Irish constituted 43.51 and 38.94 percent of the immigrants during this period while the Germans constituted 25.94 and 31.45 percent, respectively (see Table 3). If simple equality of opportunity was all that were necessary for group economic success, then the Irish should have taken up all of the jobs and available farmland when they first made contact with the American polity. The data overwhelmingly support the theory that both human capital and a system of protection are needed to ensure a group's economic success.

The Irish settled in the cities; yet, the German artisans and craftsmen who settled there during the same period fared markedly better than the Irish. For example, the Germans who settled in New York City fared better than the Irish in terms of the percentage employed in skilled occupations. Regardless of whether it was in the shoemaking category (see Table 4), peddlers (see Table 5), or carpenters, the Germans were consistent in surpassing the percentage of Irishmen in certain skilled occupations.[61]

THE SCANDINAVIANS

The forces that uprooted the Scandinavians were similar to those that uprooted the Germans some 40 years earlier. Their emigration and adjustment to American life supports one of our arguments; that is, if an

Table 3
Number and Percentage of Ethnic Groups in the United States, 1850–60

Origin	Census of 1860	Census of 1850	Proportion in 1860	Proportion in 1850
Ireland	1,611,304	961,719	38.94	43.51
Germany	1,301,136	573,225	31.45	25.94
England	432,692	278,675	10.44	12.61
British Amer.	249,970	147,700	6.05	6.68
France	109,870	54,069	2.66	2.44
Scotland	108,518	70,550	2.63	3.19
Switzerland	53,327	13,358	1.29	0.60
Wales	45,763	29,868	1.11	1.34
Norway	43,995	12,678	1.07	0.57
China	35,565	785	0.86	0.03
Holland	28,281	9,848	0.68	0.45
Mexico	27,466	13,317	0.66	0.60
Sweden	18,625	3,559	0.45	0.16
Italy	10,518	3,645	0.26	0.17
Others	60,145	37,870	1.45	1.71
Total foreign	4,137,175	2,210,866	100.0	100.0

SOURCE: Lawrence Guy Brown, Immigration (New York: Longmans,
      Green and Company, 1933), p. 81.

Table 4
Percentage of Ethnic Groups Employed as Shoemakers in New York City, 1855

Origin	Percentage of Shoemakers to Total Gainfully Employed of the Same Nationality, 1855
Germany	8.13
Poland	5.37
France	5.33
Switzerland	4.84
England	2.88
Ireland	2.04
Scotland	1.74

SOURCE: Robert Ernst, Immigrant Life in New York
        City: 1825-1863 (New York: King's Crown
        Press, 1949), p. 78.

Table 5
Percentage of Ethnic Groups Employed as Peddlers in New York City, 1855

	Percentage of Peddlers to Total Gainfully Employed of the Same Nationality, 1855
Origin	
Poland	9.06
The Netherlands	4.05
Germany	2.06
France	1.07
Scandinavia	.90
Ireland	.85
Italy	.84

SOURCE: Robert Ernst, Immigrant Life in New York
City: 1825-1863 (New York: King's Crown
Press, 1949), p. 78.

ethnic group emigrates to a physical and economic environment that approximates the one of their homeland, they will encounter little, if any, difficulty in adjusting to the new environment.

The term "Scandinavians" is used here to describe ethnic groups who emigrated from Sweden, Norway, and Denmark. Significant numbers emigrated from these countries after the Civil War and up to the 1880s.[62] These ethnic groups were able to adjust to American life much faster than the Irish and, to a certain extent, the Germans. Their rapid adjustment can be attributed to the condition of life in their homeland and the economic conditions in America during the time of emigration.

The conditions of life that uprooted the Scandinavians were preponderantly economic.[63] First, the Scandinavian countries began to lose their prestige in the mid-1860s. Denmark was defeated by the Germans in 1864, "and the rise of a new power on the Baltic destroyed the hope of growing Scandinavianism."[64] Consequently, Denmark's defeat reduced the countries on the northern continent to subordinate positions. This defeat was accompanied by three depressing years of crop failure, which destroyed Sweden's capacity as a grain-exporting country.[65]

Second, there was a reorganization of the economic and agricultural systems in these countries. In the 1830s, the Scandinavians changed from a barter economy to a money economy. The transition precipitated widespread speculation in land. This phenomenon increased the value of land in the rural districts from $5.8 million in 1833 to $67 million in the 1860s.[66] The bulk of this land was purchased through loans from mortgage associations. During the years of crop failure, the farmers were unable to pay the mortgages on their land at the same time that there was a rise in the construction of railroads and the expansion of the factory system—which demanded a large sum of capital. This new demand for capital increased the competition for money, a phenomenon that had the inevitable consequence of increasing interest rates and curtailing agricultural credit.[67] This constraint caused many farmers to go bankrupt and forced them to leave their land. Those farmers who were able to hold on to their land were forced to dispense with their hired labor and cultivate their own land as best they could with the aid of their own families.[68] This in turn created a residual number of unemployed laborers; emigration was the only reasonable alternative.

As economic conditions were the pushing forces that uprooted the Scandinavians, there also existed economic conditions that were the pulling forces in America. At the close of the Civil War, America turned its energies toward opening up the Northwest Territory and expanding the system of railroads.[69]

The tools that Congress decided to use to open up the Northwest Territory were the construction of the transcontinental railroad and the settling of farmers along the railroads lines. To achieve this end, Congress commissioned the Union Pacific Railroad Company to build the railroad, and passed the Homestead Act of 1862 to provide economic incentives to attract farmers to settle on the prairies.

One of the major purposes for constructing the railroad was to tie the western market to the main arteries of the eastern economic system. To achieve this end, Congress gave generous federal loans and grants to the railroad companies, ranging from $16,000 per mile on the flat prairie land to $45,000 for mountainous country.[70] For every mile of track laid, the government gave the railroad companies twelve square miles of land. This amounted to 640 acres of land per square mile.

In order for the railroad companies to ensure themselves a profit, they needed farmers to settle on the prairies. To achieve this goal, they sent agents to the Scandinavian countries to recruit settlers. In some instances, they offered them free transportation to America if they would agree to settle on the prairies.

When the Scandinavians made contact with the American polity, they also were handed a set of bootstraps on a silver platter. They arrived just in the nick of time to be the beneficiaries of government give-aways; that is, free land provided by the Homestead Act. This act provided for farmers to settle on 160 acres of land free. After living on it for five years and making minor improvements, they could purchase the land for the incredibly nominal fee of $10.

These government give-aways (bootstraps), coupled with the new transportation system that linked the Scandinavian farmers with the main arteries of the economic markets back east, served as a system of protection, which prevented the Scandinavians from falling victim to the culture of poverty in their initial stage of contact. Again, the government give-away of land also served as a safety net that prevented the second generation of Scandinavians also from falling victim to the culture of poverty. This land served as a set of bootstraps by which the Scandinavians were able to pull themselves up to the level of the middle-class plateau. Whatever hardships there were, they were short-lived because the farmers were part of the common-man movement, which sought release through political participation.

With the full blessing of the federal government, the Scandinavians were able to pursue their goal of becoming landowners, which was one of America's most sacred values at the time, and to improve their social and economic status. The Scandinavians were not forced to undergo a prolonged period of agony and deprivation either in their homeland or in America. Their emigration to America was precipitated not by religious persecution or political oppression but because the economic conditions in their homeland had begun to push them off the middle-class plateau onto the beaches of the culture of poverty. They did not stay on these beaches long enough to lose their skills for farming, as was typical for the Irish, or their other human capital that they had acquired.

The Scandinavians emigrated from one wheat-growing environment to another. They were, by occupation, predominantly farmers who settled heavily on the prairies of the Mississippi Valley along the railroads, as those were completed. The majority of the Norwegians settled in Wisconsin, Minnesota, Iowa, and northern Illinois. The Swedes concentrated in the upper Mississippi Valley and in the northern areas, such as St. Paul, Minnesota, and Chicago, Illinois. The Danish, who constituted 50,000, settled in Iowa, Minnesota, and Illinois.[71]

The Scandinavians did not settle in the cities, as did the Irish. Even those Scandinavians who were relatively poor upon disembarkation, and who were forced to work for the Northern Pacific Railroad at $1.50 a day, were eventually able to save enough money to purchase a farm, usually in a period of two years or less.[72] The major differences between the poor Scandinavians and their Irish counterparts was that the former had not been off the farm long enough to have lost their skills at farming. Where the Irish had been off the farm for two or more generations before emigration, the Scandinavians had been uprooted less than half of one generation. There were also tradesmen, artisans, and merchants among the Scandinavians. This group settled in the cities with little or no difficulty.

The Scandinavians were predominantly Protestant, and they supported the ideals associated with the accumulation of property and wealth, individualism, and free government based upon constitutional principles. Many values of the Scandinavian people coincided with the American value system. Success in America during this period was manifested in being an independent farmer. This the federal government handed to Scandinavians on a silver platter.

NOTES

1. See Robert Ernst, *Immigrant Life in New York City: 1825-1863* (New York: King's Crown Press, 1949), pp. 1-2.

2. Oscar Handlin, *Boston's Immigrants* (Cambridge: Harvard University Press, 1959), p. 30.

3. Brinley Thomas, *International Migration and Economic Development* (Paris: UNESCO, 1961), p. 9.

4. Oscar Handlin, *The Uprooted* (Boston: Little, Brown and Company, 1951), pp. 24-28.

5. Ibid.

6. The term "magnet" is to be understood here as the place where ethnic groups formed a pattern of settlement in their early contact with America.

7. Lawrence Guy Brown, *Immigration* (New York: Longmans, Green and Company, 1933), pp. 79-132.

8. Marcus Lee Hansen, *The Atlantic Migration: 1607-1860* (Cambridge: Harvard University Press, 1940), pp. 83-84.

9. Ibid.

10. William I. Thomas and Florian Znaniecki, *The Polish Peasant in Europe and America* (New York: Alfred A. Knopf, 1927), p. 117.

11. F. R. Bienenfeld, *The Germans and the Jews* (Chicago: University of Chicago Press, 1960), pp. 5-6.

12. Maldwyn A. Jones, *American Immigration* (Chicago: University of Chicago Press, 1960), p. 97.

13. Ibid., p. 110.

14. Hansen, *The Atlantic Migration,* chapter 5.

15. Albert Bernhardt Faust, *The German Element in the United States* (New York: Arno Press and the *New York Times*, 1969), p. 388.

16. Ibid., p. 431.

17. Ibid., p. 436.

18. Ibid., pp. 490-501.

19. John F. Kennedy, *A Nation of Immigrants* (New York: Harper Torchbook, 1964), p. 52.

20. Ibid.

21. Ibid., chapter 15.

22. Thomas A. Bailey, *The American Pageant: A History of the Republic* (Boston: D. C. Health and Company, 1956), p. 574.

23. Ibid., p. 320.

24. Faust, *The German Element,* pp. 476-477.

25. Ibid., p. 475.

26. Bailey, *The American Pageant,* p. 228.

27. Kennedy, *A Nation of Immigrants,* p. 52.

28. Oscar Handlin, *The Newcomers* (Cambridge: Harvard University Press, 1959), p. 18.

29. Hansen, *The Atlantic Migration,* p. 275.

30. See definition in Chapter 1 for an explanation of *de facto* and *de jure* systems of protection, pp. 34-35.

31. Lloyd G. Reynolds, *Labor Economics and Labor Relations* (Englewood Cliffs, N.J.: Prentice-Hall, 1970), p. 325.

32. E. Edward Herman and Alfred Kuhn, *Collective Bargaining and Labor Relations* (Englewood Cliffs, N.J.: Prentice-Hall, 1981), p. 8.

33. Reynolds, *Labor Economics,* p. 8.

34. Herman and Kuhn, *Collective Bargaining,* p. 7.

35. Ibid.

36. Marcus W. Jernegan, *The American Colonies: 1492-1750* (New York: Longmans, Green and Company, 1956), p. 310.

37. Handlin, *Boston's Immigrants,* p. 38.

38. Edmund Curtis, *A History of Ireland* (London: Methuen and Company, 1968), pp. 319-320.

39. Arnold Scrier, *Ireland and the American Emigration 1850-1900* (Minneapolis: University of Minnesota Press, 1958), p. 12.

40. Edward M. Levine, *The Irish and Irish Politicians* (Notre Dame, Ind.: University of Notre Dame Press, 1966), p. 54.

41. Handlin, *Boston's Immigrants,* p. 43.

42. See Sir Charles G. Duffy, "The Distressed Conditions of Ireland, 1847: An Irish View," in *Historical Aspects of the Immigration Problem,* ed. Edith Abott (Chicago: University of Chicago Press, 1926), pp. 116-120.

43. Levine, *The Irish,* pp. 55-56.

44. Hansen, *The Atlantic Migration,* pp. 82-83.

45. See Cecil Woodham Smith, *The Great Hunger, Ireland 1845-1849* (New York: King's Crown Press, Columbia University, 1962), chapters 1-6.

46. John E. Pomfret, *The Struggle for Land in Ireland: 1800-1923* (Princeton, N.J.: Princeton University Press, 1930), p. 23.

47. Jones, *American Immigration,* p. 121.

48. Carl Wittke, *We Who Built America* (Cleveland: Case Western Univeristy Press, 1964), p. 136.

49. Kate H. Claghorn, "The Foreign Immigrant in New York City," in United States Industrial Commission, *Reports on Immigration,* 42 vols. (Washington, D.C.: Government Printing Office, 1901), 15: 442-494.

50. Levine, *The Irish,* p. 47.

51. Ibid., p. 112.

52. Lawrence Funchs, ed., *American Ethnic Politics* (New York: Harper & Row, 1968), p. 19.

53. For a discussion of the urban triangle, see Handlin, *Boston's Immigrants,* chapter 3.

54. Levine, *The Irish,* p. 131.

55. This topic will be discussed in Chapter 8.

56. Carl Wittke, *The Irish in America* (Baton Rouge: Louisiana State University Press, 1956), p. 217.

57. Ibid.

58. Ibid., p. 222.

59. Ibid.

60. Ibid., p. 225.

61. Ernst, *Immigrant Life,* pp. 1-2.

62. Wittke, *We Who Built America,* p. 257.

63. Florence Edith Janson, *The Background of Swedish Immigration: 1840-1930* (Chicago: University of Chicago Press, 1931), p. 223.

64. Wittke, *We Who Built America,* p. 257.

65. See G. M. Stephenson, *A History of American Immigration* (Boston: Ginn and Company, 1926), chapter 2.

66. Wittke, *We Who Built America,* pp. 257-258.

67. Alfred O. Frankelsurd, *The Scandinavian-American* (Minneapolis: K. C. Halter Company, 1915), p. 35.

68. Janson, *The Background of Swedish Immigration,* p. 225.

69. Fankelsurd, *The Scandinavian-American,* p. 36.

70. See John Moody, *The Railroad Builders: Chronicles of America* (New Haven: Yale University Press, 1919).

71. Wittke, *We Who Built America,* p. 280.

72. Ibid., p. 279.

4

Italian and Jewish Immigrants, 1880–1910

In Chapter 1, it was demonstrated how scientifically fruitful it was to identify (as units of analysis) ethnic groups as substantive subsystems based on their memories of migration and colonization instead of religious denominations (normative subsystems). Such an analysis allows us to identify patterns of behavior among groups.

This chapter examines the conditions of life in the homelands both of the Italians and Jews and traces their emigration to America. The major reasons why these groups did not fall victim to the culture of poverty can be hypothesized to be because of: (1) the human capital they brought with them, (2) the system of protection that safeguarded their civil rights to acquire property and to pursue a wide range of economic opportunities in their initial stages of contact, (3) the system of protection that guaranteed them the access to society's income redistribution system, and (4) the fact that they arrived on the heels of a growing industrialized economy.

In studying immigration during the period from 1880 to 1910, we will omit all the other ethnic groups who immigrated during this period, such as the Slavs, because these groups consisted of numerous ethnic groups and data about them are incomplete. For instance, the term "Slavs" covers

Poles, Slovaks, Croatians, or Slovenians, Ruthenians or Russniak, Moravians, and Bohemians and Serbians and Montenegrins, Russians, and Dalmatians and Bosnians and Herzegovinians.[1]

The greatest difficulty lies in an attempt to assess the adjustment patterns of the Poles. The U.S. Census Bureau is not allowed to ask questions concerning religious affiliation. Therefore, a clear distinction between

Catholic Poles and Jewish Poles is almost impossible from the available data. The greatest difficulties lie with the Jews; the following passage illustrates some of the inherent difficulties in studying them:

In 1905 there entered at our ports 92,388 Jews from Austria; those who came from the Polish provinces of Russia and Austria (that is probably the greater part of them) appear in the census simply as "native of Poland" and quite distort the facts. Especially as regards concentration in cities the Polish Jews make the census figures for "natives of Poland" almost meaningless as regards Poles.[2]

Therefore, we are going to restrict our analysis to the Italians and Russian Jews, where the data are clear and complete.

CONDITIONS OF LIFE IN EUROPE

The third wave of immigrants differed markedly from the previous groups. For the first time, the immigrants did not consist predominantly of farmers. Instead, they were urban dwellers who sought non-agricultural occupations. Their immigration was precipitated both by economic and political factors. For example, the Italians' immigration can be characterized as purely economic. Their country was experiencing a severe overpopulation problem coupled with several years of a depressed agricultural industry. Many Italians emigrated to America with the idea (1) of earning a fortune and returning home to fulfill their lifelong dream of purchasing a farm, or (2) earning enough money to return home and retire in comfort for the rest of their lives. The Russian Jews' emigration, however, was characterized by political oppression and religious persecution. They became scapegoats for the economic ills that Russia was experiencing at the time.

Both the Italians and Russian Jews saw America as a place where they could escape their predicaments. They began emigrating in droves in the early 1880s and continued up to 1914, when the European countries began rumbling up their war machinery in preparation for World War I.

THE AMERICAN MAGNET

The Italians and Russian Jews emigrated to America on the heels of the "common man" movement. Out of this movement, workers managed to develop a *de facto* system of protection, which safeguarded their civil rights to acquire property and to pursue a wide range of economic opportunities. This system wrested from employers their managerial prerogatives to hire and arbitrarily dismiss their employees, or reduce their wages. Up to this period, employees' civil rights to employment rested largely on the goodwill of management instead of on a set of established procedures.[3] From this period onward, the unions, which were coming of age, shared in these decisions. Politically, the unions prevented these groups from developing the culture of poverty.

Economically, these immigrants arrived in the nick of time to ride in on the high tide of an economy that was rapidly shifting its wealth from rural areas to industrial ones. For example, in 1850, the rural districts accounted for over half of all the wealth in America. But by the 1880s this amount had decreased to 25 percent: $3 billion for rural areas compared to $49 billion for urban areas.[4]

At the end of the nineteenth century, America was emerging as a prosperous and powerful industrialized nation. In order for a nation to grow economically, there must be available an adequate supply of labor to meet the labor demand. America had a tradition of utilizing the European surplus labor to meet its labor demands and to promote its economic growth. Some scholars have argued that America's policy of turning to Europe for its labor supply (white Europeans) instead of turning to the American South for Black labor was indeed a racial policy. Also, if America had utilized the untapped southern Black labor supply, then questions of Blacks' economic status would have been solved long ago.[5] Racism did play a role in these decisions. However, there were other economic factors as well.

From an economic perspective, the American South until the turn of the century could ill afford to relinquish its labor force without significantly undermining the United States' economy. There was no conceivable way by which the South could have replaced its labor supply without seriously retarding the economy of the United States. The South produced cotton, which was indispensable to the flourishing northern manufacturing industry.

The institution of slavery had been abolished. The climate in the South was so hot that many Europeans did not have a tradition of enduring such a climate. Furthermore, there was very little unoccupied land for independent farmers. America did not need farmers at that time, but laborers to construct railroads, subways, terminals, and bridges.[6] This was the magnet that drew European immigrants to American shores during this period.

THE UPROOTED ITALIANS

The important phenomenon about the Italian peasants and their emigration to America is the condition of life that forced them off their farms. Italy, unlike other European countries, did not undergo economic development during the eighteenth century as did other European countries. As a result, the industrial development was retarded in Italy.

The lack of industrial development had a profound effect upon the economic status of the peasants. They continued to employ old methods of farming while the northern European countries were implementing new equipments and scientific techniques. The lack of the Italians' success in this area can be attributed to the system of land ownership that gave the farm tenants very little incentive to make improvements on their land, as was true with the Irish. This system was designed for the landlord to realize the greatest share of the profit. Any improvement that the farm tenant made to increase the productivity of the land went not to him, but to the landlord because the farm tenant did not have property interest rights (that is, preference) to his expired lease.

Accompanying this oppressive land system was an increase in population. The population of Italy increased from somewhat fewer than 27 million in 1871 to over 34 million in 1905.[7] Of this total population, over half the adult male population was engaged in agricultural pursuits. This class, which consisted of farm tenants and day laborers, played a very significant role in the Italian economy because the craft and trade populations were depending upon them for their existence. A decline in their productivity would automatically affect the trade and craft populations.[8]

The use of an unequal land system increased the number of common laborers in Italy during the mid-nineteenth century. Regardless of how hard they worked, the common laborers could not raise themselves above mere subsistence. The most attractive alternative for them to improve their lives was emigration.

Economically, as the population of Italy increased after 1871, the staple crops (that is, olive oil, wine, and wheat) remained stationary.[9] Italy tried to stimulate her industries through protective tariffs, but this measure only benefited the North, where industry was situated.[10] Also, the rainfall in Southern Italy was so infrequent that even the richest soil produced meager crops.

Italian farmers, despite the oppressive land system, undertook various measures to improve the productivity of their land. They employed such methods as irrigation and fertilization, but these methods proved to be ineffective because of the lack of rainfall.[11] Even the occasional rainfall had very little effect upon the crops. The soil had difficulty retaining water for any length of time due to deforestation, which the Italians had undertaken to make room for new farmland. As we shall see, the skills of irrigation, tillage, and fertilization proved to be very advantageous for the Italian farmers when they emigrated to America.

The peasants were not the only ones who were having problems surviving in Italy. As the country became more industrialized, artisans and craftsmen were being displaced by modern technology. Their products could not be matched by low-cost factory-made items. They simply could not accept the low wages offered by factory employment.[12] In the 1880s, therefore, there were two classes of unemployed Italians—the skilled workers and the peasants. The only alternative left for these classes to improve their lot was through emigration.

The Italians had begun emigrating from Italy in the 1860s. Their emigration, however, remained relatively small until the 1880s. After this period, the Italians emigrated in much larger numbers. This increase can be attributed to the Italian government, which was one of the few governments that encouraged emigration.[13] It provided a system of protection for its emigrants on their voyage to their designated country and kept a protective interest in them in their new country.[14] The Italian government found it not only socially and politically beneficial to encourage emigration, but also economically advantageous. Emigration provided the Italian government with additional revenue for its failing economy. It was estimated that the immigrants sent from $30 million to $80 million a year back to Italy to their families and relatives. This revenue boosted the Italian economy, especially in the small towns and villages. Numerous such villages emerged from poverty-stricken status to prosperous towns because of this additional revenue.[15]

The Italians' emigration was not restricted to the United States. They emigrated to almost every country that had a demand for unskilled labor. The Italians from Northern Italy preferred to emigrate to South America—Argentina and Brazil in particular. These two countries were particularly attractive to the Italians because of their favorable agricultural opportunities. The average Italian peasant who had lost his farm or was forced into day labor could emigrate to Brazil and purchase a farm for very little capital.[16] The Argentine and Brazilian governments were particularly interested in the Italian farmers because of their desire to populate the land. To facilitate their immigration to South America, the Buenos Aires Association, which was an employer organization, sent a delegation to Europe to explore various possibilities by which it could organize immigration to Argentina on a systematic basis.[17] This phenomenon created a pattern by which the Italian agricultural workers could emigrate directly from Italy to Argentina. In other words, they were emigrating from a physical environment without discontinuity in occupational life style. As has been demonstrated, this type of emigration facilitates an ethnic group's adjustment.

From 1876 to 1920, the total emigration from Italy had the following distribution: "To the Americas—North and South—about 9,000,000; to Europe, 7,500,000; to Africa, some 300,000; to Asia, about 13,000; and to Oceania, a little more than 40,000."[18] Although the Italian emigration to other countries is interesting, we are concerned primarily with their emigration to America and an examination of the economic and political linkages they fashioned between themselves and the American polity in their early stages of contact.

LINKAGES THE ITALIANS FASHIONED WITH AMERICA

The linkages that the Italians fashioned with America in their early stage of contact were with agriculture, craftsmen, artisans, contract labor, and small business.

The number of Italian farmers who emigrated to America was minute. The expanding American industry was more attractive to the class of displaced artisans and craftsmen than it was to the agricultural workers who emigrated to South America. According to the United States Bureau of the Census of 1890, 16 percent of the Italians were engaged in agriculture, and 41 percent were in domestic and personal service.[19]

The skills that the farmers developed in Italy of tilling, fertilizing, and irrigating swampy and unproductive land proved to be advantageous for those who wished to pursue farming in America.[20] They purchased swampy and unproductive land on both the East Coast and in the South and turned it into productive farmland through irrigation and fertilization. Thus, the Italians were noted for being among the first in America to use fertilizer to increase the productivity of farmland. On this previously abandoned land, they were able to raise sugar cane, corn, strawberries, peaches, and apples in eastern and southern states, such as Arkansas and Louisiana.

The fact that many Italians settled in the South seemed to refute the generally held view that emigrants refrained from emigrating to the South in the early part of the nineteenth century because they disliked the institution of slavery; and after slavery, because they disliked being associated or working closely with Blacks. The primary reason that the previous emigrants refrained from emigrating to the South was because they did not have any skills conducive to the southern agricultural industry; also there was very little, if any, unoccupied land. For example, before the mass emigration of the Italians to America, numerous Italians settled in and around New Orleans, where their main occupation was fishing, a practice that they developed in Italy. The Italians had a tendency to settle in any part of the United States where conditions allowed them to utilize their skills. They settled particularly on the abandoned farmland in the Midwest around Rockford, Davenport, Joliet, Peoria, East Moline, etc.[21]

The system of protection that the Italians used to prevent the class of unskilled workers from falling victim to the culture of poverty in their initial stage of contact was the *padroni* system. This system constituted a *de facto* system of protection, which safeguarded their civil rights to interact in three human capital environments: employment, on-the-job training, and banking.

The first task of the *padroni* system was to find work for the newly arrived immigrants. This task inadvertently elevated the system to a level where it became a system of employment and distribution of the newly arrived immigrants throughout the United States.

Employment-wise, the *padroni* system was a life-saver for the newly arrived immigrants. It facilitated their adjustment to the American polity by assisting them in finding employment and offering them financial assistance until they could find employment.[22] This system enabled the Italians to develop an employment pipeline by which workers could be transported from the shores of Italy to the main arteries of the economic system in America. For example, the Italians knew precisely where they were going in America and the type of job that was waiting for them at the end of the pipeline. This differed significantly from the Irish, who had to travel around the country from city to city looking for work.

Incorporated in the *padroni* system was a built-in system of on-the-job training, which was made possible by the pattern of immigration. The Italians of small towns and villages in Italy created a pattern of settling among other Italian immigrants from the same villages. The new immigrants seemed to pursue the same occupations as their fellow immigrants, regardless of whether or not they had skills for these occupations. This practice, in turn, served as an on-the-job training program for the unskilled workers.[23] Skilled workers from Northern Italy moved directly into the interior, where they were employed as marble cutters, miners, and mill hands. Many other immigrants were skilled mechanics, masons, stonecutters, bricklayers, carpenters, and cabinet makers. These immigrants resided in New York, where there was a high demand for their skills.[24]

In addition to employment, the *padroni* system provided services that the Italians could not get elsewhere, such as banking, letter writing, and buying and selling real estate property. Among these services, banking proved to be the most significant one. It created an environment whereby the Italians could acquire banking skills by interacting in a money-lending environment. For example, long before the Italians were able to establish their own banks, the average Italian found that he could entrust his money for safekeeping with the *padroni* system until he was ready to return home to Italy, or he could borrow money from it to purchase a farm or to establish his own business. This practice enabled some heads of *padroni* systems to turn this system into a bank, thereby becoming bankers because of the experience they gained in handling money.[25] In New York City, where the majority of the Italians resided, it was estimated by the "Big Five" banks that Italian savings constituted from 15 to 33 percent of their depositors; and they speculated that more than this amount was deposited in the Italian banks and the *padroni* system.[26]

These banks assisted the Italians in branching off to other fields of business. For example, many banks were established to facilitate the Italian saving and commercial business in America and their homeland. Some of the Italian banks established during this period still exist today; one of the largest in the country, Bank of America, has its headquarters in San Francisco.[27]

In addition to their banking system, the Italians established a significant foothold in small business. Groups' success in business, to recapitulate, is highly contingent upon (1) managerial skills they brought with them, and (2) the system of protection that safeguarded their freedom to interact in a business environment after making contact with the American polity. The Italians' success in business lends credence to this theory. For instance, the Italians were able to do better in entrepreneurship than the Irish primarily because they had the business know-how when they made contact with the American polity. They succeeded in business not by trying to pursue those businesses already developed in America, but by introducing new types of business and new concepts; for example, macaroni, artificial flowers, organ grinding, and confections.[28]

The Italians were particularly noted for introducing fruit and vegetable stands to the American small business market. This was made possible by other Italians who engaged in small farming in the outskirts of the city. They furnished the peddlers and the pushcart markets with fresh vegetables and fruits. The method of pushcart selling was somewhat new to America. At the time the Italians immigrated, greater value was placed upon the ownership of large independent farms.[29] It appears that almost all of the industries that the Italians later began to monopolize were closely related to customs and traditions of their homeland. For example, the Italians were heavily concentrated in shoemaking, tailoring, barbering, and the manufacturing of cheese. The Northern Italians were heavily concentrated in mining and masonry. The significant differences between the Northern and Southern Italians lie in manufacturing. In America, the Northern Italians constituted 4,018 of the Italian manufacturers, while the Southern Italians constituted 162 in 1910.[30] This dissimilarity can be explained by the fact that the Italian manufacturing industry was situated in Northern Italy, while the Southern Italians were predominantly farmers.

In short, the structural condition in both Italy and America restricted the Italian immigration largely to craftsmen, artisans, merchants, and a few farmers up until World War I, which placed a restriction on all immigration. After the war, the Immigration Act of 1917 restricted immigration to the skilled and literate adults.[31] It also prevented a large number of unskilled and illiterate peasants from emigrating, thus, preventing the poverty of the homeland from developing among them—a factor that the Irish-Catholics experienced for two generations. There were enough craftsmen and artisans in the *padroni* system to provide a sufficient on-the-job training program for the unskilled. It was primarily through this system that the Italians fashioned linkages between themselves and the American polity. This system was later used to transform the Italian workers into the labor unions, which provided them with a high degree of economic security. When the federal government clothed the labor unions with a system of protection and subsidized their apprenticeship programs, the Italians were catapulted onto the middle-class plateau. A full discussion of this system will be deferred until Chapter 8.

CONDITIONS OF LIFE OF THE JEWS IN EUROPE

The Jews who emigrated to the United States during the last part of the nineteenth century and the early part of the present century came largely from the Russian Empire, Austria-Hungary, and Romania. They were not uprooted from the land, as was typical of the Italians, but they were driven out of the Russian Empire because of the peculiar economic positions that they held.[32] They dominated the trade and commerce throughout the empire. At the close of the nineteenth century, Russia attempted to undergo industrial development. In order to do so, it had to take control of trade and commerce, which the Jews had controlled since the Middle Ages.[33] The Jews' concentration in these fields was due not to a calculated effort on their behalf to achieve economic upward mobility, but to their response to a set of structural conditions that foreclosed their freedom to pursue those occupations that were common to life and that society valued.

In order to fully understand how the Jews came to dominate the trade and commercial system, it is necessary to examine the social role that the ghetto played in offering the Jews a system of protection to acquire human capital in those occupations that had a propensity for producing high income in America.[34] Long before it became compulsory, the Jews found it to be socially and economically advantageous to live in separate parts of the city, primarily to preserve their religious practices and to promote their economic enterprises.[35] Through the years, the ghetto became a symbol of isolation and acted as social walls that kept them apart from the Christians. Whether by decree, law, or their own volition, the Jews developed the ghetto into a universal institution. This was particularly true in those countries that granted them full citizenship—as in the Netherlands. The Jews were forced into trade and commerce because during the medieval period the church prohibited them from engaging in occupations of prestige, such as handicrafts, artisanry, and farming.[36] These occupations were reserved for the Christians. In other words, the church forced the Jews into these occupations, which were despised but necessary.

One of the despised occupations that proved to be economically advantageous for the Jews when they emigrated to America was banking. As already mentioned, the Jews have been engaged in banking, or money-lending, even since the medieval period. At that time, they developed the concept of lending money for interest.[37] The church had long considered the lending of money for interest to be forbidden by the Scriptures and to be antagonistic to the laws of nature. Lending money had no impact upon the Jewish religion; it was simply an occupation.[38]

Besides lending money, the Jews were able to develop a system of trade and commerce unparalleled in the circle of Christians. This was in part due to the fact that the Jews were not tied to serfdom or the feudal system. Trade and commerce provided a universal institution by which the Jews could travel from one community to another to ascertain the needs and wants of the Christians. This institution in turn provided a system of secret correspondence for international commerce. The Jews consequently gained a distinctive advantage over the Christians, who were forced to rely upon the Jews for international trade.

For a long period of time, the Jews were the only link between the Orient and the Western World. They have been given credit for introducing Oriental products such as tobacco, sugar, and coffee into the West.[39] They also initiated the exchange of wool and clothing between England and Spain, which later became England's staple industry. Therefore, from the Middle Ages to the beginning of the Industrial Revolution, the Jews formed a monopoly over certain forms of international commerce. The wheels of the Industrial Revolution broke this monopoly as a new class of merchants and manufacturers emerged among the Christians, especially in England.

It may seem on the surface somewhat ironic that the Jews were able to travel from one country to another and conduct trade with the Christians, their oppressors. But the Jews considered trade an abstract phenomenon in which all emotions fell into the background. They felt free to trade with their enemies because there were no personal prejudices involved. "The less personal, the less emotional, and the more impersonal, the more abstract the attitudes of the trader, the more efficiently and the more successfully can he exercise his function."[40] From this statement, it can be inferred that the Jews created the impersonal relationships involved in business; that is, they were able to detach personal and familial ties from business, a concept that Max Weber later attributed to the Protestants.

The Jews dominated the business enterprises in almost every country in Europe until those countries began to undergo industrial development. When this occurred, the Jews were pushed out of the occupations previously reserved for them. As we have seen in Chapter 2, the origin of the Industrial Revolution, which can be traced to England, started in the late seventeenth and early eighteenth centuries. During this time, a new middle class of merchants and manufacturers emerged in England, and social prestige shifted from the aristocrats to this new middle class, who began to gain prestige in the public eye, pushing the Jews gradually out of trade and commerce, leaving them with only money-lending in England. It is worth noting here that it was precisely trade and commerce on which the British Empire flourished.[41]

The Russians, however, were almost two centuries behind the English in developing industrially. Consequently, the Jews remained in commerce and trade in Russia until the latter part of the nineteenth century. Statistics show that in 1897, the Jews constituted only 4.5 percent of the total population in the Russian Empire, but they constituted 10 percent of those engaged in manufacturing and the mechanical pursuits, and 36 percent of these engaged in commerce.[42] When compared to the rest of the Russian population, the Jews were preponderantly engaged in industry and commerce in the Russian Empire. The majority of them were concentrated in those parts of the Russian Empire where commerce, manufacturing, and mechanical pursuits took place, namely the Jewish Pale, or the "Pale of Settlement." This territory consisted of 25 provinces—10 in Poland, 3 in Lithuania, 3 in white Russia, and 9 in southwestern and southern Russia.[43]

In the Pale of Settlement, the Jews constituted 12.1 percent of the total population, 32.1 percent of all those engaged in manufacturing and mechanical pursuits, and 76.7 percent of those engaged in commerce. They also showed significant achievement in the professional services. Here, they constituted 21.7 percent of the professionals, while only 2.9 percent of the total population of the Russian Empire was engaged in these occupations, as indicated in Table 6.

Table 6
Distribution of the Jews in Occupations in the Pale of Jewish Settlement, 1897

Group occupations	Total	Jews	Percent of Total
Agricultural pursuits	6,071,413	38,538	.63
Professional services[a]	317,710	67,238	21.7
Personal services	2,138,981	250,078	11.7
Manufacturing and mechanical pursuits	1,573,519	504,844	32.1
Transportation	211,983	44,177	20.8
Commerce	556,086	426,628	76.7

SOURCE: Emigration Conditions in Europe (Washington: Government Printing Office, 1911), p. 292.

[a]In order to make these figures comparable to figures in the United States, saloon keepers are included in personal services.

The table shows that the Jews constituted the majority of the commercial class and to a certain extent a significant part of the industrial class in the Pale of Settlement. In other words, what was true of the Jewish occupations in the whole Russian Empire was increasingly true in the Pale of Settlement. They were mainly artisans engaged in the manufacturing of shoes and wearing apparel. Over half of the tailors and shoemakers in the Pale were Jews, and they constituted a high proportion of those engaged in food production, the building trades, metal working, and the wool and tobacco industries.[44] The practical political and economic importance here is that the Jews became increasingly essential to the economics of the Pale.

Russia's staple industries during the latter part of the nineteenth century were grains, cattle, furs, and hides. The majority of the Jewish merchants in the Pale were dealers in these products and the Russian peasants depended heavily upon the Jews to export their products. Where the Russian merchants were somewhat unfamiliar with the most elementary principles of trade, the Jews were more advanced in their skillful use of credit and their well-organized commercial system. Thus, the Jews played an important role in the organization of the Russian grains in the Pale and along the Black Sea.[45]

The social characteristics of Jews in the Russian Empire are of immense significance here because their status there will explain in part how they were able to achieve economic success in America at a faster rate than other ethnic groups. The Jews were mostly urban dwellers while the non-Jews were predominantly rural:

In all Russia, 51 percent of all Jews lived in incorporated towns, as against only 12 percent of the non-Jews. Though the Jews constituted 4 percent of the total population, they constituted 16 percent of the town population. In the Pale, where they constituted 12 pecent of the total population, they comprised 38 percent of the urban population.[46]

As far as social class was concerned, the Jews had a distinct advantage over the non-Jews, partially because of their urban concentration and occupational pursuits. In Russia, townsmen ranked higher in social status than the peasants, the latter constituted 86 percent of the total Russian population.

Traditionally, the urban population constituted a higher cultural standard than the rural population; and in most cases, the urban population had a higher literacy rate than the rural population. The Russian census of 1897 revealed that the Jewish population contained one-and-one-half times as many literates as the total population of Russia, which indicates that the Jews traditionally placed a higher value on education than the rest of the Russian population.[47]

The economic and social status of the Jews in Romania and Austria-Hungary was somewhat the same as it was in Russia. The principal trades in which two-thirds of the Jewish industrial workers were concentrated were "tailors, shoemakers, tanners, joiners and planers, and bakers."[48] The Jews in Romania differed somewhat from the Jews in Russia in that the former were concentrated in the glass, clothing, wood and furniture, and textile industries, they controlled these enterprises.

Socially, the Romanian Jews presented the same social characteristics as the Russian Jews. Eighty percent of the Romanian Jews lived in either towns or villages and their educational standards were somewhat higher than the former.[49] However, their standard differed from the Jews' educational attainments in that the Romanian Jews had a higher literacy rate than the total Romanian population only in the age groups above fifteen, but the Romanian urban population between the ages of seven and fifteen had a higher rate of literacy than the Jews.[50] This is attributed to specific restrictions that the Romanian government placed upon the Jews' education. It placed a 10 percent quota upon the number of Jews who could attend public schools despite the fact that the government provided only a small number of public schools. It also limited the number of private schools that Jews could establish on their own behalf. The Romanian government feared that the widespread cultivation of the majority of the Jewish population would pose a threat to the security of the state.[51] Large sums of Russian monies were spent on loan interest, armaments, new highways, and on an exceptional police force and its administration; very little money was spent for the educational needs of the people.[52]

The economic position of the Jews in Austria-Hungary, to a large extent, paralleled that of the Russian and Romanian Jews. Seventy-three percent of the Austrian-Hungarian Jews were engaged in either commerce or trade. Statistics show that 44 percent were engaged in commerce and trade and 29 percent were engaged in farming in Austria-Hungary (because the restrictions placed upon the Jews engaged in farming there were not as severe as the restrictions in Russia). In Russia, Jews were forbidden by law to buy or rent land anywhere except in towns. But in Poland these restrictions applied only to the land that belonged to the peasants. The Jews had slightly more opportunity to engage in farming in Poland than they did in Russia.[53]

Socially, the Jews in Austria-Hungary presented somewhat the same social characteristics as did the Jews in Russia and Romania.[54] In almost all of the cities that were situated in the Pale of Settlement, which constituted 40 cities with a population of over 5,000, the Jews constituted 34 percent of the total population.[55]

The examination of the occupations, education, economic functions, and social characteristics of the Jews in Eastern Europe reveals that they constituted a large proportion of the industrial class in each country. When the Jews began to emigrate to America, they differed somewhat from the Italians and the Irish in that instead of being uneducated and poverty stricken, they were predominantly literate and skilled.

THE JEWISH EMIGRATION

In the early 1860s, the Russian empire began to undertake industrial development. In order to do so, it had to reorganize its economy and bring it into conformity with the rest of the western world. Such reorganization necessitated the abolition of the feudal system and the inevitable consequences of freeing numerous peasants from the land. After Russia emancipated its serfs in 1861, the economic condition became unstable. As time progressed, the peasants' living conditions became increasingly precarious, as their government needed to raise money for the construction of highways and railroads. At just about that time, the peasants turned their attention upon the Jews (who were the merchants and the middlemen), and blamed them for the miserable conditions.[56] The peasants began a series of anti-Semitic campaigns, which erupted into a riot in 1881. In 1882, the Russian government took up the persecution of the Jews by implementing the so-called "May Laws," which placed restrictions upon Jewish worship. They also barred Jews from agriculture, industry, the professions, public office, and equal access to educational opportunities.[57] The persecution of the Jews in the Russian Empire proceeded in a systematic manner from 1881 to 1891.[58] Under the ministry of Count Ignatieff, pogroms took place on a wide scale. The pogroms resulted in 21,500 Jews emigrating from the Russian Empire. But in 1882 and 1883, when the pogroms were forbidden because of a change in ministry, the Jews' emigration from the Russian Empire dropped to 11,920.[59] In May of 1882, a law was passed that prohibited Jews from cultivating any land or residing in villages outside of Pale of Settlement. This law precipitated another large exodus of Jews from the Russian Empire. As Table 7 indicates, the number of Jews who emigrated from the Russian Empire in the period 1889 to 1899 was 24,275.[60]

The early part of 1904 marked the beginning of the Russian Civil War, which was followed by the Bolshevik Revolution. Both events significantly disorganized the economic life of Russia and had a profound effect upon the state of Jewish people. Because they were involved in trade and

Table 7
Number of Jews Emigrating to the United States from Russia, 1889-1906

Years of Emigration	Number
1889-1899	24,275
1899-1900	37,011
1900-1901	37,660
1901-1902	37,846
1902-1903	47,689
1903-1904	77,554
1904-1905	92,388
1905-1906	125,284

SOURCE: Emigration Conditions in Europe (Washington: Government Printing Office, 1911), p. 280.

commerce, they felt the impact of these events differently than the rest of the population. The anti-Semitic feelings were more extreme than previously expressed, thus encouraging thousands of Jews to emigrate from Russia. They emigrated to many parts of the world, but the majority of them came to the United States.

Table 8 indicates that over 67 percent of the Jews who emigrated to America during this period were skilled workers. If the number of professionals, merchants, and dealers was added to the figures of the skilled workers, then it could be said that 73.7 percent of the Jews were skilled workers when they first made contact with America (see Table 8).

The only other ethnic group that matched the Jews in proportion of skilled occupations during this period of emigration were the Cubans, who constituted 22,396 of the immigrants. Of the Cubans, 66 percent were recorded as skilled workers.[61]

As has been demonstrated, the Jews were forced into the industrial occupations in Europe in response to the oppressive policies applied to them by the countries in which they lived. For instance, in Germany, Russia, and Switzerland, the Jews were highly concentrated in the legal professions.[62] The Christians scorned those occupations because lawyers were looked down upon as "debt collectors," a labeling which never occurred in England and France.[63] Ever since the Middle Ages, the Jews have been referred to as "people of the Books,"[64] because they ran the printing presses in many of the European countries after the Renaissance period. These endeavors prescribed a high degree of literacy. The same is true with banking, newspapers, theaters, and stockbrokering—occupations that the Jews dominated in Europe.

Table 8
Jewish Immigrants Reporting Occupations, 1888–1910

Group	Number	Percent
Professional	7,455	1.3
Skilled laborers	395,823	67.1
Laborers	69,444	11.8
Servants	65,532	11.1
Merchants & dealers	31,491	5.3
Farm laborers	11,460	1.9
Farmers	1,008	.2
Miscellaneous	8,051	1.3
Total	590,264	100.0

SOURCE: Samuel Joseph, Jewish Immigration to the United States: From 1881 to 1910 (New York: AMS Press, Inc., 1967), p. 187.

LINKAGES THE JEWS FASHIONED WITH AMERICA

The political linkages that the Jews fashioned with the American polity in their initial stage of contact were markedly different from those fashioned by other groups. In their response to political and economic oppression in Europe, the Jews had developed an immense amount of human capital, which allowed them to align themselves with a broad segment of the American economy. For example, they were able to fashion linkages with entrepreneurship, labor unions, and the learned professions. These occupations aligned them with the mother lode of society's income redistribution system. In fact, two-thirds of them settled in the four largest industrialized cities: New York, Chicago, Philadelphia, and Boston.[65]

Since the Jews had had over 500 years' practice at entrepreneurship, it was obvious that they would pursue entrepreneurship upon their disembarkation. The scientific significance of examining the Jews' entrepreneurial pursuits is that this study will shed some light on how the Jews were able to create new jobs in America. Many of the entrepreneurial occupations that the Jews pursued were occupations that they themselves created as a result of the managerial skills they brought with them.

One of the entrepreneurial skills that the Jews brought with them was the ability to detect a need for goods and services and design a delivery system to provide them. This practice helped significantly to develop America's system of redistribution of goods. From this system, the Jews were able to create numerous jobs for themselves over a period of years. For example, the occupations of the drummer and the peddler were created as a result of this system.

As the American economy grew, the peddler and drummer business increased to the extent that the Jews were able to develop a chain of retail stores, which later came to play a major role in the American economy. The origin of many of the chain retail stores in America can be traced to the works of a peddler or a drummer. These chain stores, however, were not developed overnight. It took a generation or so to accomplish this goal. The significant aspect here is that the persons who started these stores learned their skills by interacting in a human capital environment at some point in their lives. For example, names such as Macy's, Gimbel's, Strauss, Sears, Roebuck and Co., Rosenwald, etc., can be traced back in some shape or form to an enterprising peddler or drummer.[66]

Another advantage that the Jews had over other immigrants was their experience in international trade. Over the years, they developed some unique skills in this area. When they made contact with America, they were able to utilize these skills to help other Jewish entrepreneurs to develop their businesses. In many instances, the Jewish entrepreneurs who engaged in international trade were utilizing their international connections in trade, that is, Jews were trading with Jews in other countries.

Another advantage of international trade was that it enabled the Jews to go abroad and recruit capital for business investment. Money was sought by banking families, such as "Seligman, Schiff, Loeb, Lehman, and Warburg who helped recruit overseas capital for investment in the United States."[67] With this capital, the Jews were able to start new enterprises and purchase existing ones, particularly in the garment business.[68]

Although a considerable number of Jews were engaged in business, the majority of them were employed as craftsmen, artisans, and common laborers. The significance of this class of workers is that they contributed to developing the income redistribution system through organized labor.[69] The Jews immigrated at the time the labor movement was emerging from its infant's cradle to begin influencing public policy. The American Federation of Labor (AFL) had made significant headway in wresting the power to determine individual workers' civil rights to employment from the goodwill of management and placing them on a set of *de facto* principles. The Jews arrived just in time to ride in on the high tide of this movement.

Immediately upon their arrival, the Jews formed the United Hebrew Trades with its primary aim of improving the working conditions of the Jewish workers. The Jews were very labor conscious when they made contact with America. According to Oscar Handlin:

they had the advantage—or usually it proved an advantage—of leadership by a tiny but very aggressive minority of intellectuals and intellectually-minded workers trained in the most advanced trade unions of Europe, men who brought to New York and Chicago experience learned in the Russian *bunds* and in the English labor movement. These thinkers, having escaped from European oppression to the freedom of tenement and sweatshop, were radicals, anarchists, and socialists of many varieties. They regarded the trade union as an instrument in the battle against capitalism, a means of mobilizing the laboring masses for the inevitable struggle for power.[70]

Through the United Hebrew Trades, the Jews were able to organize working in both crafts and light manufacturing, where the Jews were highly concentrated. The Jews were much easier to organize because, in many instances, both the workers and the employers were Jews.[71] The employers did not seek court injunctions to block their employees from organizing, as was the case with non-Jewish employers. "There was indeed no love lost between the 'German' manufacturer and the 'Russian' proletarian; common religion, at first, actually heightened friction. But they could at least talk with each other."[72] With this relationship, the leaders of the United Hebrew Trades were able to organize 89 unions by 1910 with a total membership of over 100,000 in the three large industrialized cities: New York, Philadelphia, and Chicago.

The United Hebrew Trades eventually merged with the AFL. The Jews became deeply involved in union politics. From their rank emerged giant labor leaders, such as Samuel Gompers, who headed the AFL from 1886 to his death in 1924. The Jews' union activities need not be rehashed here. It suffices to say that they used the unions as instruments (1) to secure political and economic gains, and (2) to protect their civil rights to acquire property and to pursue a wide range of economic and employment opportunities. As we shall see in Chapter 8, the unions catapulted the Jews on to the middle-class plateau after the federal government clothed the unions with a *de jure* system of protection.

NOTES

1. G. M. Stephenson, *A History of American Immigration* (Boston: Ginn and Company, 1926), p. 87.

2. Emily Greene Balch, *Our Slavic Fellow Citizens, Charities Publication Committee* (New York: John Wiley and Sons, 1910), pp. 457-459.

3. For a discussion of the problems that workers underwent to establish principles of collective bargaining, see Douglas L. Leslie, *Labor Law* (St. Paul, Minn.: West Publishing Company, 1979), chapter 1.

4. Solon J. Buck, *The Agrarian Crusade,* A Chronicle of America Series (New York: United States Publishers Association, 1920), p. 101.

5. The Kerner Commission, *Report of the National Advisory Commission on Civil Disorder* (Washington, D.C.: Government Printing Office, 1968), pp. 287-292.

6. Andrew F. Rolle, *The American Italians: Their History and Culture* (Belmont, Calif.: Wadsworth Publishing Company, 1972), p. 57.

7. Ibid.

8. Robert F. Forester, *The Italian Emigration of Our Times* (New York: Russell and Russell, 1968), p. 87.

9. Ibid., p. 38.

10. Stephenson, *A History of American Immigration,* p. 65.

11. Forester, *The Italian Emigration,* p. 51.

12. Lawrence Frank Pisani, *The Italian in America* (New York: Exposition Press, 1957), pp. 46-47.

13. Joseph H. Senner, "Immigration from Italy," *North American Review* 5 (June 1896): 49-57.

14. Stephenson, *A History of American Immigration,* p. 64.

15. John R. Commons, *Races and Immigrants in America* (New York: Macmillan, 1913), p. 79.

16. Stephenson, *A History of American Immigration,* p. 69.

17. Ibid., pp. 67-69.

18. The Federal Writers' Project, *Italians of New York* (New York: Arno Press and the *New York Times,* 1969), p. 43.

19. Edward P. Hutchinson, *Immigrants and Their Children: 1850-1950* (New York: John Wiley and Sons, 1956), p. 121.

20. Kate H. Claghorn, "The Foreign Immigrant in New York City," United States Industrial Commission, *Reports on Immigration,* 42 vols. (Washington, D.C.: Government Printing Office, 1901), 15: 475.

21. Daniel J. Elazar, *Cities of the Prairie* (New York: Basic Books, 1970), p. 77.

22. Pisani, *The Italian in America,* p. 85.

23. The Federal Writers' Project, *Italians of New York,* p. 2.

24. Claghorn, "The Foreign Immigrant," p. 475.

25. Ibid.

26. Ibid.

27. Pisani, *The Italian in America,* p. 99.

28. The Federal Writers' Project, *Italians of New York,* p. 2.

29. Ibid., p. 72.

30. Reports on Immigration, Statistical Review of Immigrants 1820-1910, 42 vols. (Washington, D.C.: Government Printing Office, 1920), 3:132.

31. Maldwyn A. Jones, *American Immigration* (Chicago: University of Chicago Press, 1960), pp. 269-270.

32. Major W. Evans-Gordon, *The Alien Immigrant* (London: William Heinemann, 1903), chapter 4.

33. Israel Abrahams, *Jewish Life in the Middle Ages* (London: Macmillan, 1897).

34. Louis Wirth, *The Ghetto* (Chicago: University of Chicago Press, 1929).

35. Ibid.

36. Ibid., p. 24.

37. Abrahams, *Jewish Life in the Middle Ages,* pp. 240-241.

38. Max Weber, *The Protestant Ethic and the Rise of the Spirit of Capitalism* (New York: Charles Scribner's Sons, 1958), chapters 2-5.

39. Abrahams, *Jewish Life in the Middle Ages,* p. 214.

40. Wirth, *The Ghetto,* p. 25.

41. F. R. Bienenfeld, *The Germans and the Jews* (Chicago: University of Chicago Press, 1960), p. 3.

42. Samuel Joseph, *Jewish Immigration to the United States: From 1891 to 1910* (New York: Columbia University Press, 1914), p. 158.

43. Immigration Commission, *Emigration Conditions in Europe* (Washington, D.C.: Government Printing Office, 1911), p. 265.

44. Joseph, *Jewish Immigration,* p. 44.

45. Ibid., p. 45.

46. Ibid., p. 46.

47. Evans-Gordon, *The Alien Immigrant,* chapter 5.

48. Joseph, *Jewish Immigration,* p. 49.

49. Ibid., pp. 48-49.

50. Ibid., p. 50.

51. Immigration Commission, *Emigration Conditions in Europe,* p. 280.

52. Ibid.

53. See the tables in the back of Joseph, *Jewish Immigration,* and Immigration Commission, *Emigration Conditions in Europe* for a comprehensive view of the social and economic characteristics of the Jews in the Russian Empire.

54. Joseph, *Jewish Immigration,* pp. 51-52.

55. Ibid., p. 52.

56. Commons, *Races and Immigrants,* pp. 91-93.

57. Jones, *American Immigration,* p. 201.

58. Immigration Commission, *Emigration Conditions in Europe,* p. 280.

59. Ibid.

60. Ibid.

61. See Table 20 in the appendix.

62. Thorstein Veblen, "The Intellectual Pre-Eminence of Jews in Modern Europe," in *Essays in Our Changing Order,* ed. Leon Arozrooni (New York: Viking Press, 1934), pp. 219-31.

63. Bienenfeld, *The Germans and the Jews,* p. 17.

64. Ibid., p. 9.

65. Oscar Handlin, *Adventure in Freedom* (New York: McGraw-Hill Book Company, 1954), p. 99.

66. Ibid., pp. 174-210.

67. Ibid., p. 90.

68. Ibid., pp. 92-93.

69. Ibid., pp. 174-210.

70. Ibid., p. 132.

71. Ibid., p. 136.

72. Ibid.

5

Racial Ethnic Groups: Japanese, West Indians, and Puerto Ricans

This chapter critiques the conditions of life in the racial ethnic groups' homeland (or place from which they emigrated) and the economic, political, and social linkages they fashioned with the American polity (a place of immigration) in their initial stage of contact. The racial groups to be compared here are the Japanese, British West Indians, and Puerto Ricans. We are excluding the Hispanic groups and Blacks from this discussion. The problem with the former group is the U.S. Census Bureau tends to lump all Hispanic groups together. For example, there is no distinction made between the Hispanics emigrating from South America and those migrant workers who crossed the border from Mexico to perform agricultural work. Because of the many variables to be analyzed, Blacks will be discussed separately in Chapter 6.

It will be demonstrated in this chapter that if groups are granted a *de facto* or *de jure* system of protection to interact in a human capital environment, they will acquire the necessary capital to compete successfully in a competitive society regardless of their race. This human capital will prevent the culture of poverty from developing among the first and successive generations of immigrants.

We will also examine the question that is currently being asked concerning the role that race plays in groups' economic success; specifically, social scientists are addressing the question as to why racial groups such as the Japanese, West Indians, and Chinese have shown remarkable economic success and Blacks and the Puerto Ricans have not.[1] In an attempt to answer this question, I am going to select public policy, both *de facto* and *de jure,* as my basic unit of analysis. The many pitfalls a social scientist may encounter if he selects *racism* as his basic unit of analysis has been demonstrated in Chapter 1. This variable, to recapitulate, has a tendency to cloud those public policies that operate to foreclose groups' freedom to interact in a human capital environment.

The basic argument in this chapter is that the Japanese and British West Indians did not fall victim to the culture of poverty because of the human capital they brought with them, and the system of protection they had to safeguard their civil rights to acquire property and to pursue a wide range of employment opportunities in their initial stage of contact. However, the Puerto Ricans fell victim to the culture of poverty because (1) they did not have a system of protection, either *de facto* or *de jure,* which granted them the freedom to interact in a human capital environment either in their homeland or place of immigration, and (2) there was a set of *de facto* and *de jure* public policies that foreclosed their access to the mother lode of society's income redistribution system.

THE JAPANESE

The status of the Japanese in the United States has long been anomalous because they once were considered unassimilable. Yet they have not constituted a problem of social disorganization, as has been typical of the Irish. They are not Protestants; yet they have acquired what many call Protestant values. Like the Jews, the Japanese are highly represented in the liberal professions. According to the 1970 U.S. Census, for example, they ranked high in the social mobility indicators (educational attainments and income) when compared to twelve other ethnic groups studied in this cohort. Furthermore, the Japanese have achieved a high level of economic security. Harry H. L. Kitano attempted to explain this phenomenon in the following passage:

If, however, successful adaptation to the larger society consists mainly in acculturation, measured by the ability of a group to share and follow those values, goals, and expected behaviors of the majority, then the Japanese-American group has been very successful. Japanese-American values, skills, attitudes, and behavior apparently do not differ markedly from those of the average American. "Scratch a Japanese-American and find a white Anglo-Saxon Protestant" is a generally accurate statement.[2]

Many scholars attempt to attribute Japanese success to their strong family structure.[3] These scholars have simply identified the wrong variable in determining this group's economic success. The most fruitful and scientific question that one needs to ask along these lines is: What set of structural arrangements were the Japanese responding to that enabled them to develop such a high level of economic stability? In order to answer this and other related questions, let us turn to Japan and begin examining those structural conditions that granted them the freedom to interact in a human capital environment.

CONDITIONS OF LIFE IN THE JAPANESE HOMELAND

Unlike the European emigrants, the Japanese were not uprooted in their country by political oppression. Their emigration from Japan was characterized largely by an attempt by Emperor Meiji to modernize Japan in 1868. To achieve this goal, he signed the Magna Carta of Japan, which consisted of five Articles. One of these Articles dictated that "knowledge shall be sought throughout the world, so that the foundation of the Empire may be strengthened."[4] Before Emperor Meiji came to power, approximately 43 percent of the boys and 10 percent of the girls had some kind of schooling. After he signed the Magna Carta of Japan, education was made available to all. This provided the basis for a rapid increase in the literacy rate. By 1940, every educable Japanese child had an almost total uniformity of education in the first six years of schooling. This produced a "homogeneity of popular intellectual culture which has probably never been equaled in any society of 70 million people."[5]

The Japanese families were able to internalize the Articles of the Magna Carta of Japan because of their family tradition. The whole family was politicized to work toward the improvement of the Empire. Before Meiji came to power, the Japanese government had a long-standing ban on emigration, which had lasted for three-and a-half centuries.[6] Meiji lifted this restriction in 1868, when he decided to place Japan in competition with the Western world in terms of economic and military power. In doing so, he encouraged the Japanese to travel abroad to acquire Western knowledge, that is, human capital.[7] Within two generations, the Japanese family had internalized the Magna Carta of Japan into its cultural values. When the Japanese began emigrating to America, these cultural values were naturally reflected in their behavior patterns.

THE AMERICAN MAGNET

The factors that precipitated the large immigration of Japanese were the labor vacuum in Hawaii created by the Chinese Exclusion Act of 1883 and the stagnant agricultural economy of Japan. The large sugar plantations in Hawaii were in desperate need of laborers to cultivate cane. The plantation owners sent recruiters to Japan, the West Indies, the United States, and many European countries seeking laborers.[8]

The most successful recruitment effort in Japan was carried out by Robert Walker Irwin, an American businessman living in Japan and acting as consul general to Hawaii in the 1880s. He was successful in organizing the labor supply that the sugar planters so desperately needed because of the social conditions in Japan—widespread unemployment and social unrest.[9] In the southwestern part of Japan, the population was densely settled and had to survive on an inadequate subsistence of farming and fishing. Since the sugar planters of Hawaii were seeking laborers with an agricultural background, Irwin concentrated his recruitment efforts in this area.

JAPANESE CONTACT WITH AMERICA

When the Japanese made contact with the American polity, they were not issued a set of bootstraps as was the case with the Germans and Scandinavians. Because of the structural conditions in Hawaii, they were not able to form labor unions to take their civil rights to employment opportunities from the goodwill of their employers and place them on a set of *de facto* principles, as was the case of the Jews and Italians. Instead, the Japanese emigrated into an environment that was characterized by a severe labor shortage. This shortage provided them with a system of protection that granted them the freedom to interact in a human capital environment.

Under the Irwin system, a pattern of immigration was developed between Japan and Hawaii, which lasted up until the immigration restrictions of 1924. Japanese immigration was first restricted to Hawaii. But the labor shortage created by the Chinese Exclusion Act precipitated their immigration to the western states, that is, California and Washington, to meet the labor demands in the mines, canneries, lumber camps, railroads and farms, and in the domestic industry.[10] Before 1890, the number of Japanese immigrating to America was very low. For example, between the period 1861 and 1880, only 367 Japanese were reported immigrating to America. However, between the period 1881 and 1890, their number increased to 2,270 and continued to increase up to 1907 (see Table 9).

From 1901 to 1907, the Japanese immigration reached its peak; Japanese constituted 1.74 percent of all immigrants for this period. From 1915 to

Table 9
Number of Japanese Immigrated to the United States, 1861–1940

Period	Numbers	Percent of All Immigrants
1861–1870	218	0.01
1871–1880	149	0.02
1881–1890	2,270	0.04
1891–1900	27,982	0.77
1901–1907	108,163	1.74
1908–1914	74,478	1.11
1915–1924	85,197	2.16
1925–1940	6,156	0.03

SOURCE: William Petersen, Japanese Americans: Oppression and Success (New York: Random House, 1971), p. 15.

1924, Japanese immigration to America increased to 2.16 percent of the total immigrants; 85,197.[11] This increase in percentage can be accounted for by the restrictions that World War I placed on European immigrants. From 1925 to 1940, and up to the time that Japan and America went to war, Japanese immigration to America averaged a fraction under 400 per year.

When the Japanese began immigrating into Hawaii, they were predominantly agricultural workers. Because of their long policy of isolation, the Japanese had not created a class of merchants comparable in size or aggregated wealth to that of the Western World.[12] Consequently, their early contact with America (Hawaii) was characterized by a residual of farm laborers. An examination of their subsequent concentration in entrepreneurship and skilled occupation may seem on the surface to refute one of our basic arguments—that these behavior patterns are developed by interacting in a human capital environment in their homeland. But this anomaly can be explained by examining the way in which the Japanese responded to the structural conditions of Hawaii.

In Hawaii, the Japanese were able to develop behavior patterns for skilled occupations and entrepreneurship because the conditions in Hawaii granted them the freedom to interact in an entrepreneurial environment. First, Hawaii was not an attractive place in which to live during the latter part of the nineteenth century. There was a shortage of craftsmen and artisans, who were needed for necessary construction on the island. Reluctantly, the few white craftsmen and artisans gave a limited number of Japanese the positions as assistants to skilled workers.[13] Over the years, this practice created a residual of skilled workers as the number of white skilled workers began to decrease further.

As the Japanese increased the size of their skilled workers, a law was passed in 1903 designed to foreclose their freedom to pursue skilled occupations; but it was difficult to enforce this law because of economic necessity.[14] From 1903 through World War I, American industry underwent an expansion and thus tied the majority of the skilled white workers to industrial plants in the midwestern and eastern states. As a result, it became increasingly difficult for plantation owners to recruit skilled workers to Hawaii. Consequently, they were forced to use available Japanese laborers. Over a period of two decades these conditions allowed for the emergence of a class of skilled workers.

There was a shortage of white entrepreneurs. These circumstances encouraged the Japanese to develop skills necessary for occupations in entrepreneurship.[15] First, there was a demand for goods that could be obtained only from Japan. This demand offered the Japanese opportunities to become importers and merchants. They eventually formed a monopoly in the retail grocery and dry-goods stores in Hawaii.[16] Thus, when the Japanese began emigrating to America at the turn of the present century, they had developed a class of merchants and craftsmen.[17]

MIGRATING TO THE MAINLAND

When the Japanese first emigrated to the mainland, they filled the labor shortage in domestics and personal services and farm labor. Because they had developed the skills for small intensive farming in Japan, they began buying and leasing small plots of farmland. Between 1910 and 1920, Japanese farmers owned 16,000 acres of farmland and leased another 137,000 acres in California. By 1921, they owned 1.67 percent of the cultivated farmland, while constituting only 2 percent of the total population of California.[18] This rapid increase in independent farming resulted in a decrease in the number of Japanese farmhands and an increase in competition in the produce industry.[19] Consequently, California farmers concluded that the Japanese posed a serious threat to their economic security. Because of their propensity for small farming, the Japanese recreated the labor shortage in the United States which they were brought to relieve in the 1880s.

In order to check the diminishing agricultural labor supply, the California legislature passed anti-alien laws prohibiting the "ownership or leasing of land by aliens ineligible for citizenship and the purchase of land by American-born children of such aliens under parents' guardianship."[20] The alien laws were designed to foreclose the Japanese immigrants' freedom to acquire property in his American-born child's name. However, because of the human capital they brought with them, the Japanese constantly employed various tactics to circumvent these obstacles. This was the case up to the time that their land was confiscated in 1942, when the entire Japanese population was placed in American concentration camps.[21]

The Japanese immigrants' skills for small-intensive farming enabled them to corner and monopolize the fresh vegetable market in California, which was a multimillion-dollar market at the time. For example, for those marketable crops in which they specialized, they operated 3.9 percent of all the farms in the state and harvested 2.7 percent of all the cropland. But, they produced:

— ninety percent of the snap beans for marketing; celery, spring and summer; peppers; strawberries;
— fifty to ninety percent of the following: artichokes; cauliflower; celery, fall and winter; cucumbers; fall peas; spinach; tomatoes;
— twenty-five to fifty percent of the following: asparagus, cabbage, cantaloupes, carrots, lettuce, onions, watermelons.[22]

This growing monopoly over a multimillion-dollar market was the underlying reason why the Japanese were placed in the concentration camps. If national security were the primary reason, as policy-makers stated, they would have placed the Japanese in the concentration camps until the end of the war and released them afterward. Instead, they confiscated their land and did not return it after the war.

The concentration camps did not have the same devastating effect upon the Japanese social structure as the institution of slavery had upon Blacks, as we shall see. The Japanese were stripped only of their physical capital and not their human capital. It can be argued that they were pushed off the middle-class plateau onto the beaches of the culture of poverty the same as many of the other European immigrants. But they did not remain there long enough to allow the culture of poverty to develop among them. As we have seen with the Irish, it takes over two generations to destroy human capital within an ethnic group. When the census was taken of the Japanese in 1950, they had no deficit in human capital. For example, the average percentage of professionals for this cohort was 6.2 percent; the average for farmers and farm managers was 9.7 percent; the Japanese had 15.3 percent. However, they were below the average in the craftsmen category; the cohort was 20.8 percent while the Japanese accounted for 9.7 percent. But between 1950 and 1970, the percentage of Japanese engaging in the craftsmen category surpassed that of the cohort; the Japanese had 22.2 percent and the cohort was 18.3 percent.[23]

Besides the agricultural industry, the Japanese showed remarkable gains in entrepreneurship on the mainland. "By 1919, for example, 45 percent of the hotels and 25 percent of the grocery stores in Seattle were Japanese owned."[24] The U.S. Bureau of the Census in 1930 recorded that 40 percent of the Japanese males were entrepreneurs. And, it was recorded in 1929 that the Japanese and Chinese retail stores were proportionately more numerous than those of the whites.[25] Both the Japanese and the Chinese were able to gain a foothold in the economic system despite structural barriers and racism, which were designed to foreclose their freedom to acquire property. This achievement brings into consideration the broader question of how these racial minority groups achieved success in business in America while Blacks and the Puerto Ricans are still experiencing difficulties.

The argument that has so often been advanced to explain why Blacks have been unable to achieve economic stability is this: because of racism, they were unable to obtain the initial capital to start a business. It is then reasonable to ask how the Japanese and the Chinese overcame this barrier. Both the Japanese and Chinese were able to obtain initial capital to start a business because of their ancient tradition of raising capital through a rotating credit system (human capital).[26] This method of raising money provided an opportunity for them to start their small businesses. Traces of the rotating credit system can be found in southern China, Japan, and West Africa. As we shall see, the rotating credit system will, in part, explain how the British West Indians were able to gain an economic foothold in New York City while American Blacks and Puerto Ricans were not able to do so. Let us for the time postpone further discussion of these groups and consider a full elaboration of the rotating credit system.

The concept of the rotating credit system seems to have been developed in China some 800 years ago;[27] the Japanese adopted it from the Chinese in the thirteenth century,[28] and some evidence of its existence can be found in West Africa as early as 1794.[29] The method of the rotating credit system varied in each country, but its mechanical operation achieved the same end; raising initial capital for business.

The Chinese rotating credit system was called *Hui*, the Japanese, *Ko Tanomoshi* or *Mujin*, and the West African, *Esusu* or *Dashi*. Since the principles of the rotating credit systems are basically the same, the following passage, which explains the operation of the Chinese system, will suffice to explain, generally, how the system itself works.

The Chinese have a peculiar method of obtaining funds without going to commercial banks. If a responsible Chinaman needs an amount of money, he will organize an association, each member of which will promise to pay a certain amount on a specified day on each month for a given length of time. For instance, if the organizer wants $1,300, he may ask 12 others to join with him and each will promise to pay $100 each month for 13 months. The organizer has the use of the $1,300 the first month. When the date of the meeting comes around again, the members assemble and each pays his $100, including the organizer. All but the organizer, who has had the use of the money, bid for the pool. The man paying the highest bid pays the amount of the bid to each of the others and has the money. This continues for 13 months. Each man makes his payment each month, but those who have already used the money cannot bid for it again. By the end of the 13 month period, each will have paid in $1,300 and have had the use of the whole amount.[30]

The full extent to which the rotating credit system has been used by the Chinese, the Japanese, and the British West Indians is unknown. However, the system gives us a logical explanation for their success in business in a competitive and pluralistic society where the large money-lending institutions have a tradition of not lending money to small and new businesses.[31] The greatest benefit that this system had was to widen the range of choice possibilities for groups in their initial stages of contact with America.

One of the reasons why the Japanese were able to develop skills in the craftsmen category was that they lived in states where unionization was at a minimum. It was not until the late 1960s that the labor unions made any headway in the western states, like California and Washington. These states were among the last to repeal their right-to-work laws. Therefore, the unions were unable to foreclose the Japanese people's freedom to acquire skills, as they did to Blacks in the midwestern and eastern states (see chapter 6). Consequently, the Japanese were able to perpetuate and expand their class of craftsmen.

THE BRITISH WEST INDIANS

Recently, social scientists have paraded the relatively high rate of economic success of the British West Indians as evidence that *race* is not a factor in determining groups' economic success. This is particularly true when these scientists are attempting to cast doubt on the need for an affirmative-action policy for Blacks. They quickly point out that both groups were victims of perpetual slavery. Yet, the West Indians have shown a remarkable degree of economic success while Blacks have not. This section will be directed toward offering a scientific explanation as to why the West Indians are able to succeed in spite of their skin color.

In analyzing the West Indians, the structural conditions of the islands will be compared to the structural conditions of the American South to isolate the system protection that allowed the West Indians to acquire human capital.

The argument that is advanced in this section is that the primary reason the West Indians were able to fare so well economically was because they had a system of protection both in their homeland and their place of immigration that granted them the freedom to interact in a human capital environment. Thus, the human capital they brought with them and the system of protection that America provided them to safeguard their civil rights to acquire property and to pursue a wide range of employment and economic opportunities prevented the culture of poverty from developing among them.

STRUCTURAL CONDITIONS IN THE WEST INDIES

The structural conditions in the British West Indies were not designed to foreclose the West Indians' ability to acquire the necessary human capital to compete in a competitive society, as they were in the American South. Social stratification in the West Indies displayed some basic differences when compared to the latter structure.[32]

At the top of the social hierarchy in West Indian society were the British aristocrats (plantation owners), whose primary purpose for residing on these islands was economic. Below the aristocrats were the Black masses. There was no conflict over tangible values because it was clear the aristocrats owned the land as they did in the American South.

The major difference between the aristocracy of the American South and that of the British West Indies determined in part the race relations between Blacks and whites in both areas. In the American South, the aristocrats lived on the plantation with their wives and children. But in the West Indies, the planters themselves lived on the plantation and their wives and children for the most part were tucked safely away in England, where they could enjoy the cultural and social life of their mother country. Their children attended school in England and came to the islands only on short visits.[33] As a consequence, the plantation owners' families were far removed from the threats posed by the loss of those intangible values that were an inextricable part of the white southerners' way of life; that is, white supremacy.[34]

Comparatively, the economic conditions that created a vacuum for handicrafts, artisans, and entrepreneurs in the West Indies were absent in the American South. The majority of the goods the South consumed were manufactured. Thus, items such as shoes, dresses, suits, overalls, and hats were readily available both to Blacks and whites through the plantation stores, the towns, or the mail order houses; in the West Indies, these items were made by Black artisans and craftsmen.[35]

Long before their emancipation, the structural conditions of the West Indies were re-designed to encourage the slaves to develop a propensity for economics. Society was re-structured not for any humanitarian reason but through economic necessity. The following passage epitomizes this necessity:

Administrative necessity, furthermore, induced the West Indian slaveholders to institutionalize the operation of a slave economy. This indulgence reflected the shortage of whites which relieved West Indian slaveholders of the administrators necessary to supervise subsistence farming as an organized function of the plantation.[36]

These activities created a sense of economics among slaves in the West Indies. In 1820, the British Parliament passed the Consolidated Slave Act, which required slaveholders to provide rights and land, and free time for the slaves to cultivate their own land. All slaves did not wish to cultivate land; some of them pursued a trade or a craft, which encouraged the exchange of goods and thereby created small markets.

The whites did not attempt to interfere with the slave economy. They were afraid that such interference might initiate an insurrection. Thus, slaves in the West Indies preserved elements of their African heritage that seem to have been destroyed for Blacks in the American South. It was out of necessity, however, that the plantation owners allowed Blacks in the West Indies some degree of autonomy. This was due to the absence of a large number of lower class whites. The absence of this lower class group in the West Indies and its presence in the American South was an important structural difference.

In addition to the *de jure* system of protection that encouraged the West Indians to develop a propensity for economic self-sufficiency, structural conditions operated as a *de facto* system of protection. The political significance of this system is that it granted West Indians the freedom to interact in a human capital environment after their emancipation. As a consequence, they were able to acquire the necessary skills to compete successfully in a competitive society.

The most profitable skill the West Indians acquired in their homeland that enabled them to compete successfully in America was entrepreneurship. For example, the majority of the businesses that came under the heading of ethnic demands were owned and operated by the West Indians. On the contrary, in the American South, Black entrepreneurs were confined to shoeshine stands, beauty parlors, barber shops, funeral homes, and other service enterprises that the lower-class whites considered to be below their dignity.[37]

Because there was not a white middle-class living on the islands, the West Indians had the freedom to pursue many middle-class occupations, such as liberal professionals, doctors, lawyers, civil servants, etc. However, these occupations were set aside exclusively for middle-and lower-class whites in the South by law.

In British and French West Indian society, there were few if any structural conditions designed to foreclose Blacks' freedom to acquire the necessary human capital to achieve economic stability.[38] The Black middle-class in the West Indies consisted mostly of mulattoes who were sons and daughters of the white aristocrats, or persons related to them in some other way. As the white aristocrats left the islands, they either willed or sold their land to their mulatto children.

As time progressed, mulatto and middle-class became synonymous. Being a mulatto automatically placed a person psychologically in the middle class, while being Black automatically placed him in the lower and ultimately poorer classes. But this class line did not foreclose the freedom of Blacks to elevate themselves above their lower class status. Many dark-skinned Blacks were able to elevate themselves onto the middle-class plateau by the accumulation of wealth, acquiring an education, and through personal achievement.[39]

The British West Indians' emphasis on education was in the liberal professions. Unlike the American Blacks, who were forced into "industrial education," the British West Indians were interested in the theoretical aspects of education and not solely in the practical sides.[40] Not only did they pursue the liberal professions in some of the best universities in England and in France, but:

various islands' scholarships, e.g., the Rhodes scholarships and the Cambridge scholarships, selected students of unusual ability from the elementary schools of higher education. These scholarships enabled students of poor nurture but gifted with superior intelligence to rise above the social level of which they originally belonged.[41]

Prior to emancipation, the training of Blacks for the liberal professions was confined to European universities. The school that was built in the West Indies was located in Jamaica and was designed to tutor teachers for elementary schools.[42] The elementary schools were the most important social institutions to prepare Blacks for entry into middle-class employment.

There was no public policy of racial segregation in the public schools. Consequently, the growing West Indian child was not subjected to a public policy that denoted inferiority, as was the case with American Blacks. The only separate schools in the West Indies were those schools designed to remove the language handicap for the Asiatic populations. But in the United States, however, four-fifths of all Blacks' schools of higher education were segregated by law.[43]

Unlike the American Blacks, the British West Indians were not forced into a political socialization process, which was designed to stamp a natural feeling of inferiority into their hearts and minds.[44] Becoming docile and accommodating was not a precondition for granting them their rights to enter into the mainstream of society's income redistribution system. Instead, they were "taught from early infancy to stand up for their rights."[45] As a result of this process, the British West Indians were able to develop a tradition for argumentative "aggressive-type" people, and their "program and principle of accommodation has singularly been different from that of the American" Blacks.[46] Above all, the West Indians were socialized to assert their manhood in a society, like those in America and in England, which praised "heroism" and "strength," "assertion of manhood," and which condemned weakness as personal inadequacy and inferiority.[47] Hence, there is a contradiction in the American value system. It praised heroism and strength among white males; and at the same time, it promoted personal inadequacy and inferiority among Blacks.

When British West Indians first arrived in America in the early part of this century, they vociferously opposed any manifestation of discourtesy from whites, and such

designation as "George," "Sam," which was the white American frequent manner in addressing Negro men, was so emphatically resented by the West Indians, that many employers refused to hire them on that account, complaining that the West Indians did not make good servants.[48]

In short, the structural conditions of the British West Indies offered Blacks a system of protection that allowed them to acquire the skills necessary to compete in an industrial society.

THE WEST INDIAN MIGRATION

With the war drawing a large number of white men out of the labor force and the southern whites trying to keep Blacks in the South, industry began to focus on the untapped labor force in the West Indies in general and the British West Indies in particular because the latter had one of the largest labor forces.[49]

Economic conditions in the West Indies played an important role in Black migration from this area. In the 1890s, the island's staple crops—sugar and lime—had begun to decline. The aristocrats attempted to substitute their staple crops with cotton in the first decade of the twentieth century. This new crop, however, was not enough to employ the labor surplus that emerged at the end of the first decade of the present century.[50]

The labor force in the West Indies was predominantly Black.[51] The West Indians had begun emigrating to the United States in small numbers in 1901. From 1901 to 1910, it is estimated that 15,356 Blacks emigrated to the United States. But the largest number of British West Indians emigrated to the United States between the years of 1920 and 1924: 27,373.[52]

One important factor that differentiated the British West Indians from the American Blacks and Puerto Ricans was that British West Indians were from the British Commonwealth, and they had to emigrate under the provisions of the Immigration Act of 1917. This act excluded all persons over the age of sixteen who could not read or write, or had no specific skills. The practical political significance here is that such restrictions only allowed the middle-class, skilled workers, and the upwardly-mobile West Indians to emigrate to the United States.

Of the 6,873 West Indians who emigrated between the years of 1899 and 1990, 46.8 percent of them were classified as skilled workers and 8.3 percent were in the professional occupations. If we were to compute the skilled and professionals together, we would have over 66.1 percent of the British West Indian immigrants in skilled occupations. Of the 6,873, only 6.4 percent fell into the labor category, and 35.7 percent fell into other occupational categories.[53] The latter percentage consisted mainly of women and children. The political implications here are that over 90 percent of the British West Indians who emigrated to the United States had the skills necessary for economic stability. This large number of skilled and educated individuals helped prevent the culture of poverty from developing among them in their initial stage of contact.

Because a policy of accommodation and docility was not imposed on them on the islands, the British West Indians actively pursued skilled occupations on a broad scale. They were more aggressive than American Blacks along these lines and fared much better. They had no fear of the deprivation of their life, liberty, and property at the hands of their adversaries and competitors, because they had the full protection of the federal government while American Blacks and the Puerto Ricans did not. For example, when the labor unions attempted to foreclose their freedom to practice their trades, the West Indians had the option of calling upon the British Consul, who in turn would register a diplomatic protest with the United States government. This protest won them immediate release from racial oppression and job discrimination. The American Blacks, as we shall see, did not receive such a system of protection until the passage of the Civil Rights Acts of the 1960s, and these acts were not nearly so effective as the protection that foreign subjects received under the foreign diplomatic policy.

Shielded with such a system of protection, the British West Indians were able to maintain their middle-class status. Although they experienced some discrimination, it was not systematic enough to foreclose their access to the mother lode of society's income redistribution system.

Because of the system of protection that West Indians received as foreign subjects, they were, and are still today, slow in taking out American citizenship papers. The average West Indian knows that once he gives up his foreign citizenship status, there is the grave possibility that he will be subjected to the same form of injustice and systematic discrimination as American Blacks.

In short, the analysis of the West Indians demonstrates that racism can be overcome over a period of time if a group is granted a system of protection to interact in a human capital environment. They will acquire enough human capital and property to develop a pattern of economic self-sufficience.

THE PUERTO RICAN MIGRANTS

Although the Puerto Ricans came from one of the islands in the West Indies, they were not immigrants but migrants. Their migration was not restricted to skilled and well-to-do individuals as was the case with the West Indians and, to a small extent, the Japanese. Therefore, an analysis of their migration to the States and their subsequent behavior patterns will lend credence to our basic argument that acquisition of a sufficient amount of human capital is necessary to prevent a group from falling victim to the culture of poverty.

STRUCTURAL CONDITIONS IN PUERTO RICO

The experience from which the Puerto Rican migrants emerged differed markedly from the West Indians'. The Puerto Ricans had not acquired the necessary human capital to elevate themselves onto the middle-class plateau because the island of Puerto Rico had been under Spanish control for over 400 years.[54] The island did not develop economically because Spain did not experience an industrial transformation during the eighteenth and nineteenth centuries, nor did she keep pace with the rest of the Western European countries. At the turn of the present century, Spain was an agricultural country. It had not developed its industry to can and package foodstuffs, as was typical of United States industries. The Puerto Rican merchants, however, had developed a marketing system by which they bought rice, peas, beans, and other foods in Spain in bulk supply without brand names.[55] The United States, however, had begun to move rapidly toward packaging and labeling food products.

When the United States took control of the island in 1898, there were only two or three sugar centrals, and the rest of the industries—such as repair shops, mills, and the textile industry—were on the handicraft level. These industries operated with a small number of employees and machines. There were, however, a few cigar and cigarette factories; but shortly after 1901, the American Tobacco Company set up a subsidiary on the island and gradually bought up all such factories and gained complete control of these industries. This was the beginning of the cigar and cigarette mechanization process on the island. By 1909 the American Tobacco Company had driven over 75,000 workers out of this business—consequently making Puerto Rico's own tobacco factories obsolete. Within a period of ten years only 500 persons were employed in the island's tobacco industry.[56]

After Puerto Rico was included in the United States tariff system by proclamation of the President William McKinley in 1901, their merchants began importing goods from the mainland and thereby established their first trade system with the United States. By the end of that year, the United States was supplying Puerto Rico with seven-eighths of its value import while one-eighth was supplied by Spain and the rest of the European countries.

Like all other colonized nations, Puerto Rico's economy was designed to discourage native-born economic development. After the United States gained control of Puerto Rico, the island's system of land tenure was designed to accentuate agriculture. When the sugar industry was introduced, there was a consolidation of small farms into large ones. This measure encouraged the development of a large plantation system, which flourishes on cheap and unskilled labor. The introduction of the large plantation system had the same operative effect upon the class of Puerto Ricans' artisans and craftsmen as the Industrial Revolution had upon the English peasants. That is, it discouraged the development of a class of skilled workers.

From the end of World War I up to the mid-century, only sugar mills and needle trades were operating in Puerto Rico. Needle work was the largest hand-production industry in Puerto Rico; it was operated by women, who learned the trade through the Catholic schools. These schools required all females to learn needle work. When America took control of the island, makers of linens and women's and children's clothing sent representatives to the island to contract hand-work designs with the natives. By the end of World War I, a tradition had been established whereby Puerto Rican women produced hand-work for American industry.

During the same period (1899-1930) the island experienced an astronomical population growth. In 1899, the population was 953,000; it increased to 1,554,000 by 1930—with a density of one person per square mile.[57] By 1930, Puerto Rico was one of the most overpopulated islands in the Caribbean.

As in other parts of the Caribbean, the population in Puerto Rico consisted of whites, mulattoes, and Blacks. Puerto Rico, however, differed from the rest of the Caribbean in that while other island populations were predominantly Black, Puerto Rico was 74.3 percent white and 25.7 percent Black (see Table 10).

Table 10
Population of Puerto Rico by Race, 1950

Race	Number	Percent
Whites	1,146,719	74.3
Blacks	397,156	25.7
Other races	38	

SOURCE: U.S. Census of 1930, Outlying Territories and Possessions, Table 2, p. 136.

Despite their large percentage of whites, Puerto Ricans did not fare as well as the British West Indian immigrants, who were predominantly Black. Again, this supports one of our basic arguments, that race alone does not promote or constrain a group's economic mobility. The focus of analysis must be on government action.

The basic difference between these two Caribbean groups was in educational attainment. Under United States control, the island of Puerto Rico's literacy rate did not increase to any significant degree before the 1950s. When Puerto Ricans began to migrate in large numbers to the United States after World War II, 40 percent of the population was still illiterate.[58]

The Puerto Ricans began migrating to the United States in 1908. Their numbers did not increase above 8,000 until after World War II. As has been demonstrated, whenever economic instability occurs in any given society, those who usually emigrate first are the merchants and traders, aristocrats, the political elites, or the well-to-do. From 1908 to 1930, economic and social conditions in Puerto Rico were somewhat stable. Puerto Ricans who migrated before the 1930s were small merchants involved in cigar and cigarette making. By the beginning of the 1930s, Puerto Rico had begun to feel the impact of its population growth. At the close of World War II, America experienced a period of economic prosperity that created a labor shortage. Puerto Ricans became the logical source for cheap labor because the American South had released most of its surplus labor, and the immigration laws prohibited industry from turning to Europe.

PUERTO RICANS' CONTACT WITH THE UNITED STATES

After the war, the transportation link between Puerto Rico and the

United States improved significantly. Airplane fares to New York, which had been $180, dropped to $75 on regular lines and as low as $35 on certain special flights.[59] Puerto Ricans migrated directly to New York City, where they were employed in the garment factories. In 1950, 187,000 Puerto Rican adults and 58,460 Puerto Rican children were living in New York City.[60] The greatest number of Puerto Rican migrants to reach New York City was during the period between 1952 and 1953 when over 58,507 entered the city.

One interesting factor about this transition is that there was a large vacuum in the garment manufacturing and processing industry, which allowed the women to employ skills which they had acquired in Puerto Rico. Their migration was caused in part by extremely low salaries and the spiraling cost of living in Puerto Rico. Mechanization, however, did raise the standard of living on the island, but it did not significantly improve the lot of the Puerto Ricans. As the standard of living increased, so did the demand for goods, all of which had to be imported.[61] This discouraged the development of a large class of entrepreneurs as was the case with the West Indians.

One social consequence of the Puerto Rican migration to the mainland is the number of workers who were downgraded in occupational pursuits in their initial stage of contact with the northern industrial society. As Table 11 indicates, 42 percent of the men and 34 percent of the women experienced downgrading in occupational pursuits. These migrants consisted of skilled white-collar workers, and semi-skilled workers.

The downward mobility of the Puerto Ricans was very much contingent upon the status of the American economy. Upon their arrival in New York, the Puerto Ricans were forced to accept jobs on a much lower level than the ones they had in their homeland. The downward job mobility for the Puerto Rican women was in the white-collar and skilled categories. However, there

Table 11
Last Occupation in Puerto Rico to First Occupation in New York by Sex

Direction Mobility	Men	Women
Upward	13%	15%
Stable	45	51
Downward	42	34
Total (100%)	(265)	(258)

SOURCE: C. Wright Mills and Clarence Senior, The Puerto Rican Journey (New York: Harper and Brothers, 1950).

was a large percentage of Puerto Rican workers who remained on the same occupational level they had in Puerto Rico. This group consisted of 45 percent of the men and 51 percent of the women who worked in the garment manufacturing and processing industry. This industry required precision in dexterity, and the Puerto Ricans, over the years, had developed a tradition for this in the needle-work business.

The garment manufacturing industry was among the lowest paying industries in New York. Historically, it has been attractive to almost all waves of immigrants who lacked specific skills in their initial stage of contact.

Socially, the Puerto Ricans were very slow to learn the English language, and they avoided any radical attempt to rid themselves of any stigma of Spanish culture, particularly if they were Black or mulatto. If the latter two groups rid themselves of their Spanish accent, they would automatically be considered Black by whites and be subject to the discourtesy and systematic discrimination with which white Americans were accustomed to treating Blacks. Consequently, the Puerto Ricans tried at all costs to keep at arm's distance from Blacks because to be associated with the latter was to accept all the ascriptive inferior status that white society had systematically assigned to Blacks.

The migration of the Puerto Ricans did not radically improve their social status. Possibly the most significant positive factor about their migration is that it reduced overcrowding on the island.

Economically, the Puerto Ricans did not make any remarkable showing in entrepreneurship like the British West Indians. According to Daniel P. Moynihan and Nathan Glazer, the Puerto Rican Migration Division estimated that there were over 4,000 Puerto Rican-run businesses in the city of New York.[62] They took these figures, indicative of Puerto Rican advancement in business, as showing their superiority to Blacks. But a close examination of these businesses reveals that they were on the same level, though different in form, as the businesses that Blacks owned and operated in their communities; namely, these were businesses that received little or no competition from whites. For all practical purposes, these businesses were structured to meet ethnic consumer demands; that is, businesses such as "bodegas, little Spanish American food shops, on the side streets."[63] But the majority of the grocery stores in the Puerto Rican communities were owned and operated by the white ethnic groups, as was typical of the Black community. Service businesses such as barber shops, drug stores, and pool halls that catered exclusively to Puerto Rican clientele were owned and operated by Puerto Ricans.

Their occupational pursuits were hierarchically structured at the bottom of the American economic ladder, and they were systematically excluded from many of the low-paying jobs because of language barriers. They were particularly excluded from domestic services and other low-paying jobs that carried as a prerequisite a knowledge of the English language. Other service occupations that did not require knowledge of the English language, such as unskilled jobs in the city factories, hotels, and restaurants, employed large numbers of Puerto Ricans.

The Puerto Ricans were used as buffers to undercut the wage demands of Blacks. The former were willing to work on the same job with the latter but at lower wages. This situation in itself precipitated resentment among Blacks toward Puerto Ricans.

The Puerto Ricans had some experience with trade unions when they migrated to New York. They joined the International Cigar Makers' Union and the Spanish-speaking branch of the International Ladies' Garment Workers' Union. On the whole, the Puerto Ricans did not care much for the trade unions because the unions practiced discrimination. Unlike the British West Indians, the Puerto Ricans could not call upon any foreign consul to seek release from job discrimination.

The Puerto Ricans arrived in the States after the National Labor Relations Act had been fully implemented by the labor unions. As we shall see in Chapter 7, the political significance of this act is that it took workers' property and liberty interest rights to skilled employment from the goodwill of management and placed it on a principle of law. As the unions became more powerful, they augmented their power to foreclose the freedom of Blacks and Puerto Ricans to enter into the mainstream of society's income redistribution. This exclusion provided the foundation for the development of the culture of poverty among the Puerto Ricans and Blacks.

Although America was a nation of wealth at the time of their migration, the Puerto Ricans found very little release from the yoke of poverty at the end of their voyage. There were no government-issued bootstraps waiting for them, as there were for the Germans and Scandinavians who found 160 acres of free land and free universities. Nor were they able to benefit from a system of protection provided by the unions, as did the Jews, Italians, and Poles (see chapter 8). The conditions in their homeland did not allow them to amass the necessary human capital to compete successfully in a capitalistic society, as did the Japanese and West Indians. In short, the Puerto Ricans left their homeland to escape the jaws of poverty just to be pinned down on the beaches of deprivation and degradation in America.

NOTES

1. Stanley Lieberson, *A Piece of the Pie: Black and White Immigrants Since 1880* (Berkeley: University of California, 1980), pp. 5-6.

2. Harry H. L. Kitano, *Japanese Americans: The Evolution of a Subculture* (Englewood Cliffs, N.J.: Prentice-Hall, 1969), p. 3. The acquisition of some selected middle-class values has been documented by empirical study. See Abe Arkoff, "Need Patterns in Two Generations of Japanese Americans in Hawaii," *Journal of Social Psychology* 50 (August 1959): 75-79.

3. William Caudill, "Japanese-American Personality and Acculturation," *Genetic Psychology Monographs* 45 (February 1942): 3-102.

4. William Petersen, *Japanese Americans: Oppression and Success* (New York: Random House, 1971), p. 157.

5. R. F. Dore, "Japan As a Model of Economic Development," *European Journal of Sociology* 5 (1964): 138.

6. Maldwyn A. Jones, *The American Immigration* (Chicago: University of Chicago Press, 1960), p. 204.

7. Petersen, *Japanese Americans,* p. 157.

8. Hilary Conroy, *The Japanese Frontier in Hawaii: 1868-1896* (Berkeley: University of California Press, 1953), pp. 9-13.

9. Petersen, *Japanese Americans,* p. 9.

10. Carl Wittke, *We Who Built America* (Cleveland: Case Western University Press, 1964), p. 480.

11. Petersen, *Japanese Americans,* p. 16.

12. Ibid., p. 153.

13. U.S. Bureau of Labor Statistics, *Report of the Commissioner of Labor on Hawaii: 1902* (Washington, D.C.: Government Printing Office, 1903), p. 31.

14. Ibid., pp. 45-55.

15. Conroy, *The Japanese Frontier,* p. 100.

16. Petersen, *Japanese Americans,* p. 25.

17. Ibid.

18. Wittke, *We Who Built America,* p. 481.

19. Ivan H. Light, *Ethnic Enterprise in America* (Berkeley: University of California Press, 1972), p. 9.

20. G. M. Stephenson, *A History of American Immigration* (Boston: Ginn and Company, 1926), p. 274.

21. See Edward S. Corwin, *Toward War and the Constitution* (New York: Knopf, 1947).

22. U.S. Congress, House Select Committee, *Investigation of National Defense Migration,* 77th Congress, 2d sess., 4th Interim Report (Washington, D.C.: Government Printing Office, 1953), pp. 117-118.

23. See Tables 24 and 26 in the appendix.

24. Light, *Ethnic Enterprise,* p. 10.

25. U.S. Department of Commerce, Bureau of the Census, *Fifteenth Census of the United States: 1930,* vol. 1, *Distribution,* pt. 1. "Retail Distribution" (Washington, D.C.: Government Printing Office, 1933); Table 12-C, p. 180, and Table 12-B, p. 615.

26. Shirley Ardener, "The Comparative Study of Rotating Credit Associations," *Journal of the Royal Anthropological Institute* 94, pt. 2 (1964): 201-29.

27. See Daniel H. Kulp, *Country Life in South China,* 2 vols. (New York: Columbia University Press, 1925).

28. See John F. Embree, *Suye Mura: A Japanese Village* (Chicago: University of Chicago Press, 1939).

29. Ardener, "*The Comparative Study,*" p. 209.

30. Helen F. Clark, "The Chinese of New York Contrasted with Their Foreign Neighbors," *Century* 53 (November 1896): 110.

31. Alfred R. Oxenfeldt, *New Firms and Free Enterprise* (Washington, D.C.: American Council on Public Affairs, 1943).

32. D.A.G. Waddel, *The West Indies and the Guianas* (Englewood Cliffs, N.J.: Prentice-Hall, 1967).

33. Barrington Dunbar, "Factors in Cultural Backgrounds of the British West Indian Negro and the American Southern Negro That Conditioned Their Adjustment in Harlem" (Master's Thesis, Columbia University, 1936), p. 26.

34. For a discussion on racism and white supremacy, see Thomas G. Gosset, *Race: The History of an Idea in America* (Dallas: SMU Press, 1963), chapters 1-5.

35. Dunbar, "Factors in Cultural Backgrounds," p. 7.

36. Light, *Ethnic Enterprise*, p. 38.

37. E. Franklin Frazier, *The Negro in the United States* (New York: Macmillan, 1965), chapter 13.

38. Stuart B. Philpott, *West Indian Migration: The Monserrat Case* (New York: Athlone Press, 1973), p. 65.

39. Dunbar, "Factors in Cultural Background," p. 13.

40. Ibid., p. 26.

41. Ibid.

42. Ibid.

43. Ira De A. Reid, *The Negro Immigrant* (New York: Columbia University Press, 1939), pp. 48-49.

44. See E. Franklin Frazier, *Black Bourgeoisie* (New York: Collier-MacMillan, Ltd., 1957), p. 112.

45. Reid, *The Negro Immigrant,* p. 110.

46. Ibid., p. 49.

47. See William H. Grier and Price M. Cobbs, *Black Rage* (New York: Bantam Books, 1968), chapter 4.

48. Roi Ottley and William J. Weatherby, eds., *The Negro in New York* (New York: Oceana Publications, 1942), p. 191.

49. See Table 20 in the Appendix.

50. Philpott, *West Indian Migration,* p. 27.

51. See Table 20 in the Appendix.

52. Reid, *The Negro Immigrant,* p. 236.

53. U.S. Immigration Commission, *Statistical Review of Immigration 1820-1910* (Washington, D.C.: Government Printing Office, 1911), p. 96.

54. C. Wright Mills and Clarence Senior, *The Puerto Rican Journey* (New York: Harper and Brothers, 1950), p. 43.

55. Thomas C. Cochran, *The Puerto Rican Businessman* (Philadelphia: University of Pennsylvania Press, 1959), p. 23.

56. Ibid., p. 33.

57. Martin B. Sworkis, *The Impact of Puerto Rican Migration on Governmental Services in New York City* (New York: New York University Press, 1957), p. 7.

58. Lawrence R. Chenault, *The Puerto Rican Migrant in New York City* (New York: Columbia University Press, 1938), p. 43.

59. Mills and Senior, *The Puerto Rican Journey,* p. 44.

60. Puerto Rico. Department of Labor. Migration Division. *A Summary in Facts and Figures* (New York: Commonwealth of Puerto Rico, Migration Division,

Department of Labor, April 1957).

61. Chenault, *The Puerto Rican Migrants,* pp. 124-125.

62. Ibid., p. 79.

63. Christopher Rand, *The Puerto Ricans* (New York: Oxford University Press, 1958), p. 7.

6

The Chief Cause of Blacks'
Economic Inequality

Ever since the Kerner Commission Report posed the question "Why have Blacks been unable to escape the slums as did the European immigrants?" social scientists have been busy cranking out voluminous reports and studies that try to explain the reasons why.[1] Among these reports is a body of literature that purports to present a new view of slavery.[2] The thrust of these writers, it seems, is to drive home the point that the institution of slavery had a positive effect upon Blacks; "Whatever blame there was for the unsatisfactory conditions of blacks after the Civil War thus rested with a class that no longer exists (the master class), or unfortunately, with blacks themselves."[3] This chapter, demonstrates that the present-day condition of Blacks is a function of a series of repressive public policies adopted after emancipation.

Since the theme of this work is that groups' economic success is contingent upon their civil rights to acquire property and to pursue a wide range of employment and economic opportunities resting upon a principle of law and not on the goodwill of their adversaries and competitors, we must then begin our mode of analysis at the signing of the Emancipation Proclamation and trace the conditions of Blacks' life from this period up to the time of their migration. Consequently, these groups were unable to develop a pattern for economic self-reliance from emancipation to the present day. During this same period, the federal government placed the civil rights of the immigrating European groups of the 1860s and 1870s on a principle of law; therefore, they were able to elevate themselves to the middle-class plateau.

Placing Blacks' rights on the goodwill of their adversaries and competitors contradicts the Madisonian theory of democracy for a free society. Madison argued, to recapitulate, that there can be no *liberty* either for the minority or the majority when the powers to legislate, execute, and judge are concentrated in the hands of the same individuals, whether these individuals are in the minority or the majority.[4] This theory applies equally to the freedom of groups to pursue their goal of economic self-reliance.

The question of whether or not the present-day blame for Blacks' unsatisfactory conditions should be placed on Blacks themselves or on some external factors can be settled by asking this one fundamental question: Is there sufficient evidence to support the contention that Blacks' civil rights, historically, have rested on a principle of law or instituted upon the goodwill of their adversaries and competitors? If the latter is the case, then the blame must rest with the structural arrangement of the political system that failed to safeguard Blacks' access to the mother lode of society's income redistribution system.[5]

EMANCIPATION WITHOUT A SET OF BOOTSTRAPS

In an attempt to explain the cause of inequality among Blacks, social scientists too often compare the manner in which Blacks were brought over to America to that of the European immigrants. Such comparison inevitably forces scientists to focus on family structure as an independent variable. What usually follows from such analysis is a mechanical elaboration of how the institution of slavery detribalized and annihilated Blacks as human beings, destroying the memory systems that transmit group culture and values in a positive manner from generation to generation.[6] What these scientists overlook in such an analysis is the fact that the government failed (1) to issue Blacks a set of bootstraps after emancipation, as it did the European immigrants; and (2) to provide Blacks with a system of protection that would safeguard their civil rights to enter the mainstream of society's income redistribution system.

If America had followed through with its proposal to allocate each Black family forty acres and a mule after emancipation, that would have served as a dike against the stream of the culture of poverty. This measure would have anchored Blacks at the dock of economic self-reliance within the first generation of their emancipation. The second generation of Blacks would have flourished upon the land they inherited from their parents. But the northern industrialists who held the reins of power over the southern economic system after emancipation were not interested in designing a system of protection to ensure Blacks' full enjoyment of the American democratic values; that is, income, safety, and deference.[7]

The rationale that policy-makers gave at the time for not allocating Black families forty acres and a mule was anchored in the American democratic assumption that anyone who wanted to could pull himself up by his bootstraps. Parceling out land, they further argued, would add to the huge national debt.[8] But this argument was a contradiction to the existing public policy. At the time that policy-makers were arguing against giving Blacks forty acres and a mule, Congress had passed the Homestead Act of 1862, which, as we have seen, constituted a set of bootstraps on a silver platter (i.e., free land) for the Germans and Scandinavians. Instead of offering these groups just forty acres, the government gave them 160 acres of land, under the Homestead Act, and colleges under the Morrill Act of 1862. These colleges had the operative effect of ensuring that the culture of poverty would not develop among them.[9]

Offering ex-slaves a set of bootstraps after emancipation was nothing new. When Russia freed her slaves in 1861, she not only gave them the land on which they had previously worked, but provided them with a system of protection that safeguarded their liberty and property interest rights to purchase land. Before Russian slaves were freed, Alexander II issued several "rescripts" to the nobles in Libenean providence asking them seriously to consider the possibility of emancipating their serfs, on the basis of the following mandatory principles: "(1) the right of the emancipated serf to buy the plot of land on which he lives, (2) the right to buy a parcel of land based upon his needs and ability to pay."[10] To ensure their orderly and proper adjustment to their new status, Alexander II established a statute of "temporary obligation," which allowed the newly freed slaves to enter into an agreement for a period of twenty years to purchase land from the landowners.[11] The operative effect of this time period was that it allowed the slaves to develop a sense of self-determination at their own pace.

The twenty-year period in which the Russian slaves could purchase land from their former masters is of political significance here. The time period constituted almost a generation in which the skills for economic self-reliance (i.e., acquiring human capital) could be developed among the newly freed slaves. On the contrary, the system of protection that America gave her slaves to purchase land, that is, the Confiscation Act of 1861, lasted fewer than five years.[12] The act allowed the federal government to confiscate the land of the Civil War rebels and prevented them from owning land afterward. Consequently, millions and millions of acres of land were suddenly made available for anyone, except the ex-confederates, to purchase. Blacks took advantage of this opportunity by purchasing a large portion of this land without government assistance; that is, under the Freedmen's Bureau.

THE FREEDMEN'S BUREAU AND THE QUEST FOR ECONOMIC SELF-RELIANCE

Despite the fact that the government refused to issue Blacks a set of bootstraps, unlike what it was doing for white European groups at the time, Blacks still would have achieved economic self-reliance within a generation if their property and liberty interest rights to pursue economic opportunities had been placed on a principle of law. Upon the heels of their emancipation, Blacks had an extraordinary craving for land. They perceived owning land as being a precondition for real emancipation.[13] With the aid of the Freedmen's Bureau, Blacks moved at a miraculously rapid pace in acquiring land with their own resources. The Freedmen's Bureau was "financed not by taxation but the tolls of ex-slaves; the total amount of rent collected from land in the hands of the bureau, paid mostly by Negroes, amounted to $400,000, and curiously enough it was this rent that supported the bureau during the first years."[14]

Under the Freedmen's Bureau Act of 1865, Congress gave the President the Authority to appoint a commissioner of the bureau. This act temporarily gave the ex-slaves a system of protection that safeguarded their civil rights to purchase land. The commissioner had the authority to lease unoccupied tracts of land, not exceeding forty acres, to ex-slaves and white refugees for a period of three years. At the end of this period, the tenants had the right to purchase the land.[15]

Further evidence of the ex-slaves' propensity for self-reliance was their enthusiastic support of the Freedmen's Saving and Trust Company. The bank was chartered by Congress in March of 1865. It emanated from the effort of several "Union commanders to establish banks in their departments for Negro soldiers."[16] The bank was established by a group of philanthropists.[17] This group took great care to ensure that the bank was established on solid business principles. For example, the group provided that at least two-thirds of the bank's deposits were in government securities. The bank was authorized to use any surplus funds to promote the cause of education among Blacks. Under this charter, the bank was allowed to pay a maximum interest of 7 percent.

The Freedmen's Savings Bank probably was the wealthiest and most financially secure bank in the country at the time. It was reported that in 1874 its total deposits reached approximately $57,000,000.[18] Because two-thirds of these deposits were secured by government bonds, the only way that the bank could have gone under was for the federal government itself to have collapsed, which, at the time, rested within the realm of the impossible. Again, the Freedmen's bank was the only bank in the country chartered by the federal government, and it had a captive clientele of approximately 4 million potential depositors. This factor contributed to its rapid growth in a very short period of time.

Although the bank's headquarters was located in Washington, D.C., it had 27 branches situated throughout the South and in several northern states, including New York and Pennsylvania.[19] Around the 1870s, the board of trustees of the bank changed hands and the solid foundation on which it rested began to crumble. The new trustees were attracted to the bank's enormous assets. In 1870, they introduced a bill in Congress to amend the bank's charter so that one-half of the deposits already invested in government bonds could be invested in other notes and real estate mortgages.[20] This land opened the bank's vault to predators, and the hard-earned savings of the newly freed men were lost within a period of three years.

The practical political repercussion that the bank charter amendment had upon Blacks' status is that it took their property and liberty interest rights to pursue a goal of self-reliance off a principle of law and placed them at the mercy of their competitors and adversaries. This measure helped to foreclose Blacks' freedom to purchase land on their own. Furthermore, many southern state governments opposed the branch banks in their states because they had no control over them. And they could not carry out their policy of re-instituting slavery through the guise of the Black Codes unless they could make Blacks totally dependent upon their goodwill.

To further foreclose Blacks' freedom to become self-reliant, President Andrew Johnson issued his Proclamation of Pardon for the ex-confederates. From this day onward, these individuals were able to reclaim their land. Before the pardon, they could not legally "reclaim their property until they had been pardoned and had taken the oath."[21] President Johnson had declared before the war that the large plantations would be seized and divided into small farms. But his issuance of the pardon contradicted this practice.

The condition of Blacks shortly after the issuance of the pardon began to take a nose-dive from which they were unable to recover to the present day. Blacks who had bought land with their hard-earned money were pushed off it by the Ku Klux Klan, which was created shortly after the Civil War. The influence of the Freedmen's Bureau began to diminish because Congress significantly curtailed its funds and authority. For example, in 1865, the Bureau controlled approximately 800,000 acres of land. In 1868, these acres had been reduced to fewer than 140,000.[22]

President Johnson's Proclamation of Pardon affected Blacks more than economically; it also affected them psychologically; it caused them to lose faith that the federal government would grant them a fair deal. Despite the pardoning of the ex-confederates, however, many Blacks were able to buy lands throughout the South before the Freedmen's Bank collapsed in 1874. For example,

Virginia Negroes acquired between 80,000 and 100,000 acres of land during the late sixties and early seventies. There were soon a few prosperous Negro farmers with 400 to 1,000 acres of land and some owners of considerable city property. Georgia Negroes had bought, by 1875, 396,658 acres of land, assessed at $1,263,902, and added to this they had town and city property assessed at $1,203,202.[23]

THE BLACK CODES AND THEIR EFFECT ON BLACKS

The public policy that had the most profound effect in restraining Blacks' freedom to develop a pattern of self-reliance was the Black Codes. Although the stated purpose of these codes was to regulate labor, their operative effect was to reduce the status of Blacks, that is, economically, politically, socially, and psychologically, to a subordinate position to whites both in-law and in-fact. To achieve this end, southerners attempted to divorce Blacks's minds from the land by creating conditions whereby they could be tied to the plantation system physically without becoming psychologically a part of it. This was the same status that Blacks had during slavery. The major difference between this condition and slavery was that under the former condition the slave-masters had to pay for their slaves; but afterward, they could get free labor by re-enslaving Blacks through these codes.[24]

Political Effect

The political effect that these codes had upon Blacks was that they operated to foreclose Blacks' freedom to enjoy those rights created by the Emancipation Proclamation, and the Thirteenth, Fourteenth, and Fifteenth amendments to the Constitution.[25] Second, the Black Codes became political tools by which employers fenced Blacks in on the plantations in such a way that they could not leave even if they desired to do so. For example, the codes stipulated that Blacks were free to choose their employers at the end of each year. But this was possible if, and only if, they had cleared their debts with their former employer. However, the employer had the sole authority to determine whether or not the tenants' debts were cleared; he kept the books. Any discrepancy that the tenant found in the employer's record-keeping was settled by the employer himself. Under the Black Codes, Blacks could not dispute the white man's word, because such a dispute constituted an act of disobedience and the employer had the authority to fine them $1 for every offense.[26]

The codes gave plantation owners the legal right to work Blacks a whole year without paying them a penny. There was no redress that Blacks could resort to for a denial of their basic constitutional rights. Thus, these codes institutionalized the white man's words as the law of the land as far as Blacks were concerned; a practice that lasted until the civil rights movement of the 1950s and 1960s.[27]

Social Effect

The absolute authority that the Black Codes gave whites over the lives of Blacks significantly affected their social development. They prescribed the

Black male to a caste system, which molded his social and political behavior into a Sambo or Uncle Tom personality type.[28] For example, these codes prescribed that Black males conduct themselves "properly"; that is, they demanded "obedience to all proper orders"—that his employer gave him.[29] The social significance of this law was that the term "obedience to all proper orders" was left solely up to the arbitrary and capricious interpretation of the employer. The employer had the discretion to interpret "proper orders"—ranging from leaving home without permission; to impudence, swearing, or indecent language to or in the presence of the employer, or members of his family, or his agent; to quarreling or fighting among one another.[30] Thus, the authority to levy penalties for disobedience was the tool by which employers could foreclose Blacks' freedom to develop their skills and talents. The operative effect of this practice was that the Black Codes became the catalyst that prevented Blacks from developing a sense of self-determination; and thereby creating the sense of dependency they currently have.

Economic Effect

Economically, the Black Codes were a public policy that kept Blacks legally in slavery without the economic liability that accompanied the institution of slavery. For example, the life of an adult male slave had a value ranging from $500 to $1,400. After slavery, this value was removed and the life of a Black worker became penniless to the plantation owners;[31] they were free to hang Blacks at will, while during slavery such an act would have constituted an economic loss to the slave-master.

As we have seen, Blacks had a burning desire to purchase land after their emancipation. In order to develop economically, a group must have a system to protect their freedom to interact in a human capital environment. The codes not only prevented Blacks from interacting in such an environment, but also foreclosed their freedom to take advantage of a wide range of other economic opportunities in society.

Psychological Effect

In addition to foreclosing Blacks' freedom to pursue a wide range of occupations, the Black Codes constrained the full development of their personalities, that is, discouraged the development of a sense of self-determination. These codes not only denied Blacks America's basic ideals, such as freedom of speech, assembly, petition, and expression, but also societal goal values; that is, shared power, income, safety, and deference.[32]

The American democratic values that the Black Codes denied Blacks were as important to the development of their personalities as air is to fire. The political significance of democratic values in relationship to the development of the personality has been thoroughly analyzed by Harold D. Lasswell. The whole of his writings is dedicated to analyzing the relationship between public policy and society's respect for human dignity.[33]

Lasswell demonstrates that there is a close relationship between public policy and the development of individuals' personalities. He argues that the individual's personality is developed by the degree to which the environment increases or decreases societal goal values. The personality, he argues, "is an on-going concern which is constantly relating itself as a whole to the environment in which it lives."[34] It expects to acquire societal goal values and, when certain design factors deprive it of these expectations over a given period of time, it "exhibits substitutive activities. The substitutive activities . . . will be in the direction of restoring the level of expectation which is usual for the person."[35] In analyzing the sociology of Blacks, E. Franklin Frazier found that Blacks had substituted American goal values, such as owning a home in the suburbs (appreciative goods), with purchasing conspicuous consumption goods (depreciative goods).

THE DOCTRINES OF RACISM AND THE INSTITUTIONALIZATION OF RACIAL INFERIORITY

There are two doctrines of racism that have been adopted to control Blacks: romantic racism and Social Darwinism. Both of these doctrines provided the basis for the formulation of those policies that fostered racial inequality. The doctrine of romantic racialism was adopted in the 1830s.[36] We are going to defer discussing the impact that this doctrine had in formulating public policies of repression until Chapter 8. Instead, we are going to focus on Social Darwinism, which had its greatest expression after the Civil War.

The Black Codes within themselves were not sufficient to place Blacks in a position of inferiority economically, socially, and psychologically. The southern and northern industrialists felt it necessary to adopt a doctrine of racism to achieve this end. This doctrine is better known as "Social Darwinism." The Social Darwinists extended the interpretation of the biological theory of evolution into a theory of the development of society and civilization. They argued that the status of a race in society was the product of natural evolutionary forces, which consisted of struggle and conflict in which the stronger and more advanced race would naturally triumph over the inferior and weaker race.[37]

The Social Darwinian Theory received its maximal significance in the concept of the "white man's burden" and "manifest destiny," which had the inevitable political consequence of conditioning Blacks to become docile and accommodating people. Briefly, these concepts that were advocated by social scientists and churchmen alike, argued that white Americans were destined either by natural force or by the *will of God* to rule North America and possibly the rest of the world. In addition, all non-whites were incapable of self-government. This creed, in effect, gave the white race a moral and theological justification for genocide of the non-white races.[38]

As Social Darwinism began to permeate the American thought pattern, the power elites had problems keeping Blacks in the South. These problems centered around several factors. First, there was Horace Greeley calling, "Go West, young man, go West." Second, economic conditions for Blacks had begun to worsen. With the collapse of the Freedmen's Savings Bank, Blacks were unable to secure capital to purchase land. With their inability to elevate themselves economically through the tenancy and sharecropping systems, coupled with cruel treatment by landlords and merchants, Blacks had little incentive to remain in the South. As early as 1879, Blacks began abandoning the South and adhering to Greeley's call to go West. To encourage their migration, Henry Adams of Louisiana and "Pop" Singleton of Tennessee started organizing Blacks for the westward movement. Consequently, thousands of Blacks began migrating from Mississippi, Louisiana, Alabama, Georgia, and Tennessee. "Adam claimed to have organized 98,000" Blacks from Tennessee alone.[39]

This westward movement posed a serious threat both to the southerners' and the northern industrialists' plans for economic development of the South. If left unchecked, the elites felt the movement would rob the South of its irreplaceable cheap labor force—which was necessary for growing cotton.[40] To remedy this problem, whites needed two things: a policy of social control and a Black propagandist whom they could trust and control to impose their policy on Blacks.

The purpose of the social control policy was to convince Blacks not to subscribe to Horace Greeley's urgent plea to "Go West, young man, Go West," but instead to stay in the South. To this end, the elite class recruited Booker T. Washington as the chief spokesman for the Black race.[41]

This effort to keep Blacks in the South is manifested in Washington's famous "Atlanta Compromise" speech, which he gave at the Exposition in 1895. He told Blacks:

To those of my race who depend upon bettering their conditions in foreign land, or who underestimate the importance of cultivating friendly relations with the Southern white man, who is his next door neighbor, I would say "cast down your bucket where you are"—cast down in making friends in every manly way of the people of all races by whom we are surrounded.[42]

He further sought to condone the South's wholesale violation of the civil rights of Blacks by arguing that "whatever other sins the South may be called to bear, when it comes to business, pure and simple, it is in the South that the Negro is given a man's chance in the commercial world." It is ironic that Washington would make such claims at a time when the practice of reducing Blacks to perpetual indentured servants was a way of life and lynching them for their attempts to exercise their basic civil and human rights was a common thing.[43]

The philosophy that Washington outlined in his speech was nothing new. It was simply a recapitulation of the American thought pattern of "racial adjustment," which had been brewing since the Civil War. Essentially, he argued that the solution to the race problem was for Blacks temporarily to give up three things: (1) political power, (2) insistence on civil rights, and (3) higher education of Black youth.[44] In return for surrendering these basic human and civil rights, Washington proposed to sell Blacks the notion that the solution to the race problem was the "application of the gospel of wealth" and "material prosperity."[45] He also urged Blacks to place emphasis upon self-help and racial solidarity, moral uplift, and economic development. It seemingly never occurred to Washington that these goals were unattainable as long as Blacks' liberty and property interest rights to acquire property and to seek employment opportunities rested on the goodwill of their adversaries and competitors and not on a principle of law.

The power elite was successful in elevating Washington to the level of national spokesman for Blacks at the Atlanta Exposition. This is evidenced by the fact that Washington was practically unknown when he went to the Exposition. After he left, he was identified by the white media as the "Black leader." The white media, it must be noted, had a tradition of printing news about two types of Blacks: the so-called "good nigger," and the "bad nigger." When the media wrote about the so-called "bad nigger," it was trying to depict the negative image of Blacks; and when it wrote about the so-called "good nigger," it was trying to depict the "ideal type" Black. In most cases the latter were the docile or accommodating Blacks, or "Uncle Toms," which the rest of the Blacks should model their lives after.

The political thrust of Washington's philosophy of racial accommodation was to take the civil rights of Blacks off a principle of law and place them upon the goodwill of their adversaries and competitors who, at that time, opposed any expression of economic, political, social, or educational equality.[46]

The most dynamic step that Washington took to institutionalize the Social Darwinian Theory was when he advised Blacks to forget about higher education and concern themselves with industrial and agricultural education, or "progressive education." The progressive education during that period, at its best, was preparing Blacks for:

skills that were being outmoded by the progress of the Industrial Revolution, and preparing them for lives as small individualistic entrepreneurs at a time when the philosophy of economic individuals was becoming obsolete.[47]

When Washington urged Blacks to forget about higher education, he was not only urging them to forget about thinking altogether, but foreclosing their freedom to enter into mainstream America. His emphasis upon "progressive education" coincided with lawmakers' "steady withdrawal of aid from institutions for higher learning."[48] Shortly after the Civil War, the Peabody Fund was established to aid Black education. As a precondition for receiving funds, Blacks were "expected to conform to the racial policy of the foundation." This policy was designed to shape not only their philosophy of racial adjustment but also their "general social philosophy according to the social philosophy of the northern philanthropic foundation."[49]

During the time when the Peabody Fund was doling out pennies to the Black colleges, Congress was doling out to white colleges "more than a quarter of a billion dollars"[50] in the form of grants and land under the Morrill Act of 1862.[51] The political significance of this act is that it recognized "the principle that every citizen is entitled to receive educational aid from the government and that the common affairs of life are proper subjects with which to educate or to train men."[52] This principle, however, applied only to whites and European immigrants during the period between 1862 and 1920. Education was made available to prevent the culture of poverty from developing among them. Black schools, for the most part, depended largely on donations from whites who insisted that Black students adopt a philosophy of racial adjustment.[53] This policy was overseen by Booker T. Washington.

After he convinced Blacks temporarily to give up their political rights and to place them on the goodwill of their adversaries and competitors, Washington became the unidirectional political link between Blacks and the American power structure nationally. He had quasi-dictatorial power to suppress dissent among those Black leaders who overtly criticized his philosophy as one of accommodation. Although Washington resided in Tuskegee, Alabama, he could still use his quasi-dictatorial power to have a Black fired from a civil service job in New York if that Black "published some disparaging remarks about [his] leadership."[54] Economically, Washington controlled the purse strings—and the decision-making mechanism—for the majority of those programs designed to improve the status of Blacks. Any program that did not conform to his ideas of racial adjustment did not receive financial support, because the philanthropists who funded these programs would consult Washington to make sure that the recipients of these programs were safe, or conformed to the policy of docility, before they would support them.

Devoid of a system of protection to safeguard their civil rights to an education, Blacks could not increase the relative size of their middle class; that is, increase the number of Black lawyers, doctors, and businessmen. Any attempt to do so was undermined by the southern system of injustice and the repressive nature of the plantation system. From the end of the Reconstruction Period to the passage of the civil rights laws of the 1960s, the white man's word was the law in the South and in many parts of the North. Often, Blacks were forced to take the judgments and opinions of whites as the law of the land. Southern whites felt it to be their moral obligation to punish, violently, any Black who disputed a white man's word.[55]

Hence, the deprivation of these civil rights that Washington forced Blacks to give up in the 1890s kept them pinned down on the beaches of the culture of poverty until the culture itself began to develop among them. Once developed, it became a self-perpetuating cycle up to the implementation of affirmative action in the mid-1960s. The affirmative action, as we shall see in Chapter 8, took the civil rights of Blacks to seek employment opportunities off the goodwill of their competitors and adversaries and placed them on a principle of law.

STRUCTURAL CONDITIONS OF THE AMERICAN SOUTH

After the Reconstruction Period, economic and political life of the American South continued in a somewhat modified form, as it was, before the Civil War. The social structure there was a classic example of the feudal system in which the aristocracy (landowners) dominated both the economic and political life of the South, and the lower class whites (land tenants) and Blacks (mostly sharecroppers) were left to compete for the meager tangible and intangible benefits that were left. The lower class whites served as a buffer to minimize the conflict between the masses of Blacks and the aristocrats.[56]

The conflict that often emerged between the lower class whites and the Blacks centered around the distribution of tangible and intangible benefits or values, more of the latter than the former. The tangible values centered around the ownership of property, and there was very little conflict here because it was clear that the aristocrats owned the majority of the land.[57] The real conflict emerged in the struggle for the intangible values, which were manifested in the control of those social and political institutions that were an intimate part of the old caste system of the antebellum South. The whites had come to control these institutions either through their own achievements or through inheritance, more often the latter. When Blacks became emancipated and the carpetbaggers from the North invaded the South during the Reconstruction Period, Blacks began to pose a threat to those intangible values that whites had come to believe to be theirs by birthright—values such as control of the social and political institutions. More important, when Blacks started competing for these positions, they began to destroy the false sense of racial superiority that the lower class whites felt toward Blacks. The lower class whites, for the most part, owned very little land or property. If Blacks were put in the same social status as whites, they would not have anyone to feel superior to in the eyes of their wives and children.[58] Therefore, it was a concerted effort on the part of the antebellum South to design an environment, both politically and economically, governed by race and class.

The practical consequence of these cleavages was that they prevented Blacks from acquiring the human capital that was indispensable for their competition in the northern industrial society. They were prevented from entering the economic system by law. Race prejudice (attitude) was not enough to keep Blacks from entering the economic system on a competitive basis. There were also specific laws (government actions) that foreclosed Blacks' freedom to take advantage of a wide range of economic activities that would have enabled them to elevate themselves up off the beaches of the culture of poverty.

By the time Blacks started migrating North, they had fully developed a pattern of non–self-determination. This pattern significantly impeded their rapid adjustment to an urban environment.

THE BLACK MIGRATION

The dominant forces that precipitated the Black migration from the American South were very much like those that uprooted the European peasants. Both groups were freed from a feudal system that had kept them tied to the land. The European feudal system differed from the plantation system in the American South in that the South continued to hold Blacks in slavery on the plantations even after emancipation in a modified form.

The forces that broke bonds that held the European peasants to the land were related to the rise of the Industrial Revolution during the seventeenth and the whole of the eighteenth centuries. Industrialization did not evolve in America until the nineteenth century. When it did, it surfaced primarily in the North and did not significantly influence the South. The South's economy was restricted primarily to growing cotton and tobacco. At the height of this economy, it supplied over three-fourths of the world's cotton needs. The South continued to supply the world with cotton up to the turn of the present century, when America began to receive competition from abroad and the manufacturers started shifting to synthetic fibers.[59]

The Black labor supply was indispensable to the United States economy because it was irreplaceable. As mentioned before, in order for a country to develop economically, there has to be a supply of cheap labor available. When industrial development began in America, the majority of Blacks were locked into the institution of slavery. If they had been freed in 1830 and had migrated North to fill the labor demand, it would have severely affected the American economy both in the North and the South. Cotton was needed by the North as raw material for manufacturing clothing. The northern clothing factories could not have survived without it. To promote northern industries and the southern economy, manufacturers and southern planters cooperatively adopted a policy of social control. Blacks were confined to the South, as we have seen, to support the southern economy, and whites were recruited from abroad for northern industries.

The advent of World War I and the passage of the Immigration Act of 1917 significantly curtailed the flow of European labor to America. This curtailment occurred when American industry was at its peak and when European countries depended on America for food and war materials. Northern industries turned for the first time to the untapped labor force in the South.

Northern industries would not have been so successful in recruiting Blacks if the economic conditions of the South had not begun to free Blacks from the land some fifteen years earlier. There were several factors that helped to loosen the bonds that had kept Blacks tied to the plantation since Reconstruction.

Southern crops were suffering from floods and the effect that boll weevils had upon the cotton crop. The first crop disaster occurred in 1892, when boll weevils from Mexico attacked cotton in Texas. They spread 160 miles a year, until they had invaded all the southern states except for the Carolinas and Virginia.[60] The boll weevils significantly lowered the profits of the plantation owners. Before the boll weevil invasion, the South produced approximately 400,000 bales of cotton a year; after the invasion, the production of cotton was cut in half. It was estimated that the South lost $250,000 worth of cotton in the first three years of the boll weevil invasion.[61]

With the curtailment in the production of cotton, plantation owners had less money to buy supplies for their tenants. Merchants accustomed to lending money to the plantation owners began to curtail the merchants line of credit, because the former saw no bright future in the southern staple crop. "This, of course, means financial depression, for the South is a borrowing sector and any limitation to credit there blocked the wheels of industry."[62]

The amount of damage the boll weevils could inflict upon the cotton depended heavily upon the amount of rainfall the crop received. The South experienced its heaviest rainfalls in the summer of 1915, when thousands of Blacks were left destitute. With a curtailment in cotton production and constraint on credit, many plantation owners were reluctant to continue investing in the cotton industry. As a consequence, many Blacks were left homeless and out of work for the first time since the end of Reconstruction, thus creating the southern labor surplus.

When the northern industries began recruiting the southern labor surplus, they received a labor force with a predominantly agrarian background.

They recruited both Black and white laborers. Although whites were recruited, the bulk of the labor supply consisted largely of Blacks whose ties to the plantation system had been broken by the effect of the boll weevils.

The most compelling force expediting the Black Migration northward was the "Work or Fight" order issued by the War Department during World War I.[63] With this order, the war economy forced the labor unions to suspend their systematic discriminatory policies against hiring Blacks in workshops. For the unions to act to the contrary would have depicted a degree of disloyalty to the war effort. Thus, for the first time labor unions felt external pressure to relax their anti-Black policies.[64]

Before the war, Blacks had very little incentive to migrate North, even if they could escape the restrictions of the Black Codes of the South. The labor unions had systematic discriminatory policies. But with the whites going off to war, as a result of a direct response to the Draft Act requiring all males between the ages of 18 and 45 to register, there was a large vacuum left in the labor force, which was filled by Blacks.[65]

As large numbers of Blacks began to abandon the South, the plantation owners became alarmed and tried to curtail the migration by passing strict ordinances designed to constrain the recruiting agents' efforts in facilitating Blacks' migration. In many cases, these agents offered free passage North.[66] Mississippi, Florida, Georgia, and Alabama were the hardest hit by the Black migration. Some of these states required the recruiting agents to post $1,000 licenses or be subjected to 60 days in jail or a $600 fine.[67] But the state of Georgia had one of the stiffest laws designed to discourage recruitment. For instance, the City Council of Macon passed an ordinance requiring license fees of $25,000 and demanded that the labor agent be recommended by ten local ministers, ten manufacturers, and twenty-five businessmen. It has been estimated that over one million Blacks left the South in 1918.[68]

CONTACT WITH THE NORTHERN CITIES

When the American Blacks made contact with the northern cities, there were more jobs available than people to fill them. The war economy had created greater demands for goods than industries could produce. Unlike the Irish, who had a similar background, Blacks did not have to rove around the country from city to city seeking employment. They found work at the end of their journey. However, when the country began to shift from a war to a peacetime economy, the situation changed.

During the war, Blacks were fully employed in the economy. However, they did not have a system of protection to safeguard their property rights to employment, that is, protection against arbitrary layoffs and dismissals as did the European immigrants. When white soldiers returned home from the war, Blacks were either fired outright or asked to work for lower wages than whites. Thus, the temporary foothold they had gained in the economy was wiped out during this period and during the great depression in the 1930s.[69]

At the close of the war, once again a conflict erupted between Blacks and whites who were competing for the same jobs. The political and social consequences of this conflict resulted in the construction of barriers to foreclose Blacks' freedom to take advantage of a wide range of employment opportunities. These constraints were manifested in the so-called "Job Ceiling" that had an effect on Blacks' upward employment mobility similar to that of the Black Codes in the South.[70]

The job ceiling prevented Blacks from elevating themselves to the middle-class plateau by their own bootstraps. To their dismay, they found that Booker T. Washington's philosophy of "progressive education" led them directly to a stone wall. Under this system of education, Blacks subscribed tenaciously to the Protestant work ethic, that is, working hard and delaying present gratifications for future ones, just to learn that their skin color was the sole criterion foreclosing their freedom to elevate themselves to the middle-class plateau. In the Black colleges, for example, Blacks acquired skills as artisans and craftsmen (human capital), just to find these occupations foreclosed to them in the North. They were systematically excluded from entering into the unions of their trade. Those Blacks with

trades either gave them up and hired out as waiters or laborers, or they became job workmen and floating hands, catching a bit of carpentering here or a little brick-work or plastering there at reduced wages.[71]

Through unionization, whites were able to keep Blacks out of job competition with them. They attempted to derive the same psychological gratification of being better off than Blacks as did the southern whites. The greatest opposition that Blacks encountered in joining the labor unions came from the Irish, who entertained anti-Black sentiment because Blacks monopolized the service occupations during the 1840s, 1850s, and 1870s, while the Irish were just a level below them.[72] For instance, it was the Irish who launched the race riot against Blacks before the Civil War.

Unlike the British West Indians, Blacks did not have the protection of the federal government to safeguard their liberty and property rights to seek a wide range of employment opportunities. The American Black male was deprived of the freedom of expressing any of the signs of aggressiveness of the West Indians. Any attempt to depict such behavior in the North was met with a system of oppression geared to put him back in his so-called "place," as was the case in the South. In the South, for example, the Black male found that the average white citizen had the legal authority to deprive him of his life, liberty, and property rights without due process of law. In the North, he found this task had been relegated to the police. Regardless of whether they were in the North or South, Blacks did not receive a system of protection to safeguard their life, liberty, and property rights until the passage of the civil rights laws of the 1960s. These laws were not nearly as effective as the system of protection that foreign subjects received from the federal government, because foreign relations laws are questions of diplomatic relations with foreign countries. Any tampering with these policies precipitated intervention by officials from Washington.

BLACKS LACKED A PATTERN OF ENTREPRENEURSHIP

Unlike the British West Indians, Blacks were not able to develop a class of entrepreneurs after their migration because they did not have the necessary human capital to do so. As we have seen, the British West Indians acquired the human capital for entrepreneurship in the West Indies because they did not have a white middle and lower class with which to compete on the islands. However, Blacks had these classes of whites to compete with in the South. Therefore, when the Black professionals were confronted with racial discrimination, they did not have the human capital with which to turn inward and start their own businesses. Consequently, they were subjected to demotion, arbitrary layoffs, and dismissals. Many Black professionals, such as lawyers, teachers, etc., were forced to seek employment in the Post Office system.

Because of their lack of experience in management know-how, Blacks were unable to establish businesses in their community to any marketable degree. The majority of the businesses were owned by the West Indians. For example, a survey taken of Black businesses in Harlem in the late 1950s revealed that a high proportion of the black-owned and operated businesses were owned by West Indians.[73] There were some successful American Black businessmen in Harlem other than in the service businesses, but their numbers were not commensurate with the numbers of successful West Indians.

It could be argued that American Blacks were not able to obtain a foothold in business in Harlem because of the competition with the West Indians and whites. But the West Indians were confined to the East Coast (mostly in New York and Boston), and Blacks' poor showing in business is systematic throughout the northern cities. If we look at the Blacks who migrated to Chicago, which had very few West Indians, we see the same picture as in New York.

Blacks who migrated to Chicago were unable to establish competitive businesses with whites as the West Indians did. As St. Clair Drake and Horace Clayton have pointed out, Blacks in Chicago were highly concentrated in the service businesses before the Big Migration. As far back as 1885, there were over 500 enterprises and 27 fields in which Blacks owned and operated businesses.[74] These businesses were in the service fields, with barber shops and moving and storage establishments forming the majority of the enterprises.

The number of Black-owned and operated businesses increased in

Chicago because the Big Migration created a market for them. Although the number of such enterprises increased during this period, the enterprises themselves were similar to those owned by Blacks in Harlem, namely businesses in which Blacks received little or no competition from whites (see Table 12).

Table 12
Ten Most Numerous Types of Black-Owned Businesses in Chicago, 1938

Type of Business	Number of Units
Beauty parlors	287
Grocery stores	257
Barber shops	207
Tailors, cleaners, and pressers	163
Restaurants	145
Coal and wood dealers	87
Taverns	70
Undertakers	50
Shoe repairing	48
Dressmakers	42
Total	1,356

SOURCE: St. Clair Drake and Horace R. Clayton, Black Metropolis (New York: Harper and Row, 1962), p. 438.

The most noticeable large Black businesses were the two banks and four insurance companies. They drew the majority of their capital "from within the Negro community to lend money for the purchase of homes."[75]

Social scientists have offered many explanations for why Blacks fared so poorly in business during their initial stage of contact in the northern cities. For example, Drake and Clayton give the following reasons:

(1) difficulty in procuring capital and credit, (2) difficulty in getting adequate training, (3) inability to secure choice locations on the main business street, (4) lack of sufficient patronage to allow them to amass capital and to make improvements, (5) inability to organize for co-operative effect.[76]

The difficulty of procuring capital and credit brings into consideration the broader question of the problems involved in securing initial capital for establishing new businesses.

One major argument that has been advanced to explain Blacks' lack of success in business is that the lending institutions have systematically discriminated against Blacks.[77] On the surface, this argument seems to have some validity. But a close examination of lending institutions conducted by Alfred R. Oxenfeldt in *The New Firms and Free Enterprise,*[78] reveals that these institutions rarely lend money to small and/or new enterprises. Oxenfeldt further argues that small and new enterprises are financed primarily by owners, their relatives and friends, and by suppliers of materials and equipment; only slight accommodation is extended to small businesses by banking institutions. Therefore, raising capital to start up new businesses is a problem faced by all groups; they must obtain such funds from other places.

As we have seen, the West Indians, Chinese, and Japanese were able to raise initial capital for business through their traditional rotating credit system. Hence, it seems that the all important variables for a group to succeed in business include first the freedom to interact in a human capital environment where individuals can have the opportunity to acquire managerial skills, and second, developing a process for raising the initial capital.

In short, the chief reason Blacks were unable to escape the slums, as did the European immigrants, has been because the government has consistently refused to provide them with a system of protection that safeguarded their civil rights to enter into the mother lode of America's income redistribution system. It has historically placed their civil rights to acquire property and to pursue employment and economic opportunities on the goodwill of their adversaries and competitors. These individuals have acted in the same manner in which Madison predicted in his *Federalist* papers. They have oppressed the minorities.

NOTES

1. See especially Robert Fogal and Stanley Engerman, "The Economics of Slavery," *The Reinterpretation of American Economic History* (New York: Harper and Row, 1971), pp. 311-341; *Time on the Cross: The Economics of American Negro Slavery,* 2 vols. (Boston: Little, Brown and Company, 1974).

2. Nathan Glazer, "A New View of Slavery," *Commentary* 58 (August 1974): 68-72; and *Affirmative Discrimination* (New York: Basic Books, 1975).

3. Herbert G. Gutman, "The World Two Cliometricians Made: A Review-Essay of F + E = T/C," *The Journal of Negro History* 60 (1975): 107. For a critique of the revisionist historians, read the entire essay, pp. 53-277.

4. For a discussion of the Madisonian theory of democracy, see Robert A. Dahl, *A Preface to Democratic Theory* (Chicago: The University of Chicago Press, 1956), chapter 1.

5. The federal government failed to provide Blacks with a minority veto over the tendency of tyranny by the majority.

6. E. Franklin Frazier, *Black Bourgeoisie* (New York: The Macmillan Company, 1957), p. 114.

7. For a discussion of American goal values, see Harold Lasswell, *The World Revolution of Our Time* (Stanford: Stanford University Press, 1951).

8. W.E.B. Du Bois, *Black Reconstruction in America* (New York: Russell & Russell, 1935), p. 602.

9. Edwin E. Slosson, *The American Spirit in Education* a series of *The Chronicles of America* (New Haven: Yale University Press, 1921), chapter 15.

10. Paul Miliukov, *History of Russia* (New York: Funk & Wagnalls, 1969), p. 10.

11. Ibid.

12. See Forrest G. Wood, *The Era of Reconstruction* (New York: Thomas Y. Crowell Company, 1975), chapter 1.

13. Du Bois, *Black Reconstruction in America,* p. 601.

14. Ibid., p. 602.

15. Ibid, p. 221.

16. Martin Abbott, *The Freedmen's Bureau in South Carolina* (Chapel Hill: University of North Carolina Press, 1967) p. 109.

17. See Arnett G. Lindsay, "The Negro Banking," *Journal of Negro History* 14 (1929): 156-201.

18. Walter L. Fleming, *Documentary History of Reconstruction* (New York: McGraw-Hill Book Company, 1966), chapter 5.

19. Ibid.

20. Du Bois, *Black Reconstruction in America,* p. 600.

21. John Hope Franklin, *Reconstruction* (Chicago: University of Chicago Press, 1961), p. 34.

22. Du Bois, *Black Reconstruction in America,* p. 603.

23. Ibid.

24. For a discussion of the Black Codes, see Rayford W. Logan, *The Negro in the United States* (Princeton: D. Van Nostrand Company, 1957), pp. 109-110.

25. Fleming, *Documentary History,* chapter 4.

26. Logan, *The Negro in the United States,* p. 110.

27. For a discussion of how brutal the white man was toward Blacks, see Allison Davis et al., *The Deep South* (Chicago: University of Chicago Press, 1965), chapter 11.

28. For a discussion of how the "Sambo" personality type developed as a result of interacting under absolute authority, see Stanley Elkins, *Slavery* (Chicago: The University of Chicago Press, 1965).

29. Logan, *The Negro in the United States,* p. 110.

30. Ibid.

31. Fleming, *Documentary History,* pp. 259-312.

32. See Harold Lasswell, *The Analysis of Political Behavior: An Empirical Approach* (New York: Oxford University Press, 1947), pp. 195-234.

33. Ibid.

34. Ibid., p. 207.

35. Ibid.

36. George M. Fredrickson, *The Black Image in the White Mind* (New York: Harper & Row, 1971), pp. 97-129.

37. See Thomas F. Gosset, *Race: The History of an Idea in America* (Dallas: SMU Press, 1963), p. 145.

38. Louis Knowles and Kenneth Prewitt, *Institutional Racism in America* (Englewood Cliffs, N.J.: Prentice-Hall, 1969), p. 10.

39. John Hope Franklin, *From Slavery to Freedom* (New York: Alfred A. Knopf, 1974), pp. 291-292.

40. Ibid.

41. See Du Bois, *The Souls of Black Folk* (Greenwich, Conn.: Fawcett Publications, 1961), chapter 3.

42. Arthur P. Davis and Saunders Redding, eds., *Cavalcade: Negro American Writing from 1760 to the Present* (New York: Houghton Mifflin Company, 1971), pp. 158-161.

43. Davis et al. *The Deep South,* chapter 11.

44. Du Bois, *The Souls of Black Folk,* p. 48.

45. August Meier, *Negro Thought in America: 1880-1915* (Ann Arbor: University of Michigan Press, 1968), p. 100.

46. Gilbert Osofsky, *Harlem: The Making of a Ghetto* (New York: Harper and Row, 1963), p. 164.

47. Meier, *Negro Thought,* p. 93.

48. Du Bois, *The Souls of Black Folk,* p. 49.

49. Frazier, *Black Bourgeoisie,* p. 85.

50. Slosson, *The American Spirit in Education,* p. 226.

51. Ibid., p. 225.

52. Ibid., pp. 232-233.

53. Frazier, *Black Bourgeoisie,* p. 85.

54. Osofsky, *Harlem: The Making of a Ghetto,* p. 164.

55. Davis et al., *The Deep South,* chapter 11.

56. Pierre Van der Berghe, "The United States Is a 'Herrenvolk' Democracy," *Nation of Nations: The Ethnic Experience and the Racial Crisis,* ed. Peter I. Rose (New York: Random House, 1972), p. 213.

57. Davis et al., *The Deep South,* chapter 11.

58. See Gunnar Myrdal, *An American Dilemma* (New York: Harper and Row, 1962), chapter 4.

59. Leon F. Litwack, *North of Slavery* (Chicago: University of Chicago Press, 1961), pp. 64-112.

60. Carter G. Woodson, *A Century of Negro Migration* (New York: Russell and Russell, 1969), p. 171.

61. Ibid.

62. Ibid., p. 172.

63. Thomas A. Bailey, *The American Pageant: A History of the Republic* (Boston: D. C. Heath and Company, 1956), p. 740.

64. See Litwack, *North of Slavery,* for a discussion of the economic repression of Blacks in the Northern cities, pp. 153-186.

65. Bailey, *The American Pageant,* p. 740.

66. St. Clair Drake and Horace R. Clayton, *Black Metropolis* (New York: Harper and Row, 1962), p. 58.

67. Ibid.

68. Ibid., p. 59.

69. Drake and Clayton, *Black Metropolis,* pp. 77-98.

70. Ibid.

71. W.E.B. Du Bois, *The Philadelphia Negro* (New York: Benjamin Blom, 1967), p. 130.

72. Oscar Handlin, *Boston's Immigrants* (Cambridge: Harvard University Press, 1959), p. 70.

73. Osofsky, *Harlem: The Making of a Ghetto,* p. 133.

74. Drake and Clayton, *Black Metropolis,* p. 436.

75. Ibid.

76. Ibid., p. 437.

77. Myrdal, *An American Dilemma,* pp. 314-418.

78. Alfred R. Oxenfeldt, *The New Firms and Free Enterprise* (Washington, D.C.: American Council on Public Affairs, 1943), p. 46.

7

Assessment of Groups' Economic Linkages and Income Inequality

The previous five chapters consist of a critical examination of the structural conditions in groups' homelands and the economic and political linkages they fashioned with the American polity in their early and initial stages of contact. The task of this chapter is to assess the impact of these linkages in the period between 1920 and 1970 in order to determine subsequent group behavior.

The data that have been used in this assessment are drawn from the various U.S. Census reports from 1920 to 1970. Data between 1970 and 1980 are not to be used because during this period the civil rights of Blacks, that is, the right to acquire property and to pursue economic opportunities, was temporarily taken from the goodwill of their adversaries and competitors and placed on a principle of law, that is, affirmative-action and civil rights laws of 1960s.

ECONOMIC LINKAGES OF EUROPEAN IMMIGRANTS, 1920-1970

As demonstrated in previous chapters, European ethnic groups came over and fashioned economic linkages with the American polity. The data in Table 13 indicate that these groups have not deviated significantly from these linkages. These data allow us to trace the occupational rank order for seven white ethnic groups in the period between 1920 and 1970.[1]

The year 1910 marked the beginning of the decline in agriculture from America's dominant occupation. At the beginning of that year, 32.5 percent of the workers in the labor force were engaged in agricultural work.[2] Table 19 in the appendix indicates that agriculture constituted the highest percentage (37.6 percent) of all workers engaged in the labor force among this cohort. These data are limited to the extent that they cover only six states (Massachusetts, New York, Pennsylvania, Michigan, Minnesota, and Wisconsin), and do not represent the total population in America for each group. These states were selected by the Immigration Commission because they had the largest numbers of foreign-born workers employed in the occupational categories selected for this table.

The data are not as complete as they are in Tables 24, 25, and 26. However, they are sufficient to give us some indication of the occupational status of groups in 1920.

In Table 13, four occupational categories (professional, managerial, craftsmen, and farming) were selected in an attempt to trace occupational mobility among the seven white ethnic groups represented during the period between 1920 and 1970. The first three categories were selected because they represent the occupational trend between 1920 and 1950.[3] The farming category was selected because it represents the dominant occupation in which the Protestants were engaged in 1920.

The data in Table 13 seem to indicate that the English were maintaining economic linkages similar to those they fashioned with the American polity during the colonial period. Their occupational rank order in 1920 indicates the following: farming, 18.1 percent; craftsmen, 13.8 percent; managerial, 5.6 percent; and professional, 0.8 percent. The highest percentage of the English were engaged in the coal mine operative category (41 percent).[4] By 1950, however, the Census Bureau had ceased recording this category. The jobs previously included in this category were re-classified and assigned to the craftsmen and operative categories. The coal mine operative category of 1920, therefore, is not a good indicator for making a strong inference about groups' occupational status. For this reason, this category will be ignored when discussing the rest of the groups.

During the period between 1920 and 1950, there was a shift in occupational services. Agriculture continued to decline as America's dominant occupation. It was replaced by managerial, professional, and craftsmen categories, respectively. As the English left the farms, they moved into the craftsmen category (17 percent), and this remained their dominant occupation until 1970. Between the years 1950 and 1960, the English began increasing their percentages in the professional category. This category remained their second occupational preference up to 1970, with craftsmen at 20.5 percent; professional, 19.6 percent; managerial, 16 percent; and farming, 2 percent.

An examination of the economic linkages of immigrants of the 1830s and 1850s will reveal that the occupations they fashioned for themselves in their initial stage of contact followed the same general patterns in 1920, approximately three generations later. As has been demonstrated, the vast majority of Germans moved directly into the interior and settled on farms, while the Irish-Catholics settled in the cities.

Table 13
Occupational Mobility of Race and Ethnic Groups, 1920–70

Years		English		Germans		Irish		Italians		Russian Jews		Norwegians		Swedes	
1920	1	Farm.[a]	18.1	Farm.	64.6	Crafts.	18.5	Crafts.	10.2	Crafts.	11.5	Farm.	87.3	Farm.	81.4
	2	Crafts.[b]	13.8	Crafts.	8.1	Farm.	13.5	Mgrs.	2.8	Farm.	4.1	Crafts.	11.3	Crafts.	10.3
	3	Mgrs.[c]	5.6	Mgrs.	2.8	Mgrs.	8.3	Farm.	0.9	Prof.	3.8	Mgrs.	0.5	Mgrs.	1.3
	4	Prof.[d]	0.8	Prof.	0.8	Prof.	0.8	Prof.	0.7	Mgrs.	2.8	Prof.	0.05	Prof.	0.09
1950	1	Crafts.	17.0	Crafts.	16.2	Crafts.	16.3	Crafts.	28.4	Mgrs.	25.5	Farm.	22.4	Crafts.	14.1
	2	Mgrs.	14.6	Farm.	14.8	Mgrs.	12.4	Mgrs.	11.1	Prof.	15.3	Crafts.	12.3	Mgrs.	13.3
	3	Prof.	11.2	Mgrs.	12.5	Prof.	9.7	Prof.	6.0	Crafts.	12.0	Mgrs.	11.4	Farm.	13.0
	4	Farm.	5.7	Prof.	7.3	Farm.	2.8	Farm.	1.1	Farm.	4.9	Prof.	7.5	Prof.	10.3
1960	1	Crafts.	17.7	Crafts.	23.1	Crafts.	18.6	Crafts.	23.4	Mgrs.	23.3	–		Crafts.	22.9
	2	Prof.	15.1	Mgrs.	12.7	Prof.	13.3	Mgrs.	11.6	Prof.	20.0	–		Mgrs.	14.8
	3	Mgrs.	15.0	Farm.	11.7	Mgrs.	12.7	Prof.	9.6	Crafts.	12.0	–		Prof.	13.1
	4	Farm.	3.2	Prof.	9.8	Farm.	1.5	Farm.	0.8	Farm.	3.5	–		Farm.	9.7
1970	1	Crafts.	20.5	Crafts.	22.0	Prof.	17.6	Crafts.	23.7	Prof.	25.4	Crafts.	21.5	Crafts.	22.0
	2	Prof.	19.6	Prof.	14.3	Crafts.	17.5	Mgrs.	13.7	Mgrs.	23.5	Prof.	14.4	Prof.	16.7
	3	Mgrs.	16.0	Mgrs.	13.4	Mgrs.	15.0	Prof.	12.5	Crafts.	12.0	Mgrs.	14.3	Mgrs.	16.2
	4	Farm.	2.0	Farm.	8.0	Farm.	0.7	Farm.	0.6	Farm.	2.4	Farm.	11.5	Farm.	6.7

The percentages in this table were taken from Tables 19, 24, 25, and 26 in the appendix, and they do not represent the total percentage of each group who are engaged in the labor force. For the total occupational percentage for each period, see Tables 19, 24, 25, and 26 in the appendix. Data for Norwegians was not available in 1960.

Notes: These occupational categories (Craftsmen,[a] Professional,[b] Managerial,[c]) were selected because they had the greatest percentage of expansion between 1920 and 1970. See E. P. Hutchinson, Immigrants and Their Children (New York: John Wiley and Sons, 1956), pp. 197–218. The farming category[a] was selected because it was considered to be the dominant occupation in the 1920s for the Protestants (Ibid.).

In 1920, the Germans had the following occupational order: farming, 64.6 percent; craftsmen, 8.1 percent; managerial, 2.8 percent; and professional, 0.8 percent.[5] Thus around 1950, as the process of urbanization continued to increase, and numbers of second-generation Germans began to enter the labor force, they began to enter the craftsmen category. Their occupational order shifted to the following between 1920 and 1950: craftsmen, 16.2 percent; farming, 14.8 percent; managerial, 12.5 percent; and professional, 7.3 percent. By 1970, the highest percentage of Germans in the labor force was in the craftsmen category (22 percent), followed by professional, 14.3 percent; managerial, 13.4 percent; and farming, 8 percent.

The Irish-Catholics, however, settled in the cities between 1830 and 1860 and were still in the cities in the 1920s. In 1920, for example, 13.5 percent of the Irish were engaged in farming. It must be noted, however, that a large proportion of farmers tabulated here were Scots-Irish rather than the Irish-Catholics. The census did not make a distinction between the two groups. Besides, many of the farmers can be assumed to be Scots-Irish because of the linkages that groups established with the American polity in their initial stage of contact.

The significant aspect of the Irish-Catholics' occupational status is that the occupational categories in which they were concentrated were those traditional urban occupations (that is, municipal jobs) which have been traditionally associated with political patronage. Many of the municipal jobs are classified as managerial in the census. Hence, the Irish had the following occupational rank order in 1920: craftsmen, 18.5 percent; farming, 13.5 percent; managerial, 8.3 percent; professional, 0.8 percent. In 1950, the Irish had the following occupational rank order: craftsmen, 16.3 percent; managerial, 12.4 percent; professional, 9.7 percent; farming, 2.8 percent.

By 1970, the highest percentage of the Irish males were employed in the professional category (17.6 percent) and craftsmen (17.5 percent), followed by managerial (15 percent). The professional and managerial categories in which the Irish were concentrated are closely related to their tradition of pursuing jobs in the public sector. In looking at all of the European ethnic groups in this cohort that were employed in the government bureaucracies in 1970, we find the Irish were mostly represented in the local government agencies (12.6 percent) in comparison to other white males. (The rest of the white males had less than 7.7 percent employed in this category. See Table 30 in the appendix)

The Scandinavians who immigrated during the 1860s and 1870s followed the same general pattern in adjustment and occupational pursuits as did the Germans. In 1920, the Scandinavians were still highly concentrated in farming. By 1950, they had begun to leave their farms and to move to the cities, if we assume that non-farming occupations are urban occupations.

The Norwegians began to leave the farms at a much slower rate than the

Swedes. Around 1950, the occupational rank order of the Norwegians had the following composition: farming, 22.4 percent; craftsmen, 12.3 percent; managerial, 11.4 percent; and professional, 7.5 percent. However, the Swedes' occupational rank order was as follows: craftsmen, 14.1 percent; managerial, 13.3 percent; farming, 13 percent; and professional, 10.3 percent.

The data for the Norwegians in the 1960s were not made available in the census. But in the 1970s, the occupational rank order of the Norwegians and the Swedes was basically the same while their percentages differed slightly (see Table 13). There was a higher percentage of Norwegians on farms than Swedes in the 1970s. Between 1960 and 1970, the Swedes began gradually to move out of the managerial category into the professional, thereby placing farming at the bottom of their list of occupational preferences.

The data in Table 26 seem to indicate that the majority of Italian males were concentrated in the craftsmen category. As we shall see in the next chapter, the majority of the craftsmen in the northern cities were in some way associated with the labor unions. Therefore, we can reasonably assume that the largest percentage of Italians concentrated in the craftsmen category in 1970 were members of the labor union (see Table 26 in the appendix); and the linkages they fashioned with the American polity in their early stage of contact constituted the same general pattern that they were currently following.

The data in Table 30 in the appendix indicate that Italian males have not pursued government jobs at the same rate as the Irish. As we have seen, the Italians did not fashion linkages with the government in their initial stage of contact. Therefore, the Italians' employment in municipal jobs exceeds the average percentage among this cohort by a mere 1.2 percent (the average percentage, 7.3 percent; the Italians, 8.5 percent). The highest percentage of the Italians in the working class category are either in the self-employed category (11.3 percent) or among the private wage and salary workers (72 percent).[6]

We have already seen that the primary reason the Jews were kicked out of the Russian Empire was that they dominated the trade and commerce industries and, to a certain extent, the liberal professions. In order for the Russians to undergo economic development, they felt it necessary to seize control of these industries—thus displacing the Jews. When they emigrated to America, they pursued many of the same occupations they had held in Russia. As we have seen, the underlying reason that Jews came to dominate these occupations in Europe was because they were looked down upon by the Christians. But in America, these occupations constituted the core of the mother lode of the income redistribution system. Consequently, the Jews were able to catapult themselves upon the middle-class plateau faster than most groups.

In pursuing occupations in America, the Jews no doubt faced some form of discrimination. However, this discrimination did not operate to foreclose their freedom to acquire property and to take advantage of a wide range of economic opportunities as it did for Blacks. Because of the human capital they brought with them, they were able to turn inward and draw upon their resources by establishing new businesses and developing educational institutions—thus adding to the economic growth of the country.

Around 1920, the Russian Jews had the following occupational rank order: craftsmen, 11.5 percent; farming, 4.1 percent; professional, 3.8 percent; managerial, 2.8 percent. Table 13 does not give us an adequate picture of the occupational distribution of Russian Jews for 1920. In Table 19 in the appendix, the Russian Jews are shown highly concentrated in the clerical category (25 percent) and the coal and mine operative category (33.9 percent). But the most significant aspect of the Russian Jews' employment is that they constituted the highest percentage among this cohort in the professional category (3.8 percent). The professional category since 1920 has been expanded to cover a wide range of professionals. The figures in the 1950 census seem to present a better picture of the occupational rank order of the Russian Jews. By 1950, the percentage of the Russian Jews in the managerial category had increased from 2.8 percent to 25.5 percent. As we have seen, the managerial, professional, and craftsmen categories had the greatest percentage increase since 1920. The Jews, therefore, had the highest percentage of increase for males in the managerial category. In 1920, craftsmen ranked number one as the Jews' occupational preference listed in Table 13. But by 1950, this craftsmen category had moved to third and remained there into the 1970s. Between 1950 and 1960, the Russian Jews were highly concentrated in the professional and managerial categories, and their percentage in the craftsmen category remained at almost the same percentage point as they had in 1920: 11.5 percent in 1920, and 12 percent in 1970.

The percentage of the Russian Jews employed in government jobs (local, state, and federal) is far below the average for the thirteen groups computed. The highest percentage of Jewish males is concentrated among the private wage and salary workers, 66.4 percent, and the self-employed category, 20.2 percent (see Table 30 in the appendix).

Among the racial ethnic groups, we have the Japanese, Chinese, American Blacks, British West Indians, Spanish, and Puerto Ricans. The data on the Spanish and Puerto Ricans are not complete because in many instances the U.S. Census Bureau lumped all Spanish-speaking immigrants together and did not make a distinction between Puerto Ricans and those who emigrated from Mexico. Therefore, this group is referred to occasionally, but the primary focus is on the Japanese, Chinese, Blacks, and West Indians.

We have seen that the Japanese were able to develop skills as merchants and craftsmen in Hawaii because the structural conditions existing at that time served as a system of protection that allowed them the freedom to interact in a human capital environment. When they made contact with the states, they were highly represented in the entrepreneurial and craftsmen categories. We have also seen how they monopolized the green vegetable market on the West Coast before their land was confiscated by the government during World War II. Despite this confiscation, they were still highly concentrated in the farm and farm manager categories (15.3 percent) in the 1950 census.[7] The next most prestigious occupation in which they were concentrated was the craftsmen category (9.7 percent) and managerial (8.6 percent).

The data on the Japanese in the 1950s were not so complete as in the 1960s because, during the former period, they had just been released from the concentration camps. Turning to the data collected in the 1960s, we find that the Japanese had the following occupational rank order: craftsmen, 20.1 percent; professional, 12.6 percent; farming, 12 percent; and managerial, 9.5 percent. Of all the ethnic groups that pursued farming during their initial stages of contact, the Japanese had the highest percentage of males employed in this category in 1960. They were followed by the Germans (11.7 percent), and the Swedes (9.7 percent).[8] By the 1970s, the Japanese occupational rank order had risen to the same level as other ethnic groups despite their oppression here during World War II. Their occupational rank order was as follows: craftsmen, 22.2 percent; professional, 20 percent; managerial, 13.8 percent. In looking at the Class of Workers of the Native Population in Table 30 in the appendix, we see the Japanese are highly concentrated in the private wage and salary workers (63 percent) and self-employed categories (17.3 percent). Hence, the Japanese did not deviate significantly from the occupational linkages they established with the American polity in their early stage of contact.

As we have seen, the British West Indian and Chinese immigration to America was constrained by the Immigration Act of 1917. This act restricted immigration to the skilled and the well-to-do. The Chinese who were able to emigrate to the United States after the Exclusion Act of 1882 were highly skilled and in the professional category.[9] In 1970, the occupational rank order of the Chinese was the following: professional, 27.7 percent; managerial, 14 percent; craftsmen, 10.5 percent.[10] Professionally, the Chinese lead other groups, having the highest percentage for their males concentrated in the professional category (27.7 percent) followed by the Russian Jews (25.4 percent) and the Japanese (20 percent).[11] The percentage of the rest of the ethnic groups employed in the professional category is below 20 percent.

In the working-class category, the West Indians are highly concentrated in local and federal government; 16.6 percent and 11 percent, respectively.[12] Discrimination in the private sector of the economy, that is, foreclosing a wide range of employment opportunities, has driven racial ethnic groups disproportionately to public employment where the rules for hiring, promotion, and layoffs rest on a principle of law. In looking at this sector in Table 30 in the appendix, Blacks, West Indians, Chinese, and Japanese have a higher percentage of males employed in government than the average for all groups. The Mexican or Spanish and the Puerto Ricans are hard to trace because of the method the Census Bureau used in collecting data. But where the ethnic identification is consistent, we can find a pattern of racial minority groups highly concentrated in those government agencies where the decision for hiring and promotion rests on a principle of law.

EDUCATIONAL ATTAINMENTS

According to the 1970 U.S. Census, the Russian Jews had the highest level of educational attainment with 12.8 median school years completed, followed by the Chinese with 12.7, and the Japanese with 12.6 (see Table 29). The English and West Indians are equal in the number of school years completed, 12.4, but the English surpass the West Indians if we consider the groups with the highest percentage of four or more years of college education; English, 17.5 percent; and West Indians, 14.8 percent.[14]

An examination of all those groups in this cohort with 17 percent or more of their males employed in the professional category reveals a close correlation between educational attainment and occupational status. For example, all groups with median school years completed of 12.4 or higher have over 17 percent employed in the professional categories; the Russian Jews, Chinese, Japanese, English, and British West Indians. A similar pattern can also be found among the groups concentrated in the craftsmen category with 12.1 or less median school years completed—except for the Japanese, who have 12.6 median school years completed. However, there is a disparity in the educational attainment among the Catholics (Irish and Italians). A closer look at the occupational categories in which these groups are concentrated reveals that 23.7 percent of all Italian males in the labor force were employed in the craftsmen category, while the Irish males were evenly scattered throughout the professional (17.6 percent), managerial (15 percent), clerical (12.3 percent), and craftsmen (17.5 percent) categories (see Table 26).

The craftsmen category does not prescribe the same level of educational attainment as the professional and managerial categories.[14] However, the craftsmen occupations prescribe a higher level of median family income than education. The Italians have a family median income slightly higher than the Irish ($11,857 and $11,776, respectively). It may appear that the differences are inconsequential; but they are highly significant when we take into consideration the size of both groups (Italian families, 1,314,594; Irish families, 423,888). Again, the Italians have a higher percentage of families earning incomes of $10,000 or more: 62.3 percent and 60.3 percent, respectively (see Table 23 in the appendix).

Educationally, the professional and managerial occupations in which the Irish are concentrated are governmental bureaucracies prescribing a higher level of education, but lower income, than the craftsmen occupations. There are slightly more Irish males employed in white-collar occupations (41 percent) than Italian males (33.7 percent). (White-collar occupations consist of professional, managerial, and sales workers. See Table 26.)

The Protestants are also employed in the craftsmen occupational categories, as are the non-Protestants. But there is a disparity in median income. This disparity can be explained when we introduce region as an independent variable. As Table 14 indicates, less than 30.2 percent of all Protestants (English, Swedes, Germans, and Norwegians) studied here are concentrated in the nine standard metropolitan areas. However, all of the non-Protestants—except the Italians—are highly concentrated in the large metropolitan areas in the eastern states. The Irish, the Italians, and the Russian Jews are highly concentrated in the New York metropolitan area. The Poles are the only ones who seem to be dispersed throughout the New York, Chicago, and Detroit areas.

The Italians, however, are scattered around the eastern states in cities such as Newark, New Jersey, Buffalo, New York, and other surrounding metropolitan areas.

Statistically, the regional and occupational variables seem to explain conclusively the socioeconomic disparity among the Protestants and non-Protestants. They also explain why certain racial groups are doing considerably better than the Protestants and Catholic groups. The West Indians, Japanese, and Chinese are highly represented in those occupational categories that prescribe high incomes. Again, these groups are concentrated in large metropolitan areas or in heavily industrialized states, where the economic structures prescribe a high level of income. For example, 54.8 percent of the West Indians reside in New York, 21.1 percent of the Chinese reside in San Francisco, and 16.3 percent of the Japanese reside in Los Angeles (see Table 14).

The lower percentage of the groups in the latter two cities must not be taken here to represent flaws in my theory. There exist two phenomena operating to support this argument. First, California's economy depends heavily on its defense industries. Under the Davis-Bacon Act, defense contractors are required by law to pay union wages even if the shop is non-union. Second, the peculiarity of the state's geological characteristics (providing a high potential for earthquakes) necessitated the building of numerous suburbs (that is, before the 1970s) that catered predominantly to those workers who fall in the professional, managerial, and craftsmen categories. Hence, although the Chinese and the Japanese are scattered throughout the state of California, they are concentrated in those industries that prescribe a high level of income.

Furthermore, the downward mobility of the Protestants and upward

Table 14
Population by Nativity, Parentage, and Race for Nine Selected
Standard Metropolitan Areas

	Total and Percent	New York	Chicago	Detroit	Milwaukee
English	1,778,951 (33.1)[a]	130,449 (7.3)	57,964 (3.2)	62,026 (3.5)	17,058 (0.9)
Irish	1,198,844 (50.1)	230,619 (19.2)	72,682 (6.0)	14,920 (1.2)	2,792 (0.2)
Italians	3,232,245 (48.2)	724,897 (22.4)	143,644 (4.4)	66,008 (1.2)	11,639 (0.2)
Polish	1,232,246 (50.1)	248,224 (13.3)	214,863 (11.8)	125,938 (10.5)	34,463 (1.9)
Russians	1,497,733 (54.2)	380,153 (25.7)	76,138 (5.1)	34,003 (2.3)	9,038 (0.6)
Swedes	679,068 (21.3)	21,383 (3.2)	52,934 (7.4)	8,302 (1.2)	4,086 (0.6)
Norwegians	517,406 (18.4)[a]	24,252 (4.7)	22,149 (4.3)	4,165 (0.8)	5,968 (1.1)
Mexicans	1,579,362 (27.2)	5,629 (0.4)	60,255 (3.8)	10,013 (0.6)	3,690 (0.2)
Blacks	22,539,362 (27.2)	1,620,693 (7.2)	1,214,922 (5.3)	748,078 (0.4)	105,467 (0.4)
West Indians	149,157 (68.6)	81,826 (54.8)	2,804 (1.9)	1,395 (0.9)	319 (0.2)
Japanese	273,554 (28.0)	1,936 (1.6)	7,159 (2.6)	1,699 (1.0)	342 (0.1)
Chinese	167,111 (51.5)	21,936 (13.1)	4,295 (2.5)	1,699 (1.0)	320 (0.2)
Germans	2,789,070 (29.5)	203,782 (7.3)	166,507 (6.0)	68,871 (2.5)	73,467 (2.6)

	Cleveland	San Francisco	Pittsburgh	Philadelphia	Los Angeles
English	23,029 (1.3)	44,784 (2.5)	40,254 (2.3)	78,070 (4.4)	86,311 (4.8)
Irish	13,669 (1.1)	28,535 (2.3)	20,859 (1.7)	71,795 (6.0)	28,177 (2.3)
Italians	47,488 (1.1)	65,633 (2.0)	93,207 (2.9)	181,973 (5.6)	85,752 (2.6)
Polish	48,180 (1.1)	10,708 (0.6)	54,566 (3.0)	70,491 (3.8)	47,376 (2.6)
Russians	29,200 (1.4)	21,217 (1.4)	18,350 (1.2)	90,551 (6.1)	96,110 (6.4)
Swedes	3,550 (0.5)	16,203 (2.2)	4,148 (0.6)	5,129 (0.7)	29,052 (4.2)
Norwegians	1,169 (0.2)	11,394 (2.2)	611 (0.1)	3,088 (0.6)	19,244 (3.7)
Mexicans	1,084 (0.06)	44,388 (2.8)	1,087 (0.06)	1,131 (0.6)	302,511 (19.1)
Blacks	329,554 (1.5)	323,110 (1.4)	167,112 (0.7)	828,845 (3.6)	745,551 (3.3)
West Indians	644 (0.4)	1,676 (1.1)	643 (0.4)	4,093 (2.7)	4,847 (3.2)
Japanese	664 (0.2)	15,181 (5.5)	343 (0.1)	2,280 (0.8)	44,507 (16.3)
Chinese	844 (0.5)	35,379 (21.1)	596 (0.3)	2,035 (1.2)	15,724 (8.8)
Germans	40,740 (1.5)	46,404 (1.6)	46,300 (1.7)	73,281 (2.6)	88,311 (4.8)

SOURCE: Calculated from: U.S. Bureau of the Census, Census of the Population: 1970, Subject Reports, Final Report PC (2)-1A, National Origin and Language (Washington: Government Printing Office, 1973).

[a]Protestants.

mobility of the non-Protestants can also be seen as a shift in the mode of production. When the American economy began to feel the impact of auto-mation, the Germans and Scandinavians were still largely on the farm. The impact of automation was felt more heavily in the industrial states where industries were flourishing. When automation shifted into high gear, the non-Protestants were in those industrial cities and states that benefited from this shift in economic growth. As automation increased, the standards of living in these industrial states and cities rose more rapidly than they did in the non-industrial states.

The Black and Spanish males, however, are considerably less well off educationally and economically because they are under-represented in those occupational categories that prescribe high incomes (see Table 16). All of the ethnic groups that have achieved economic security among this cohort have done so because they have established an economic base in the three high-income occupational categories: professional, managerial, and craftsmen. Each of these groups has 43.6 percent or more of their males concentrated in these occupational categories. Only 23.8 percent Blacks and 33.7 percent Spanish are concentrated in these same occupational categories. In other words, 76.2 percent of the Black males are concentrated in those occupational categories that do not prescribe high income.

TOWARD A THEORY FOR MEASURING INCOME DIFFERENCES

The attempt to explain the chief cause of income differences has preoccupied social scientists since the 1960s. Many arguments have been advanced and models constructed to isolate and identify the independent variables that can best explain this difference with the maximum degree of certainty. As we have seen in the Introduction, Thomas Sowell has identi-fied age, geographic distribution, and fertility as independent variables. These are not independent variables, but merely a citation of statistical incidences. They tell us very little, if anything, about society's income redistribution system.

One of the greatest pitfalls that social scientists fall into when they attempt to measure groups' income differences is that they attempt to lump all white ethnic groups together and compare race, that is, Blacks, whites, and others. Such comparison invariably forces them to assume that race itself, that is, the biological make-up of the groups, has functional economic and political characteristics. Because the assumption is false, the scientists' conclusions are inevitably false, thus adding very little, if anything, to the understanding of the cause of income differentials.

To avoid these pitfalls, this study measures the socioeconomic characteristics of groups on a one-to-one basis. For example, we will compare the total percentage of income above $10,000, the median income for this cohort in the 1970s, with occupational categories.

Using the 1970 U.S. Census data in looking at the wealthiest ethnic groups in this cohort, we can see that the Japanese stand at the top of the totem pole, with 73.6 percent of their families earning incomes of $10,000 or more, followed by the Jews with 71.2 percent, the Poles with 64.5 percent, and the Chinese with 64.3 percent (see Table 15).

Table 15
Percentage Distribution of Ethnic Groups with Family Incomes of
$10,000 or More, 1970

Ethnic Groups According to Rank Order	Percentage $10,000 or More
Japanese	73.6
Russian Jews	71.2
Poles	64.5
Chinese	64.3
Italians	62.3
Irish	60.3
English	57.5
Swedes	53.4
West Indians	53.1
Norwegians	48.8
Germans	46.1
Spanish	34.7
Blacks	23.3

SOURCE: These percentages are taken from Table 23 in the
appendix.

It must be pointed out here that a certain percentage of the Poles are in fact Jews. The U.S. Census does not make this distinction between Poles and Jews because it is not allowed to ask individuals questions about their religious affiliation. However, in 1975, Andrew Greeley conducted a study of the Polish Catholics. His study showed that they had a median family income of $11,298.[15] The U.S. Census reported their income to be $12,274. This discrepancy in median income suggests that a large percentage of Jews were included among the Poles in the census survey.

There does not appear to be a close correlation between the ethnic groups with the highest economic achievement and those groups with the highest educational attainment. When median school years completed are compared among this cohort, we get a different rank order than we did in family incomes. At the top of the totem pole, we have the Russian Jews, with 12.8 median school years completed, followed by the Chinese with 12.7

percent, the Japanese with 12.6 percent, and both the English and the British West Indians with 12.4 percent (see Table 29).[16]

The above data indicate that the racial minorities—except for Blacks and some Hispanics—and the non-Protestant ethnic groups overall are doing much better economically and educationally than the Protestants. There appears to be an economic disparity between the Protestants and the non-Protestants. This disparity was first brought to the attention of students of group mobility by Greeley. He interpreted this disparity as an indication of a reverse in the Protestant work ethic theory, and he saw no obvious reason for its reversal.[17]

What Greeley was looking at in his study were subsystems (religious groups) capable of prescribing only normative behavior patterns (social norms) and not economic and educational behavior. Until the 1970 Census was taken, students did not have sufficient data to allow them to separate the influence of the Protestant work ethic and the Protestants' economic achievement—which social scientists freely use to explain Blacks' lack of success. Scientists have assumed tht the Protestant work ethic was an independent variable influencing groups' economic success. This is exemplified in the "lack-of-values" argument. Here we can better understand Max Weber's statement that Protestantism was not responsible for the Protestants' economic success but was a product of it.[18] These Protestants were concentrated in an economic environment prescribing the rapid accumulation of wealth and property; namely, merchants, traders, and manufacturers (see Table 16).[19]

Therefore, income disparity can best be understood by comparing the percentage of group income above $10,000 to the occupational categories in which their males are concentrated. This proposition is based on the assumption that occupational categories have prescriptive-behavioral characteristics, that is, they prescribe income levels. In Table 15, we rank according to their percentage of families earning income above $10,000. In Table 16, we rank them according to their total percentage in the three major occupational categories in which groups are concentrated: professional, managerial, and craftsmen categories.

At the top of the totem pole, we have the Russian Jews with 60.9 percent of their male work force employed in these three categories. They are followed by the English, 56.1 percent; Japanese, 56 percent; Swedes, 54.9 percent; Chinese, 52.2 percent; Poles, 50.6 percent, etc.

There are several conclusions that can be drawn from tables 15 and 16. First, all groups with 60 percent of their family earning income of $10,000 or more have over 35 percent of their male work force employed in the professional or craftsmen categories. With the exception of the Russian Jews, Chinese, and Irish, all groups that have over 50 percent of their families earning income above $10,000 have over 20 percent of their male work force concentrated in the craftsmen category. As we shall see in

Table 16
Occupational Categories Which Prescribe High Group Income

Groups	Professional	Managerial	Craftsmen	Total
Russian Jews	25.4	23.5	12.0	60.9
English	19.6	16.0	20.5	56.1
Japanese	20.0	13.8	22.2	56.0
Swedes	16.7	16.2	22.0	54.9
Chinese	27.7	14.0	10.5	52.2
Poles	15.5	11.5	23.6	50.6
Norwegians	14.4	14.3	21.5	50.2
Irish	17.6	15.0	17.5	50.1
Italians	12.5	13.7	23.7	49.9
Germans	14.3	13.4	22.0	49.7
West Indians	17.3	8.6	16.7	42.6
Hispanics	6.7	5.1	21.9	33.7
Blacks	5.6	3.0	15.2	23.8

Source: Table 26 in the appendix.

Chapter 8, the craftsmen category prescribes a high level of income because it is highly subsidized by the federal and state governments. Government subsidies include such items as fringe benefits, union scale wages, apprenticeship programs, guaranteed weekly wages, and the mandates of the Davis-Bacon Act.

The professional category also prescribes a high level of income. Both the Russian Jews and Chinese have over 25 percent of their males employed in this category; 25.4 percent, 27.7 percent respectively. Both groups have the lowest percentage concentrated in the craftsmen categories: 12 percent, and 10.5 percent respectively.

Blacks and Hispanics have a disproportionately low number of their males employed in all three categories: Blacks have 5.6 percent concentrated in the professional categories, 3 percent in managerial, and 15.2 percent in craftsmen. The Hispanics have 6.7 percent concentrated in the professional, 5.1 percent in managerial, and 21.9 percent in craftsmen categories. Hence, the low income is a function of groups not being concentrated in those occupational categories that prescribe high income.

What the figures in Tables 15 and 16 demonstrate is that occupational categories are the best indicators to explain group income differences. The downward mobility of Protestants and the upward mobility of the non-Protestants and some racial minority groups can be explained by the geographic areas and occupational categories in which these groups are concentrated.

The data in Table 16 indicate that the occupational categories in which ethnic groups are concentrated have a more positive relationship in determining income differences than educational attainment, as has been commonly thought. Therefore, the pattern of downward mobility of the Protestants and the upward mobility among the Catholics and racial minority groups can be understood partly by looking at the occupational categories in which each group is employed. The shift in the American economy from agriculture to industrialization, coupled with the various labor laws, also had a determinative impact on the economic and social status of these groups. As we shall see in the next chapter, there are high levels of government subsidies embedded in the professional and craftsmen categories.

As stated earlier, the Germans and the Scandinavians were still on the farm in the 1950s when automation began to have an impact upon the American economy. Automation had its greatest impact, perhaps, in those industrial states where industries were flourishing. Thus, when automation was shifted into high gear, the non-Protestants were there in the cities to seize control of those economic sectors that were highly subsidized by the federal government and which prescribed high income, as will be demonstrated in the next chapter. As automation increased, the standards of living in these industrial states rose higher than they did in the less industrial states. The Protestants (particularly the Swedes, the Norwegians, the Germans, and the Scots-Irish) had originally settled in those states where industrial development and government subsidies were less pronounced. The English were scattered throughout the industrial and non-industrial states, particularly in the South. Thus, their downward mobility can also be viewed not so much as their having moved downward, but that the other groups have caught up with and surpassed them. As we shall see in the next chapter, the primary cause for this change in mobility is that the system of income redistribution shifted between the 1940s and 1970s while the Protestants stayed put.

The disparity in the educational attainment between the Catholics, that is, the Irish-Catholics and the Italians, can best be understood if we look at the occupational categories in which each group is concentrated. Of the Italian males 23.7 percent are employed as craftsmen, while the Irish are evenly scattered in the professional (17.6 percent), managerial (15 percent), clerical (12.3 percent) and craftsmen (17.5 percent) categories. The craftsmen category does not prescribe the same level of education as does the professional and managerial categories. Since many of the professional and managerial jobs are in the public sector or other related bureaucracies, it is obvious why the Irish have higher educational attainments than the

Italians. There are slightly more Irish employed in white-collar occupations (professsional 17.6 percent and managerial 15 percent) than Italians (professional 12.5 percent and managerial 13.7 percent). Again, the Irish are employed in those occupational categories that have very low positive statistical relationships in determining median family income (management and clerical and kindred workers); it follows then that the occupational categories in which the Irish have established an economic base prescribe a higher level of education than income—the opposite is true for the Italians.

The Protestants are also employed in the same craftsmen occupational categories as the non-Protestants; but, the difference here is that the former groups are concentrated in non-industrial states and the latter groups are concentrated in industrial states. There is good reason to believe that if the costs of living in the industrial states were compared with those of the non-industrial states there would be very little difference in the percentage of family income among these groups. This is merely a suggestion, and a full exploration of the subject is beyond the scope of this study.

The underlying reasons why some racial minority groups are doing considerably better than some Protestants and the Catholic groups is that the former groups are concentrated in those occupational categories and geographic areas that prescribe high income.

However, Black and the Spanish males are doing considerably less well educationally and economically because they are under-represented in those occupational categories that have a determinative impact on income. Over 76 percent of Black males are employed in those occupational categories that have a very low income.

In summary, this chapter has examined the economic linkages that groups fashioned with the American polity between the years 1920 and 1970. It has been revealed that groups maintained the same linkages they established in their initial stages of contact. It has also been demonstrated that income inequality can best be explained by comparing geographic areas in which groups are situated to the occupational categories in which they are concentrated. Such comparison will present a pattern of behavior among groups. There does not seem to be a close correlation between educational attainment and income. Education is relevant insofar as it serves as a ticket to enter those occupational categories that prescribe high income. In the next chapter, we will examine those factors within the occupational categories that prescribe high income.

NOTES

1. In Table 13, there are four occupational categories. At particular times, the seven ethnic groups were more heavily concentrated in one or more of these categories than they were at other times. Therefore, I rank each category according to the higher percentage of each group's males engaged in each category for that time

period. Subsequent reference to these occupations will be stated as to "occupational rank order."

2. See Table 13 for subsequent references to data on occupational rank order.

3. E. P. Hutchinson, *Immigrants and Their Children: 1850-1950* (New York: John Wiley and Sons, 1956), pp. 197-218.

4. See Table 19 in the appendix.

5. See Table 19 in the appendix for an overall picture of the Germans' occupation distribution.

6. See Table 30 in the appendix for the data previously cited.

7. See Table 24 in the appendix.

8. See Table 25 in the appendix.

9. Lawrence G. Brown, *Immigration* (New York: Longmans, Green and Company, 1933), chapter 14.

10. See Table 26 in the appendix

11. Ibid.

12. See Table 30 in the appendix.

13. See Table 29 in the appendix.

14. See, for instance, Peter M. Blau and Otis D. Duncan, *The American Occupation* (New York: John Wiley and Sons, 1967), p. 27; Otis D. Duncan, David L. Featherman, and Beverly Duncan, *Socioeconomic Background and Achievement* (New York: Seminar Press, 1972).

15. Andrew M. Greeley, "Ethnicity, Denomination and Inequalities," A Bicentennial Report to the Ford Foundation, Center for the Study of American Pluralism, National Opinion Research Center, Chicago, 1975, p. 88.

16. See Table 29 in the appendix.

17. Greeley, "Ethnicity, Denomination and Inequalities," p. 46.

18. Max Weber, *The Protestant Ethic and the Spirit of Capitalism* (New York: Charles Scribner's Sons, 1958), pp. 35-36.

19. Henri See commented that it was "only because the English have become merchants and traders that London has surpassed Paris in extent and in the number of its citizens: that the English can place 200 warships on the sea and subsidizes allies." Henri See, *Modern Capital* (New York: Adelphi, 1928), p. 87.

8

How Did the European Immigrants Escape the Slums?

This chapter is directed toward answering the underlying question that was raised in Chapter 1: "Why were Blacks unable to escape the slums as did the European immigrants?" This question can best be answered by restating it in the following manner: "How did the European immigrants escape the slums?"[1]

The primary reason why the European immigrants were able to leave the slums, to recapitulate, was because the government offered them a *de jure* system of protection to safeguard their civil rights: (1) to interact in a human capital environment, and (2) to enter into the mother lode of society's income redistribution system. The primary reason why Blacks, and other oppressed minority groups, have not been able to escape the slums has been that the federal government has historically refused to offer them the same system of protection to acquire property and to pursue a wide range of economic opportunities, as it did for whites.

These propositions superimpose all of the traditional arguments advanced thus far, such as groups' "accepting or rejecting the Protestant work ethic,"[2] the "weak family structure,"[3] "Blacks' inability to delay present satisfactions for future ones,"[4] "fertility rate,"[5] "IQ deficiency,"[6] "groups' culture and not discrimination determines who get ahead,"[7] and so on.

What all of these traditional arguments have in common is that they ignore that groups' behavior is a function of those public policies that grant or deny groups the freedom (liberty interest rights) to take advantage of a wide range of economic opportunities that exist within society's income redistribution system. In this chapter, it will be demonstrated (1) that embedded in this income redistribution system is an awesome structure of government subsidy; and (2) that income difference among groups is a function of unequal access to this awesome system of subsidies.

Students of group mobility are quick to point out that the white ethnic groups were able to escape slums through hard work and adhering tenaciously to the Protestant work ethic.[8] When these immigrants arrived, to repeat, they accepted dirty and low-paying jobs such as those in the garment districts, worked hard, and subsequently pulled themselves up by their own bootstraps. These students then proceed to ask the following question: "Why can't Blacks do the same?" Students who advance this argument overlook the role that the government played in helping European groups to escape the slums and, at the same time, blocked Blacks' freedom to do the same. Before continuing, let us restate the thesis of this book.

As has been argued earlier, in order for a group to pull themselves up by their bootstraps, they must have two things: a pair of boots and a set of bootstraps. The boots are something that groups or individuals can acquire on their own by working hard, and delaying present satisfactions for future ones, as Edward Banfield argues.[9] Groups can acquire a set of boots under a *de facto* system of protection. However, only a minute number among each group is going to be able to elevate themselves from the beaches of the culture of poverty onto the middle-class plateau. In order to elevate themselves onto the middle-class plateau collectively, a group must have a set of bootstraps that are government issued. Otherwise, groups will make the same mistakes as Blacks made from emancipation to the mid-1970s; that is, working hard, delaying present gratifications for future ones only to discover that their freedom to job upward mobility has been foreclosed by a set of structural arrangements—that is, governmentally- sanctioned "job ceilings."[10] It has been well documented that Black parents, and Black students themselves, have worked hard to send their children to college only to find that the only white-collar and high-paying jobs they could obtain were as clerks in the Post Office. Non-white-collar employment—as janitors, elevator operators, dishwashers (all of which were low-paying), etc.—was readily available. The political irony here is that they could have gotten the same jobs without obtaining even a high school education.[11] Before fully developing this argument, let us pinpoint the time and methods the government used to subsidize white ethnic groups to escape the slums.

In order to add conceptual clarity to the assessment of groups' socioeconomic status, it is necessary to go beyond simply measuring Blacks' income in relation to whites; for example, Blacks' income is 60 percent that of whites. Such measurement is tantamount to little more than a recitation of statistical incidences. It tells us nothing about how groups are structured within the income redistribution system. In order to get a clearer picture of this system, it will be scientifically fruitful to compare the increase in group income on a one-to-one basis among the thirteen race and ethnic groups for a twenty-year period. The figures in Table 17 are an attempt to achieve this goal.

Table 17
Percentage of Increase in Family Income Above Median, 1950 and 1970

Ethnic Groups	Percentage of family Income above median[a]		Percentage increase above median from 1950 to 1970
	1950	1970	
Japanese	18.8	73.6	54.8
Chinese	15.8	64.3	48.5
Russian Jews	33.2	71.2	38.0
Italians	27.3	62.3	35.0
Poles	32.0	64.5	32.5
Irish	28.6	60.3	31.7
English	28.5	57.5	29.0
Spanish	9.4	34.7	25.3
Swedes	32.4	53.4	21.0
Norwegians	28.5	48.8	20.3
Blacks	3.4	23.3	19.9
Germans	27.9	46.1	18.2

SOURCE: See Tables 22 and 23 in the appendix.

[a] The median income for the entire cohort was $2,245 in 1950
and $11,374 in 1970. However, the median income for 1970
falls somewhere between $10,000 and $14,999. From $9,999 to
$25,000, the U.S. Bureau of the Census used intervals of four
thousands and nine thousands. Since it is difficult to locate
the median income between $10,000 and $14,999, $10,000 or more
is used to compute the percentage above the median for this
cohort.

The figures in this table measure the percent increase of groups' income above the median for this cohort. The median income for this cohart was $2,245 in 1950 and $11,374 in 1970 (see tables 22 and 23 in the appendix). In 1970, the United States Census Bureau used intervals of four digits ($9,999 to $14,999) to compute group income. From this tabulation, we cannot locate the median income of $11,374. Therefore, in Table 17, we selected $10,000 or more as group median income for 1970, and $2,500 or more as group median income for 1950. We then tabulated the percentage of each group with income above this figure. For example, 73.6 percent of the Japanese families in the work force were earning incomes above $10,000 in 1970. They were followed by the Russian Jews, 71.2 percent; Poles, 64.5 percent; Chinese, 64.3 percent; etc. In 1950 the percentage of Japanese families earning incomes above the median ($2,500) was 18.8 percent. By 1970, that percentage had increased (that is, percentage of $10,000) to 73.6 percent. Hence, the Japanese experienced a 54.8 percent income increase from their average in 1950.

THE MOST UPWARDLY MOBILE GROUP BETWEEN 1950 AND 1970

There have been some questions raised regarding which ethnic group has achieved the highest rate of social upward mobility during the period between 1950 and 1970. This period is significant here because it epitomizes the era in which the New Deal programs instituted an income redistribution system for the lower class.[12] Groups that had a system of protection that granted them the freedom to participate fully in this system showed a marked socioeconomic upward mobility between the years 1950 and 1970. Groups that were excluded showed a marked decline in the same area (see Table 18).

From the data in Table 17, we can see that the most upwardly mobile group during this period was the Japanese, followed by the Chinese, the Russian Jews, and the Italians. There are two basic reasons for the miraculous increase in the Japanese and Chinese income percentage during this period. First, they are highly concentrated in those occupational categories that prescribe high income (that is, professional, managerial, and

Table 18
Percentage of Group Income Above and Below Average Median, 1950 and 1970

Ethnic Groups	Percentage above or below average median[a]	
	1950	1970
Japanese	- 0.9	34.1
Russian Jews	13.5	31.7
Poles	12.3	25.0
Chinese	- 3.9	24.8
Italians	7.6	22.8
Irish	8.9	20.8
English	8.8	18.0
Swedes	12.7	13.9
Norwegians	8.8	9.3
Germans	8.2	6.6
Spanish	-10.3	- 4.8
Blacks	-16.3	-16.2

SOURCES: Tables 22 and 23 in the appendix.

[a] The total percentage of families above the median income for this cohort was 19.7 percent in 1950 and 39.5 percent in 1970.

-Below the median average.

craftsmen; hereafter, high-income occupational categories). For example, in 1950, 6.4 percent of Japanese males were engaged in the professional category. By 1970, this figure had increased to 20 percent. In the managerial category, the figure was 8.6 percent in 1950 and increased to 13.8 percent by 1970. The largest increase for the Japanese was in the craftsmen category, which increased from 9.7 percent in 1950 to 22.2 percent in 1970 (see tables 24 and 26 in the appendix).

The Chinese had 6.3 percent of their males concentrated in the professional category in 1950. By 1970, that figure had increased to 27.7 percent. However, they experienced a decline in the percentage of males engaged in the managerial category: from 22.2 percent in 1950 to 14 percent in 1970. As we saw in the last chapter, the managerial category has a very low correlation in determining median income. The Chinese showed a marked increase in the percentage of their males engaging in the craftsmen category; from 3.3 percent in 1950 to 10.2 percent in 1970. Therefore, the high income increase for the Chinese can be explained by their marked increase in the professional and craftsmen categories.

The second reason for the Chinese and Japanese increase in the percentage of families earning income above the median was because they were concentrated in highly industrialized states and cities. As has been demonstrated in the previous chapter, the Japanese and Chinese are highly concentrated in California and other western states. California is included among the highly industrialized states because of its economic expansion after World War II and its defense industries. Again, California happens to be one of those states in which the Scandinavians and Germans did not settle in the 1860s and 1970s. These groups did not migrate to the western states, as did the Irish and Italians, who traditionally followed public works projects.

Table 17 offers further evidence that geographic areas are factors in determining income difference. Embedded in these geographic areas are those industries that have built-in income redistribution systems prescribing high income. For example, the Russian Jews have 60.9 percent of their males concentrated in occupational categories that have a strong correlation with high income. However, 25.7 percent of the Russian Jews are concentrated in New York City; followed by Los Angeles, 6.4 percent, Philadelphia, 6.1 percent; and Chicago, 5.1 percent (see Table 14 in Chapter 7).

The West Indians also have a high percentge of their families earning incomes above $10,000, 53.1 percent (see Table 15 in Chapter 7). They are also concentrated in New York City; for example 54.8 percent of them live in New York City alone. Embedded in the occupational structures in New York City are many professional jobs that prescribe high income and contain a high structure of government subsidies. For instance, the Russian Jews have 25.4 percent of their males concentrated in the professional category and 23.5 percent in the managerial category. By the same token, the West Indians have 17.3 percent and 8.6 percent of their males in the same categories, respectively.

The Chinese have 52.2 percent of their males concentrated in the three high-income occupational categories. They are also concentrated in the most industrialized cities in America, 21.1 percent in San Francisco, and 13.1 percent in New York City. The Japanese are spread throughout the western states (see Table 14 in Chapter 7). Their highest concentration is in Los Angeles, 16.3 percent, and San Francisco, 5.5 percent. However, they are also scattered throughout the state of Washington, which also has a large defense industry.

As will be demonstrated, the mere concentration of groups in the three high-income occupational categories is not within itself a guarantee of high income. As Table 16 in Chapter 7 indicates, 56.1 percent of the English males and 54.9 percent of the Swedes are concentrated in these categories. However, the percentage of these groups' families earning incomes above $10,000 for 1970 was not so high as some of the other racial ethnic groups and the Russian Jews; for example, the number of English families earning incomes above $10,000 equaled 57.5 percent; the Swedes, 53.4 percent (see Table 17). The English had only 30.2 percent of their group living in the nine metropolitan areas that were compared in this study (see Table 14 in Chapter 7).

It is obvious from this analysis that the income redistribution systems embedded in these occupational categories can offer a better explanation for groups' income differences than other non-measurable factors such as, the Protestant work ethic, fertility rate, age, etc. An examination of these systems will be the focus of the next section. The groups concentrated in the high-income occupational categories seem to have improved their condition over the years. For instance, very few Black and Hispanic males were concentrated in the professional and managerial categories in 1970; 8.6 percent and 13.8 percent, respectively. These data strongly indicate that these two groups were being excluded from the income redistribution system at a time when the government was pumping billions of dollars annually into the economy in the form of federal subsidies.

In Table 17, we have seen that all groups within this cohort experienced an increase in the number of families earning incomes above the median between the period of 1950 and 1970. For example, in 1950, 6.9 percent of all Black families engaged in the labor force were earning incomes above the median income for this group. By 1970, this figure had increased to 23.3 percent—with a net gain of 16.4 percent.

If we tabulate the total number of families for this cohort earning incomes above the median for 1950 and 1970, we obtain a better picture of how well Blacks and Hispanics fared in relation to the other groups. For instance, the total figure of families earning incomes above the median

($2,245) in 1950 for this cohort equaled 19.7 percent. In 1970, this number had increased to 39.5 percent, a 19.8 percent increase. In Table 18, we compared each group's median income with the average for both 1950 and 1970. In 1950, median income of the Japanese, Blacks, Chinese, and Hispanics was below the average median for this group. But by 1970, the Japanese and Chinese had caught up with the rest of the group. In fact, the Japanese surpassed the entire group, showing a 31.5 percent increase above the median for this cohort (see Table 18).

The most astonishing finding among this group is the decline in the status of Blacks. Instead of gaining percentage points above the median, they actually lost ground. In 1950, Blacks were 12.8 percentage points below the average. In 1970, they were 18.6 percentage points below this average, thus falling 5.8 percent further behind the rest of the groups in the twenty years since 1950. The relatively downward mobility of Blacks seems somewhat ironic when we consider the tremendous amount of literature purporting to show that Blacks are doing considerably better than they were in the 1950s. The data do not support such arguments.

As Table 18 indicates, Blacks, Japanese, Chinese, and Hispanics had incomes below the median in 1950. The Japanese and Chinese closed this gap by 1970. The Japanese lead this cohort in widening the gap between themselves and the median, while Blacks lost ground. The Hispanics closed the gap slightly, but still fell below the median for this group. The question that emerges here is, what factors can be attributed to Blacks' decline in the percentage of family income below this cohort while the European groups experienced an increase? This question will be addressed in the next section.

COMBINATION IN RESTRAINT OF TRADE

The most important single factor to account for the European immigrants' ability to escape the slums while Blacks remained was the enactment of the various national labor laws between the years 1930 and 1960. Before the passage of the first national labor laws in 1932, employers kept union workers pinned down on the beaches of the culture of poverty. They used a legal tool known as *combination in the restraint of trade,* which was prohibited by the Sherman Antitrust Act of 1890. This act was originally designed to prevent businesses from forming monopolies for the purpose of restraining trade. But in 1908, the United States Supreme Court ruled, in *Loew v. Lawler*, that this act made "every contract, combination, or conspiracy in restraint of trade illegal," regardless of whether the entities were businesses, farmers, or labor unions.[13] From this year to 1932, employers used the Sherman Anti-Trust Act to undermine the efforts of the unions to organize. For example, whenever unions attempted to organize and strike for better working conditions and higher wages, employers would go to federal court seeking an injunction to thwart the unions' activities.

Because of the standardized "form of pleadings" and "vaguely worded affidavits, injunctions were often issued *ex parte* and tended to be cast in such broad terms as to include the permitted with the proscribed. While a full hearing on the appropriateness of continuing the injunction would eventually be held, usually this came too late to help the union, whose strike, boycott or other activity had been effectively 'broken'."[14]

With the power of an injunction, employers effectively restricted unions' freedom to organize and to protect the civil rights of their members to bargain for high wages and better working conditions.

Because of the use of injunctions, labor unions experienced a marked decline in membership and strength between World War I and the 1930s, from 5 million members in 1920 to fewer than 3 million in 1933.[15] At the beginning of the depression of the 1930s, the permanent demise of the unions seemed imminent. The unions were unable to protect workers' civil rights to employment security during this period; consequently, employers were extravagant with their use of injunctions to curb union activities.

In an attempt to get the country out of the depression, Congress passed the Norris-LaGuardia Act of 1932.[16] This act took away the legal weapon that employers had to restrict the growth of unions; that is, it removed the power of the federal courts to issue either temporary or permanent injunctions in labor disputes. But this act did not make a significant improvement in the lot of workers. This improvement did not take place until Congress passed the Wagner Act (National Labor Relations Act) in 1935. Essentially, this act threw the weight of the federal government behind unionism and collective bargaining.

NATIONAL LABOR RELATIONS ACT AND BOOTSTRAPS

The National Labor Relations Act was more than a law governing the relationship between labor and management. It constituted: (1) a system of protection that took union members' civil rights to employment and economic opportunities off the goodwill of management and placed these rights upon a principle of law, and (2) a set of bootstraps in the form of high wages and fringe benefits that were subsidized by the federal government.

Before the National Labor Relations Act gave unions the right to collective bargaining, the European ethnic groups who immigrated during the last two decades of the nineteenth century were pinned down on the beaches of the culture of poverty alongside Blacks. But with collective bargaining, these groups were able to elevate themselves onto the middle-class plateau.

PROPERTY RIGHTS TO EMPLOYMENT

The political significance of collective bargaining is that it took the decisions concerning wages, hiring, layoffs, and seniority off the goodwill of management and placed it upon a principle of law. This law allowed these decisions to be made jointly by both employers and unions. It also bestowed upon union members property interest rights to their continuous employment. Employers could no longer arbitrarily lay off an employee or reduce his wages. With collective bargaining, this decision was subjected to procedural due process, which is a constitutionally protected right.

Under the federal collective bargaining laws, unions had the authority to negotiate property rights and fringe benefits for their members. Among these rights were hours of employment, wage employment guarantees (WEG), supplementary unemployment benefits (SUB), and other conditions of employment. The most significant of these to groups' upward mobility was WEG, which constituted job security. The purpose of this provision was "to ensure employees a specified minimum amount of work or compensation for a predetermined period of time. The existing guarantees range from one week to a year or more."[17] The provisions of the WEG varied with different contracts; but, the following clauses exemplify a form of job security that the unions could possibly negotiate for their members: "All employees within the terms of this agreement shall be guaranteed not less than 40 straight time hours of work per week."[18] "Every permanent employee who reports for work regularly every day during the work week will be guaranteed 40 hours of pay for the week."[19] "All regular employees shall be guaranteed a minimum of 36 hours of work or pay in lieu of work per week."[20]

Accompanying WEG were the supplementary wage benefits (SUB). The purpose of the SUB was to provide weekly supplements to government unemployment benefits to workers in case of layoffs. The amount of SUB varied among states and contracts unions were able to negotiate. However, these benefits ranged from 55 percent to 95 percent of the worker's weekly salary.[21] SUB was financed by the employers through one of the following methods: "individual account fund, single-employer pooled fund, multi-employer pooled fund, and unfunded plans."[22]

The method used to fund SUB is of little political significance to our argument here. What is germane is that under the federal collective bargaining laws these benefits were negotiable as property interest rights to employment and they could not be arbitrarily and/or capriciously taken away from the employees by management. They were safeguarded through procedural due process.

The overall political significance of WEG and SUB was that they constituted income security. In terms of group mobility, this form of security is more important than high income. With it, the European immigrants were able not only to catapult themselves up off the beaches of the culture of poverty and onto the middle-class plateau, but also to land themselves and their children in the middle of the mainstream of society's income redistribution system. For example, income security qualifies the individual to take advantage of a wide range of other economic benefits that significantly enhance group upward mobility, such as good credit ratings, low group insurance, group discounts, and easier qualification for conventional loans. Without job security, these benefits are more likely improbable.

JOB SECURITY AND UPWARD MOBILITY

It has often been argued that European groups left the beaches of the culture of poverty because of their adherence to the Protestant work ethic. The corollary to this is the racist argument that the primary reason why Blacks have not left the beaches of the culture of poverty (slums) is that they are too lazy to work. Or, as Nathan Glazer has implied it, they are there by choice.[23]

European immigrants, to repeat, did not make it to the middle-class plateau because of their hard work, but because they had the full blessing of the federal government to negotiate income security for their members by: (1) enlarging job opportunities, (2) controlling access to jobs, and (3) providing supplementary income for workers out of work. The latter has already been discussed.

ENLARGING JOB OPPORTUNITIES AND MOBILITY

Enlarging job opportunities for members of their own group was a practice that was widely used by European immigrants after the passage of the NLRA. This process can explain groups' mobility better than the Protestant work ethic theory. Through enlarging job opportunities, groups' mobility is characterized more by horizontal mobility than by vertical. Before continuing, an explanation of the various forms of group mobility is in order.

Pitirim Sorokin, who was a pioneer student in this area, constructed a model that divided group mobility into two schema; *horizontal* and *vertical*. Horizontal social mobility explains how individuals move from one social group to another on the same social stratum. Vertical social mobility describes how individuals descend and ascend from one social stratum to another in a society.[24] Sorokin developed this model in 1927, and "modern analysis has not gone far beyond"[25] his accomplishment.

Modern students have interpreted groups' mobility as being predominantly vertical in America. This is evident in Joseph A. Kahl's study on intergenerational mobility. He attempted to measure the importance of technological change on social mobility by comparing the changes in occupational standings of sons to their fathers for the period from 1920 to 1950.[26]

For conceptual clarity in this study, groups' upward mobility can be divided into a dichotomy of *ascriptive-based means* of success (vertical mobility) and *prescriptive-based means* of success (horizontal mobility).

Ascriptive-means of success are characterized by individual success; that is, an individual who makes it in spite of the adversitites confronting his group. For example, within the den of the Ku Klux Klan in Birmingham, Alabama, there emerged a Black millionaire in the 1950s, A. G. Gaston. And there are numerous other Blacks who have achieved millionaire status in spite of racial discrimination. However, through ascriptive-based means of upward mobility, we can reasonably expect only a minute number of individuals to succeed. In order to move up from the beaches of the culture of poverty collectively, groups have to utilize horizontal mobility; that is, prescriptive-based means of success.

Prescriptive-based means of success is the method the European immigrants used to elevate themselves onto the middle-class plateau. They seized control of certain sectors of the economy through the means of collective bargaining and established rules and regulations that protected jobs for themselves and their offspring. They parceled out jobs via primordial attachment; that is, individuals obtained jobs in their sector not on the basis of merit and qualifications, but through whom the applicant knew. Through primordial attachment, the group could prevent other groups from obtaining jobs in that sector that they controlled.

With collective bargaining giving them the right to participate in establishing rules and procedures for recruitment, the European immigrants were able to create an environment whereby fathers could virtually guarantee jobs for their sons at their respective place of employment. When jobs were not available, they created them through the process of *enlarging job opportunities.*

The notion of enlarging job opportunities did not just appear on the scene after the national labor law was passed. This law simply strengthened the hands of the unions to utilize this method. Essentially, enlargement job opportunities resulted from unions restricting the outputs of production; that is, making work last. As part of their conditions of work, the unions would negotiate the minimum as the "maximum, impressing upon its members that to produce more throws someone out of a job."[27] The unions were further able to enlarge job opportunities through job classifications and jurisdiction. For example, in a theater the unions would require the employer to hire separate workers to handle the curtains, property, or lights. If the theater was not unionized, all of these tasks could be handled by one person.[28]

Hence, the job enlargement process undermines the argument that the European immigrants made it because of hard work or their adherence to the Protestant work ethic. Hard work proved to be more of a disadvantage in collective bargaining than an advantage.

PRIORITY RIGHTS TO JOBS

Priority rights to jobs was another method European groups used to maintain their standing on the middle-class plateau. This method consisted of equal division of labor and seniority. Both concepts are basically the same. The major difference is the sequence of operation. Equal division of labor occurs when work is persistently irregular. When the work is slow, employees are laid off according to seniority. But the burden of layoff is shared with all workers, not concentrated with a few. Seniority comes into play in a reverse manner when the work load increases. That is, the last to be laid off are the first to be rehired.

Seniority also gives workers preference to new and high-paying jobs. Whenever a new position is made available, a senior person bidding for the position has preference for the job even if he is not the best qualified for it.

In short, through the practice of enlargement of job opportunities and priority rights to jobs, both supported by the federal government, white ethnic groups were able to elevate themselves onto, and maintain themselves on, the middle-class plateau. After they made it to the plateau, they began to establish rules and procedures to foreclose Blacks' and Puerto Ricans' freedom to elevate themselves to the same plateau, thus keeping them pinned down on the beaches of the culture of poverty until the implementation of affirmative action. The following section will be a discussion of these practices.

KEEPING BLACKS PINNED DOWN ON THE BEACHES OF THE CULTURE OF POVERTY

In their opposition to affirmative action, white ethnic groups are quick to argue that this policy penalizes them, who at no time victimized Blacks. The operative effect of this argument is to shift the blame for the present-day conditions of Blacks back to the institution of slavery or to some other factor, rather than fixing it on anything the late-nineteenth-century European immigrants have done. This line of argument overlooks two major factors: (1) the politics of inequality, and (2) the actions that European groups took to foreclose Blacks' freedom to elevate themselves from the beaches of the culture of poverty.

The cause of the present-day income inequality among Blacks can be attributed not to what happened to them during slavery, but to what happened to them from the passage of the National Labor Relations Act in 1935 to the implementation of affirmative action. As we have seen in Table 18, Blacks experienced a decline in median income among this cohort during the period between 1950 and 1970. There are two basic factors that can account for this decline. First, Congress refused to place Blacks' civil rights to acquire property and to pursue employent opportunities on a principle of law, as it did for white ethnic groups. Second, there was a dramatic increase in the amount of federally subsidized programs that benefited union workers and white workers.

GOVERNMENT REFUSAL TO OFFER BLACKS
A SYSTEM OF PROTECTION

With the exception of the licensing laws, the unions' power to foreclose Blacks' freedom to take advantage of a wide range of skilled occupations up to 1935 constituted *de facto* government action.[29] After the passage of the various national labor laws, their power consisted of *de jure* government action.

Politically, the national labor laws gave white ethnic groups the power authoritatively to allocate property and liberty interest rights to members of their groups on the basis of rights and privilege by law. (A skill within itself, it must be noted, is a property interest right. To have the freedom to pursue training for this skill is a liberty interest right.) Therefore, the NLRA gave labor unions the exclusive power (through its cardinal principle of exclusive jurisdiction) to allocate skilled jobs in those sectors that produced high income.[30] More important, this act gave the unions exclusive control over who could and could not enter the skilled trades (see section following on Federal Subsidy Programs). The unions used this power to exclude Blacks from the mainstream of society's income redistribution system.

BLACKS' ATTEMPT TO ATTACH AN
ANTI-DISCRIMINATION CLAUSE TO NLRA

The unions' legal exclusion of Blacks from the mainstream of society's income redistribution system did not constitute a policy of "benign neglect" as Daniel P. Moynihan alleged in 1972.[31] Black leaders foresaw the political repercussions of this act.[32] For example, when the NLRA was being debated in Congress, members of the National Association for the Advancement of Colored People (NAACP) and the National Urban League lobbied hard to get Congress to include into the bill a system of protection for Black workers: that is, they wanted to attach an anti-discrimination clause to it.[33] The purpose of this clause was to deny any union the protection of the federal government for collective bargaining if it had a policy of racial discrimination. Senator Robert Wagner, who sponsored the bill, had this clause written into the original draft. But the AFL, which was dominated by the late nineteenth-century immigrants, exerted its power in Congress and had the clause removed from the bill. Thus, the fight over the bill boiled down to two Black advocate organizations that were weak in resources and numbers, and the powerful AFL, which was strong in both respects. Even President Franklin D. Roosevelt, with his charismatic leadership, was unable or unwilling to withstand the pressure of the powerful AFL. Thus, from the passage of the NLRA to the implementation of the various civil rights laws, the unions not only had the power to deny Blacks their liberty interest rights to pursue a higher standard of living, but also were able to do so with the full blessing of the federal government; that is, *de jure* government action.

The power to exclude blacks from the labor market had both economic and social implications. Socially, the unions had the power to elevate or to reduce individuals' social status in society. As far as the social status of Blacks, the unions kept them pinned down on the beaches of the culture of poverty until the implementation of affirmative action. This ensured whites that Blacks would never achieve a social status equal to theirs; that is, the social equality that they historically opposed.

One of the most widely used methods by which whites maintained economic and social inequality was job encroachment and Blacks' removal from the job market. For example, if the economy was flourishing, there was a high probability that Blacks could find work in non-union shops. But as soon as there was a recession, the unions were in a position legally to move into non-union shops and use their exclusive bargaining power to force employers to dismiss Blacks and hire whites in their place. Economically, this practice significantly reduced the status of Blacks.

With the cardinal principle of exclusive jurisdiction clothed in the protection of federal law, the unions moved to foreclose a wide range of employment opportunities for Blacks from 1935 to 1970. For instance, the Brotherhood of Electrical Workers in Long Island City, New York, in the 1930s decided to expand its jurisdiction over the electrical supply shops that had employed several dozen Blacks. With a policy of racial exclusion, the Brotherhood Union moved in and organized these shops. Their first order of business was to force the employers to dismiss all Blacks. This practice was not confined only to New York but was carried out throughout the country. In St. Louis, for instance, employers found to their dismay that they could not employ even one skilled Black to build the $2 million Homer Philip Hospital in the heart of the Black community. When the General Tile Company of St. Louis attempted to hire one highly trained Black worker as a tile setter, all of the AFL's men walked off their jobs and held up construction for two months,[34] thus causing the employer to suffer irrevocable economic loss. This strike had a ripple effect upon the employment status of Blacks throughout the country, particularly in the northern cities. It touched the central nervous system of the business world and forced many employers to think twice before they employed Blacks in any capacity. For instance, the building committee of the St. Louis Board of Education refused to hire Blacks to perform maintenance work on the seventeen schools in the Black community in fear of white workers suddenly turning up sick or having to take off from work to take care of personal business. The political significance of these maintenance jobs was that they paid the "prevailing" union wages, which were covered by the Davis-Bacon Act, discussed later.

Before the passage of the NLRA, jobs in the building service areas were traditionally filled by Blacks. But when the Building Service Union was formed in the 1930s, it began to organize hotels, restaurants, and office buildings. Once these entities were unionized, white groups forced employers to discharge all Black waiters, elevator operators, and other service workers and to hire whites. There were a number of instances in which the AFL moved in to an open shop, such as the Wehr Stell Foundry of Milwaukee, organized the workers, and made one "blanket demand": fire all of your Blacks.[35] The power of the unions to make "blanket demands" on companies to fire Blacks lasted for twelve years—from 1935 to 1947. The Taft-Hartley Act of 1947 stripped the power unions of the power to make "blanket demands" on employers. By this time, the practice had taken its toll in reducing the numbers of skilled Black workers in society between 1935 to 1970.

The unions were adamant in using the instrumentalities of the government to foreclose Blacks' freedom to pursue skilled occupations. In 1963, Myrna Bain conducted a study of organized labor and Blacks. She found the unions to be extravagant in their use of collective bargaining to push Blacks out of high-paying and skilled jobs. She wrote:

When the International Brotherhood of Electrical Workers became the collective bargaining agent at the Bauer Electric Company in Hartford, Connecticut, in the late forties, the union demanded and got the removal of all Negro electricians from their jobs. The excuse was advanced that, since their union contract specified "white only," they could not and would not change this to provide continued employment for the Negroes who were at the plant before the union was recognized. Similar cases can be found in the Boilermakers' Union and the International Association of Machinists at the Boeing Aircraft Company in Seattle.[36]

From the latter part of the 1940s to the mid-1950s, the competition over recruiting members by the AFL and the Congress of Industrial Organization (CIO) offered Blacks a temporary system of protection to compete freely in skilled occupations. The CIO emerged as a strong competitor for the AFL. The CIO was able to grow fast because it recruited workers, skilled and unskilled alike, who were already on the job, including Blacks. However, the AFL used the cardinal principle of exclusive jurisdiction to recruit only skilled workers.

The AFL soon recognized that the CIO's method of recruitment was to build a strong union. If left unchecked, the former feared the latter would eventually drive them out of business. To undermine the CIO's strength, the AFL altered its racial policies and began recruiting Black workers.[37]

Although the CIO recruited Blacks, its members did not accept them on an equal basis with whites. They confined Blacks to low-paying jobs and prohibited them from participating in the upgrading and seniority systems. It was able to restrict Blacks' upward mobility by keeping a separate seniority roster.[38] The CIO also attempted to isolate Blacks into segregated locals, both in the South and the North. For example, in the North, white workers walked off their jobs when the CIO attempted to upgrade Blacks and sign them to what had been traditionally considered a "white man's job." Thus, from the end of World War II up to the merger of the AFL and CIO, Blacks' promotion and employment were related highly to competition between these two unions for membership. In the South, for instance, the CIO lost several bargaining units to the AFL largely because of their racial policies. However, the AFL lost several areas to the CIO in the North for the same reason.[39]

The competition between the AFL and CIO in recruiting Black members inadvertently offered Blacks a system of protection for employment. But when these unions merged in 1956, Blacks lost this protection and the unions resumed their policy of foreclosing Blacks' freedom to take advantage of a wide range of skilled career opportunities. Consequently, from this date up to the implementation of affirmative action, the relative numbers of skilled Blacks began to decline markedly.

The unions were able to keep the number of skilled Blacks at a significantly low number by its systems of seniority and primordial attachment. The latter system eliminated Blacks from entering skilled occupations by its method of recruitment. Skilled jobs were parceled out to individuals on the basis of kinship ties. Since Blacks had previously been excluded from skilled jobs, they were automatically excluded from the recruitment process.

The seniority system worked to the detriment of upward mobility and employment of Blacks. For example, during periods of prosperity, this system allowed Blacks to enter the labor market at the lower strata of the economic ladder. Whenever a recession sets in, the seniority system comes into play and workers are laid off according to seniority; this automatically forced Blacks to give up their low-paying jobs to whites; hence, Blacks became the victims of the revolving door.

Hence, with the full blessing of the federal government, the European immigrants were able to keep Blacks pinned down on the beaches of the culture of poverty while, at the same time, they sought to elevate themselves onto the middle-class plateau through various federally subsidized programs.

FEDERAL SUBSIDIES AND BOOTSTRAPS

As the data indicate in the tables in this chapter, all of the ethnic groups in this cohort, except Blacks and Puerto Ricans, were able to escape the slums. They were able to elevate themselves to the middle-class plateau not by hard work and their acceptance of dirty and low-paying jobs, but by the system of protection and the various federal subsidy programs (bootstraps).

This section will examine the bootstraps that the government offered white ethnic groups under the various labor laws.

The first set of bootstraps took the form of collective bargaining, which we have already discussed. Collective bargaining was the political link that connected these groups to the mainstream of society's income redistribution system. Through unionization, European groups were able to set wages by law. To further raise their standards of living, they fought successfully for the passage of the Davis-Bacon Act, which significantly raised their standard of living.

Under the Davis-Bacon Act, companies that had contracts with the government were required to "pay" 'prevailing' wages and fringe benefits to workers on federal government contracts for the construction of public buildings or public work."[40] The act served as the cornerstone for various other federally assisted programs. By 1970, the "prevailing" wages concept had spilled over to approximately 57 other federally assisted projects. The political significance of the "prevailing" wages law is that wages were determined not by the free market, but by law. This law artificially raised workers' income higher than that earned in the manufacturing and non-agricultural industries. For example, for the year 1969-1970, workers' income in the manufacturing industry increased about 5.3 percent. In the construction industry, it increased 9.2 percent.[41]

Because there was no anti-discriminatory clause to place Blacks' civil rights to employment opportunities on a principle of law, the unions foreclosed their freedom to seek jobs in the high-paying construction industry. The extent to which the unions were able to exclude Blacks has been well documented by Herbert Northrup, in *Organized Labor and the Negro*,[42] and Ray Marshall, in *The Negro and Organized Labor*.[43] Such documentation need not be rehashed here. However, there are some points that do merit discussion to shed some light on the magnitude of the unions' capacity to promote income inequality among Blacks.

Between 1941 and 1964, the executive branch attempted to police discrimination in the defense industries by issuing various executive orders. President Roosevelt established the Fair Employment Practice Commission (FEPC); Truman, the Committee on Government Contract Compliance; Eisenhower, the Presidential Committee on Government Contracts (PCGC); and Kennedy and Johnson, the Committee on Equal Employment Opportunity (EEO).[44]

These commissions had no more than investigative functions. Between 1953 and 1956, the PCGC investigated only complaints of discrimination against Blacks, except in one instance that was a complaint filed by a Hispanic against the railroad. The following passage summarizes some of the charges that the PCGC investigated:

The specific charges included denial of membership to Negroes, thereby forcing companies to discharge them; refusal by a company to hire a Negro because he could not get in the union; restricting Negroes to certain departments and excluding them from apprenticeship training programs; violation of seniority rights; providing in the contract for separate lines of progression for Negroes and whites; failure of a union to protest seniority violations; refusal to file charges against the company for failing to promote or hire Negroes in categories other than laborers and janitors. Also, a construction local was accused of rejecting an agreement with international union representatives which provided that eight or ten Negroes would be employed on a project; the result was that Negroes were denied work on the project.[45]

All of the above charges, collectively, took their toll upon the status of Blacks. But the one that had the most detrimental impact on job upward mobility was the unions' refusal to admit Blacks. When the above-mentioned commissions charged the unions with racial discrimination, the unions not only admitted that they discriminated against Blacks, but also defended their right to do so. They went so far as to include discriminatory clauses in their contracts, thus throwing the force of federal law behind their decision to foreclose Blacks' freedom to job upward mobility. For example, Blacks in Philadelphia charged a company and union with "blocking their promotion to higher jobs; the company said it would promote . . . [Blacks] if the union would agree."[46] The union flatly refused to adhere to the agreement. They argued that the FEPC did not have the legal authority to force them to allow the company to promote Blacks.

Since there were no anti-discriminatory laws in employment, the incident in Philadelphia was duplicated, if not multiplied, throughout America during the period between 1940 and 1970. Companies that attempted to hire Blacks in union shops were forced to dismiss them when the unions refused to admit them. When the FEPC found a local plumbers' union guilty of discrimination in Chicago, its officials argued that it was the prerogative of a union to discriminate.[47]

THE APPENTICESHIP PROGRAM

In addition to the NLRA and the Davis-Bacon Act, the public policy that perhaps was the next most instrumental in promoting income inequality among Blacks and the other groups in this cohort was the National Apprenticeship Act of 1937. This act was institutionalized by the apprenticeship programs in America. It had many provisions, but the one that is germane here is that which authorized the Secretary of Labor to "bring together employers and labor to create apprenticeship programs."[48] The AFL seized control of this program and began to establish rules and recruitment procedures to favor the offspring of union members. Since the unions had a long-standing policy of Black exclusion, this provision of the act allowed them to exclude Blacks with the full cooperation of the law.

Although the Bureau of Apprenticeship and Training was established to administer the program, it did little to prevent the unions from excluding

Blacks. Its director took the position that his function was largely promotional and that he had no power to eliminate discrimination in the program. The AFL objected to any attempt to force the admission of Blacks to the program. Furthermore, the U.S. Commission on Civil Rights in 1961 reported that over the period of 24 years in which the program had been in existence, the craft unions generally controlled admission to the program and they excluded Blacks on account of race.[49]

It has often been argued that one of the major reasons why Blacks have not made it is because they were latecomers and all of the skilled jobs were taken when they arrived. This argument overlooks two major factors. First, Blacks migrated North during the two world wars when the country was undergoing industrial development. Blacks experienced one of the highest periods of employment during the two wars and after World War II. Second, these arguments overlook the role that the federal and state governments played in subsidizing the apprenticeship programs for white workers.

The level of government subsidy cannot be overemphasized when one discusses the lack of skilled workers among Blacks. There was a drastic increase in government subsidies for job training between the period 1940 and 1950. For example, the number of "apprentices in training in registered programs increased from 17,300 on January 1, 1941, to 40,571 on January 1, 1945, 131,217 on January 1, 1947, and to 230,832 at the beginning of 1950."[50] Between 1950 and 1962, the number decreased to 151,490 for a variety of reasons. One reason was that there already existed a large number of trained individuals; and second, there was a recession between 1955 and 1962. Between 1962 and 1964, this number increased to 156,000.[51]

Most of the cost of the apprenticeship program was paid for by the federal government. The government reimbursed job instructor fees, paid for instructional supplies, provided consultation and advice on training problems, assisted in developing training programs, recruited job applicants, and arranged for area-wide training programs.[52] In 1962, the apprenticeship program cost the federal government $4 million annually. By 1964, this amount had increased to $5 million.[53]

The apprenticeship program covered more than the trades. It extended into the health professions, including occupational therapists, physical therapists, medical record librarians, medical technicians, X-ray technicians, and practical nurses.[54]

In addition to apprenticeship programs, there were other government subsidized programs from which the European immigrants benefited. These programs were intertwined within the three occupational categories that prescribed high income; that is, professional, managerial, and craftsmen. The level of federally subsidized programs had increased dramatically by 1972.

In 1972, Senator William Proxmire held a hearing on the economics of federal subsidy programs. At this hearing, it was discovered that federal subsidy programs constituted $63 billion of the total federal budget. This figure does not include "welfare payments, old age benefit payments" and free government services.[55] It includes programs that are fed through the private market to stimulate economic activities.

In short, groups that are locked into the mainstream of the American income redistribution system are more likely to exhibit high incomes. The white ethnic groups have been in this mainstream from its very inception. Blacks and Puerto Ricans have been on the outside. From the analysis in this chapter, it can be concluded that groups' income inequality is a function of the unequal access to the mother lode of society's income redistribution system. The government has provided some groups with a system of protection to this system and has denied the same to others on account of race.

NOTES

1. It is commonly thought that the European immigrants made it to the middle-class plateau by accepting dirty and low-paying jobs, adhering to the Protestant work ethic, and working hard. Social scientists too often overlook the role played by government in assisting these immigrant groups.

2. See Andrew M. Greeley and William C. McCready, *Ethnicity in the United States* (New York: John Wiley & Sons, 1974), chapter 11.

3. Daniel P. Moynihan, *The Negro Family* (Washington, D.C.: Department of Labor, Policy Planning and Research 1965).

4. Edward C. Banfield, *The Unheavenly City* (Boston: Little, Brown and Company, 1968), chapter 3.

5. Thomas Sowell, *Markets and Minorities* (Boston: Basic Books, 1981), chapter 1.

6. Arthur R. Jensen, "How Can We Boost IQ and Scholastic Achievement?" *Harvard Educational Review* 39 (Winter 1969): 1-123.

7. Thomas Sowell, "Culture—Not Discrimination—Decides Who Gets Ahead." *U.S. News & World Report* 91 (October 12, 1981): 74-75.

8. Larry Lavinsky, "DeFunis Symposium." *Columbia Law Review* 75 (1975): 520-535.

9. Banfield, *The Unheavenly City,* p. 49.

10. St. Clark Drake and Horace R. Clayton, *Black Metropolis* (New York: Harper and Row, 1962), chapter 9.

11. W.E.B. Du Bois, *The Philadelphia Negro* (New York: Benjamin Blom, 1967), p. 130.

12. For a discussion of the economic philosophy behind the New Deal programs, see John Kenneth Galbraith, *The Affluent Society* (Boston: Houghton Mifflin Company, 1969), chapter 8.

13. *Loew v. Lawler,* 208 U.S. 274 (1908); 52 L.ed. 488.

14. Douglas L. Leslie, *Labor Law* (St. Paul, Minn.: West Publishing Company, 1979), p. 4.

15. E. Edward Herman and Alfred Kuhn, *Collective Bargaining and Labor Relations* (Englewood Cliffs, N.J.: Prentice-Hall, 1981), p. 18.

16. This was the first federal law designed to protect labor; it is known as the Anti-Injunction Act.

17. *Supplemental Unemployment Benefit Plans and Wage Employment Guarantees* (June 1965), Bulletin 145-3 (Washington, D.C.: United States Department of Labor, Bureau of Labor Statistics).

18. Herman and Kuhn, *Collective Bargaining,* p. 405.

19. Ibid.

20. Ibid.

21. Ibid, p. 407.

22. *Jobs? or Jobless Pay? The Real Issue Behind the New Guaranteed Wage Proposals* (Washington, D.C.: Chamber of Commerce of the United States, 1954), p. 3.

23. Nathan Glazer, "Blacks and Ethnic Groups: The Difference, and the Political Difference It Makes." *Social Problems* 18 (1971): 444-461.

24. Pitirim A. Sorokin, *Social and Cultural Mobility* (New York: Free Press, 1959).

25. Celia S. Heller, ed., *Structural Social Inequality* (London: Macmillan and Company, 1969), p. 310.

26. Joseph A. Kahl, *The American Class Structure* (New York: Holt, Rinehart and Winston, 1961), pp. 251-257.

27. Herman and Kuhn, *Collective Bargaining,* p. 440.

28. Stanley B. Mathewson, *Restriction of Output Among Unorganized Workers* (New York: Viking Press, 1969), p. 173.

29. The National Labor Relations Act of 1926 was the first piece of national labor legislation enacted by Congress. An amended version of this act can be found at U.S. Code, Title 45, chapter 8.

30. G. Wilson Randle, *Collective Bargaining Principles and Practices* (Boston: Houghton Mifflin Co., 1951).

31. Moynihan, *The Negro Family.*

32. *Apprenticeship Past and Present,* United States Department of Labor, Manpower Administration, Bureau of Apprenticeship and Training (Washington: Government Printing Office, 1964).

33. See Raymond Walters, "Closed Shop and White Shop: The Negro Response to Collective Bargaining, 1933-1935," in *Black Labor in America,* Milton Contor, ed. (Westport, Conn: Negro Universities Press, 1969).

34. Frank W. McCulloch, *The National Labor Relations Board* (New York: Praeger Publishers, 1974).

35. Walters, "Closed Shop and White Shop," p. 143.

36. Myrna Bain, "Organized Labor and the Negro Worker," *National Review* (June 4, 1963), p. 455.

37. Horace R. Clayton and George S. Mitchell, *Black Workers and the Unions* (College Park, Md.: McGrath Publishing Co., 1969), chapter 11.

38. Ray Marshall, *The Negro and Organized Labor* (New York: John Wiley and Sons, 1965), p. 45.

39. Ibid., p. 56.

40. Congress of the United States, Joint Economic Committee, *The Economics of Federal Subsidy Programs* (Washington, D.C.: Government Printing Office, 1972), p. 165.

41. Ibid., p. 166.

42. Herbert Northrup, *Organized Labor and the Negro* (New York: Harper, 1944), chapter 1.

43. Marshall, chapters 2 and 3.

44. Ibid., p. 219.

45. Ibid., p. 221.

46. Ibid., p. 215.

47. Ibid.

48. U.S. Department of Labor, *Federal Labor Laws and Programs* (Washington, D.C.: Government Printing Office, 1971), p. 194.

49. "Employment," *1961 Report of the U.S. Commission on Civil Rights,* pp. 104-111.

50. Summer H. Slichter, James J. Healy, and E. Robert Livernash, *The Impact of Collective Bargaining on Management* (Washington, D.C.: The Brookings Institution, 1960), p. 69.

51. *Appendix: The Budget of the United States Government* (Washington, D.C.: Government Printing Office, 1962), p. 823.

52. United States Department of Labor. Bureau of Apprenticeship and Training, Manpower Administration, "Apprenticeship Program," 1963.

53. *Appendix: The Budget of the United States Government* (Washington, D.C.: Government Printing Office, 1962), p. 603.

54. National Manpower Council, *A Policy of Skilled Manpower* (New York: Columbia University Press, 1955), p. 205.

55. Congress of the United States, Joint Economics Committee, *The Economics of Federal Subsidy Programs,* p. 4.

9

Summary and Conclusions

Although I am confident that this book has added conceptual clarity to the study of the causes of racial inequality, it only represents the tip of the iceberg in understanding the complexities of the inherent problems involved in this area of inquiry. I am acutely aware of the many topics omitted. The intent of this study was not to cover all of the subject areas, but to develop a conceptual framework whereby a systematic interpretation of the cause of racial inequality can be analyzed. Within this framework, we are now able to formulate a set of propositions that can explain the cause of racial inequality with conceptual clarity and empirical accuracy.

Proposition 1: The majority of the European immigrants were victims of physical poverty and not the culture of poverty. The widely held thought pattern that holds that immigrants typically came over to America poor and poverty stricken, accepted dirty and low-paying jobs, worked hard and subsequently climbed the economic ladder is little more than partisan exaggeration. Implied in this argument is the notion that is currently being advocated by the critics of affirmative action; that is, the primary reason why Blacks and Puerto Ricans are disproportionately represented in the unemployment and welfare statistics is because they choose to be there.

Proposition 2: To make it to the middle-class plateau collectively, a group needs two things: a pair of boots and a set of bootstraps. A pair of boots consists of human capital in the form of education, job training, and knowledge of how the economic and political systems work. It is something that an individual can acquire on his own initiative by delaying present gratifications for future ones. However, only a minute number of individuals can make it by utilizing this method. This phenomenon is cross-cutting in that students can find evidence of success among all race and ethnic groups.

But to make it to the middle-class plateau collectively, a group needs a set of bootstraps that must be government issued. These bootstraps must consist of a system of protection that takes the civil rights of groups to acquire property and to pursue a wide range of economic opportunities off the goodwill of their competitors and adversaries and places them on a principle of law. Without such a system of protection, groups are destined to remain pinned down on the beaches of the culture of poverty by their competitors and adversaries until the culture of poverty itself begins to develop among them. Once developed, it becomes self-perpetuating.

The political significance of a set of government issued bootstraps is that it not only safeguards a group's civil rights to acquire property, but also offers its members economic inducements to fashion linkages with the mother lode of society's income redistribution system. Evidence to this effect can be found in the literature from the colonial period to the present day. These economic inducements consisted of: (1) the headright system during the colonial period, (2) Land Act of 1800 (amended 1804 and 1820), (3) the Homestead Act of 1862, and (4) the system of protection the government offered workers (the guild system and the labor unions) to safeguard their civil rights to economic opportunities. These factors prevented these groups from falling victim to the culture of poverty in their initial stages of contact with the American polity.

Proposition 3: European ethnic groups that immigrated between the period 1880 and 1910 only began to climb the economic ladder after the government issued them a set of bootstraps in the 1930s and 1940s. These straps consisted of various labor laws, such as the National Labor Relations Act and the National Apprenticeship Act. These laws (1) clothed their jobs with a system of job security (collective bargaining), and (2) locked them into the income redistribution system.

The collective bargaining laws constituted a system of protection that took white ethnic groups' property and liberty interest rights to employment opportunities off the goodwill of management and placed them on a principle of law. Accompanying the collective bargaining laws was a system of subsidies in terms of supplementary income and fringe benefits. This system of subsidies played a dominant role in preventing the culture of poverty from developing among them, for it connected them to the mother lode of society's income redistribution system.

Proposition 4: The basic cause of racial inequality in America can be attributed to the politics of racial inequality. These politics consist of the government failing to offer racial groups, that is, those that have fallen victim to the culture of poverty, a system of protection that would grant them the freedom: (1) to interact in a human capital environment, and (2) to enter into the *mother lode of society's income redistribution system.*

Proposition 5: Racial discrimination does not constrain group economic growth and development per se. Groups can overcome the effects of discrimination if they are granted a system of protection to safeguard their civil rights to acquire a sufficient amount of human capital to compete successfully in a competitive society. This is evidenced by the success of the British West Indians, Chinese, and Japanese.

These propositions encompass many of the arguments already advanced as to how groups are able to elevate themselves to the middle-class plateau. They do not, however, address the arguments centered around the role that group values and family structure play in the success of these groups. These arguments have been deferred to another study because they are beyond the scope of this one. A major problem with these arguments is that students too often attempt to discuss group work values and family structure without conducting a systematic analysis of the relationships between these and other political variables, such as public policy and the theory of socialization. It would be senseless, as it seems, for scientists to discuss a group's lack of work values and family structure without selecting as their basic unit of analysis those public policies that grant or restrict a group's access to the agents of socialization.

Until the passage of the 1964 Civil Rights Act and the implementation of affirmative-action policy, Blacks' civil rights to acquire property and to pursue a wide range of employment opportunities rested on the goodwill of their competitors and adversaries. According to James Madison, this political construction is the exact meaning of tyranny. He defined "tyranny" as every severe deprivation of natural rights. The civil rights laws placed external checks on the tyrannical tendency of the adversaries and competitors of Blacks to deprive them of their natural rights to enter society's income redistribution system.

Without a system of protection, a group's civil rights to enter the mother lode of society's income redistribution system rests on the goodwill of their competitors and adversaries. The term "goodwill" is not to be understood here as mere political rhetoric. Its essence is deeply rooted in traditional Western philosophical and theological thought. An elaboration of the essence of the "will" requires more space than this study allows. It is a subject that needs to be discussed in relation to the affirmative-action policy as a system of protection that grants Blacks and other racial minority groups a right to acquire property.

In short, the socioeconomic status of Blacks and the Puerto Ricans will become progressively worse as long as their property and liberty interest rights to acquire property and to pursue a wide range of employment opportunities rest on the goodwill of their competitors and adversaries. Such political status will foster and perpetuate racial inequality.

Appendix

Table 19
Employment Status and Major Occupation of Foreign Males Ten Years Old and Over in Certain Selected States, 1920

Subject	Total	English[a]	Germans	Swedes	Norwegians	Irish	Italians	Russian Jews
Males employed	289,292	24,065	67,457.	27,665	27,568	12,612	53,708	12,559
Percent	100.0	100.0	100.0	100.0	100.0	100.0	100.0	100.0
Agricultural: Farmers	37.6	18.1	64.6	81.4	87.3	13.5	0.9	4.1
Coal Mine Operatives	31.2	41.0	8.0	3.9	0.2	18.5	50.2	33.9
Managerial, Foreman, etc.	2.5	5.6	2.8	1.3	0.5	8.3	2.8	2.8
Skilled Mechanics: Carpenters	9.2	13.8	8.1	10.3	11.3	18.5	10.2	11.5
Laborers:								
Blast Furnaces	10.0	8.0	6.0	1.4	0.03	15.8	16.4	16.2
Steam Railroad	4.1	2.0	1.6	0.5	0.04	8.6	13.4	2.8
Professional: Physicians and Surgeons	0.6	0.8	0.8	0.09	0.05	0.8	0.7	3.8
Clerical: Salesmen	6.0	10.5	8.0	0.8	0.4	15.8	5.2	25.0

SOURCE: Immigrants and Their Children, pp. 283-84.

[a] The English category encompasses all of the groups from the United Kingdom (Scots, Welsh, and English) except the Irish.

Notes: The data in this table are limited to the extent that they cover only six states (Massachusetts, New York, Pennsylvania, Michigan, Minnesota, and Wisconsin), and do not represent the total population for each group. However, these states were selected because they had the largest numbers of foreign-born employed in occupations selected.

Table 20
Occupation of Ethnic Groups by Sex and Age

Race or People	Total 100%	Males	Females	Under 14 yrs.	14-45 yrs.	Over 45 yrs.	Total 100%	Professional	Commercial	Skilled	Unskilled
African (Black)	3,786	62.2	37.8	9.1	86.8	4.1	2,921	3.0	2.6	45.6	48.8
Armenian	1,895	75.1	24.9	11.8	84.3	3.9	1,390	3.4	5.1	38.5	53.0
Bohemian & Moravian	12,958	57.3	42.8	20.7	73.9	5.4	7,985	1.3	1.2	43.6	53.9
Bulgarian, Serbian, & Montenegrin	11,548	96.2	3.8	1.9	96.2	1.9	11,025	0.1	0.3	3.7	95.9
Chinese	1,485	94.1	5.9	4.5	81.5	14.0	1,261	6.9	66.0	1.5	25.6
Croatian & Slovenian	44,272	86.5	13.5	3.8	94.1	2.1	40,125	0.1	0.1	3.7	96.1
Cuban	5,591	67.4	32.6	17.2	73.2	9.6	2,842	10.3	19.1	55.9	14.7
Dalmatian, Bosnian, & Herzegovinian	4,591	95.1	4.9	1.7	96.3	2.0	4,373	0.1	0.3	7.7	91.9
Dutch & Flemish	9,735	67.0	33.0	17.6	76.4	6.0	5,849	5.2	7.9	30.1	56.8
East Indian	271	93.0	7.0	5.5	90.5	4.0	222	9.9	52.7	5.4	32.0
English	45,079	62.1	37.9	13.5	75.3	11.2	28,249	10.8	13.5	51.3	24.4
Finnish	14,136	67.4	32.6	7.1	90.8	2.1	11,959	0.4	0.3	7.2	92.1
French	10,379	57.1	42.9	8.6	81.7	9.7	6,823	16.5	12.9	31.3	39.3
German	86,813	59.2	40.8	15.1	78.6	6.3	55,095	4.3	6.7	29.7	59.3
Greek	23,127	96.3	3.7	3.1	95.9	1.0	21,615	0.5	2.6	9.4	87.5
Hebrew	153,748	52.1	47.9	28.3	66.3	5.4	76,605	1.4	5.6	66.7	26.3
Irish	40,959	50.9	49.1	4.6	90.9	4.5	35,387	1.7	2.9	15.1	80.3
Italian (North)	46,286	78.9	21.1	8.6	87.9	3.5	36,980	1.4	2.3	19.4	76.9
Italian (South)	240,528	79.4	20.6	11.1	84.3	4.6	190,105	0.4	1.3	16.0	82.3

Table 20 *(continued)*

Race or People	Total 100%	Males	Females	Under 14 yrs.	14-45 yrs.	Over 45 yrs.	Total 100%	Professional	Commercial	Skilled	Unskilled
Japanese	14,243	89.6	10.4	1.0	97.1	1.9	11,797	2.2	10.3	2.8	84.7
Korean	127	81.1	18.9	16.5	81.1	2.4	90	6.3	15.0	2.5	76.2
Lithuanian	14,257	66.1	33.9	8.9	89.5	1.6	11,568	0.2	0.2	9.2	90.4
Magyar	44,261	71.8	28.2	9.0	87.5	3.5	34,559	0.6	0.5	9.3	89.6
Mexican	141	66.0	34.0	14.9	74.5	10.6	65	23.1	35.4	24.6	16.9
Pacific Islander	13	76.9	23.1	7.7	76.9	15.4	9	33.3	0.0	66.7	0.0
Polish	95,835	69.3	30.7	9.3	88.5	2.2	77,437	0.2	0.2	7.7	91.9
Portuguese	8,729	58.4	41.6	20.9	70.7	8.4	5,815	0.5	1.1	4.8	93.6
Romanian	11,425	92.5	7.5	2.0	94.0	4.0	10,759	0.2	0.2	2.5	97.1
Russian	5,814	82.7	18.3	10.0	86.8	3.2	4,591	3.2	2.4	10.8	83.6
Ruthenian	16,257	75.7	24.3	3.6	93.9	2.5	14,899	0.1	0.0	2.7	97.2
Scandinavian	58,141	62.1	37.9	9.1	86.4	4.5	47,352	1.8	1.6	23.5	73.1
Scottish	16,463	66.1	33.9	12.9	78.8	8.3	11,207	5.7	9.9	62.8	21.6
Slovak	38,221	69.6	30.4	8.9	88.4	2.7	29,817	0.0	0.1	4.9	95.0
Spanish	5,332	83.6	16.4	7.1	84.6	8.3	4,211	5.7	19.2	44.4	30.7
Spanish American	1,585	69.7	30.3	17.0	74.4	8.6	790	23.7	37.1	21.1	18.1
Syrian	5,824	70.4	29.6	15.2	80.9	3.9	4,023	1.1	11.1	19.9	67.9
Turkish	2,033	95.7	4.3	1.9	96.0	2.1	1,914	1.5	4.4	8.3	85.8
Welsh	2,367	70.1	29.9	12.5	78.2	9.3	1,639	4.9	6.7	62.4	26.0
West Indian	1,476	58.9	41.1	14.8	76.1	9.1	900	7.6	15.0	49.4	28.0
Other Peoples	1,027	94.5	41.1	14.8	76.1	9.1	932	1.2	4.1	18.0	76.7
Total	1,100,735	69.5	30.5	12.4	83.0	4.6	812,275	1.8	3.1	21.7	73.4

SOURCE: Reports of Commission-General of Immigration, 1906, Table 8, p. 28.

174

Table 21
Population of the Caribbean Area by National Affiliation and Race, 1936

Political Area	National Affiliation	Total	Colored	White	Others
Total		12,397,222	8,084,778	3,862,058	451,376
Bahamas	Great Britain	62,697	48,697	13,000	1,000
Barbados	Great Britain	180,055	162,055	18,000	--
Bermuda	Great Britain	29,896	17,862	11,684	350
Cuba	Republic	4,011,088	1,300,000	2,444,000	268,088
Grenada	Great Britain	78,662	62,919	15,576	157
Guadeloupe	France	267,407	213,925	52,948	534
Haiti	Republic	2,650,000	2,646,000	3,500	500
Jamaica	Great Britain	1,090,269	1,040,269	20,000	30,000
Leeward Islands	Great Britain	132,973	106,378	26,330	265
Martinique	France	234,695	187,756	46,470	469
Puerto Rico	United States	1,623,814	473,664	1,150,000	150
St. Lucia	Great Britain	62,000	49,600	12,276	124
St. Vincent	Great Britain	47,961	44,549	2,173	1,239
Santo Domingo	Republic	1,478,121	1,444,621	30,000	3,500
Trinidad	Great Britain	425,572	265,572	15,000	145,000
Virgin Islands	United States	22,012	20,911	1,101	--

SOURCE: Ira De Reid, The Negro Immigrant (New York: Columbia University Press, 1936), p. 238.

Table 22
Family Income by Ethnic Origin, 1950[a]

	Total	English	Germans	Origin Irish	Italians	Norwegians	Poles	Russian Jews
All persons	25,559,964	1,306,685	3,558,005	1,766,335	2,774,495	618,925	1,771,245	1,459,520
Percent	100.0	100.0	100.0	100.0	100.0	100.0	100.0	100.0
Percent of persons with income	62.4	6.4	63.0	63.1	63.2	65.3	65.4	61.5
Under $500	12.3	9.0	9.3	7.7	5.8	9.8	5.9	6.0
$500 to $999	9.4	7.5	7.6	7.6	5.6	8.0	5.4	4.5
$1,000 to $1,499	7.3	5.6	5.8	5.6	6.4	6.6	6.7	4.9
$1,500 to $1,999	6.6	5.5	5.5	5.9	7.8	6.6	6.7	4.9
$2,000 to $2,499	7.0	6.6	6.5	7.4	9.9	6.1	9.3	6.7
$2,500 to $2,999	5.3	5.0	5.6	6.5	8.2	7.0	8.8	6.0
$3,000 to $3,999	7.7	11.0	10.6	11.4	11.9	10.6	14.2	10.2
$4,000 to $4,999	3.0	5.3	5.1	5.0	4.0	5.0	4.9	5.4
$5,000 to $5,999	1.5	2.8	2.6	2.5	1.6	2.4	1.9	4.2
$6,000 and over	2.2	4.4	4.0	3.2	1.6	3.5	2.2	7.4
Median income	$2,245	$2,322	$2,245	$2,309	$2,137	$2,475	$2,775	$2,887
Not reported	6.1	5.3	4.7	5.5	5.1	3.7	4.6	5.5
Percent above $2,500	19.7	28.5	27.9	28.6	27.3	28.5	32.0	33.2

Table 22 *(continued)*

	Spanish	Swedes	Blacks	Puerto Ricans[c]	Japanese[b]	Chinese[b]
All persons	566,540	820,870	10,505,185	216,830	109,410	90,615
Percent	100.0	100.0	100.0	100.0	100.0	100.0
Percent of persons with income	55.2	66.0	61.3	56.8	62.7	56.7
Under $500	13.2	8.0	18.7	6.0	8.8	6.9
$500 to $999	10.9	6.5	13.1	8.7	9.0	8.1
$1,000 to $1,499	8.6	5.5	8.8	10.1	8.0	8.1
$1,500 to $1,999	6.6	5.7	7.1	11.5	8.0	8.3
$2,000 to $2,499	6.1	7.3	-	9.7	9.7	8.8
$2,500 to $2,999	3.8	6.4		4.6	6.0	4.7
$3,000 to $3,999	4.2	12.3	2.8	-	7.6	6.1
$4,000 to $4,999	0.9	6.3	0.4	0.4	2.3	2.3
$5,000 to $5,999	0.2	3.1	-	0.5	1.2	1.2
$6,000 and over	0.3	4.3	0.2	0.7	1.7	1.5
Median income	$1,200	$2,483	$952	$1,654	$1,839	$1,799
Not reported	5.7	4.2	7.6	-	6.9	10.4
Percent above $2,500	9.4	32.4	3.4	6.2	18.8	15.8

[a]Calculated from: U. S. Bureau of Census, U. S. Census of Population: 1950, vol. 4. Special Reports, Part 3, Chapter A, Nativity and Parentage (Washington: Government Printing Office, 1954), pp. 13-45, 56-83.

[b]Calculated from: U. S. Bureau of Census, U. S. Census Population: 1950, vol. 4, Special Reports, Part 3, Chapter B, Nonwhite Population by Race (Washington: Government Printing Office, 1953), pp. 14-20, 30-40.

[c]Calculated from: U. S. Census of Population: 1950, Continental United States (Washington: Government Printing Office, 1953), chap. 2.

Table 23
Family Income by Ethnic Origin, 1970

	Total	English	Germans	Origin Irish	Italians	Poles	Russian Jews	Swedes
Total family heads	10,375,309	590,853	949,127	423,888	1,314,594	740,112	635,270	277,584
Percent	100.0	100.0	100.0	100.0	100.0	100.0	100.0	100.0
Under $1,000	3.8	1.3	1.8	1.3	1.3	1.0	1.1	1.3
$1,000 to $1,999	5.0	2.1	3.9	2.0	1.3	1.3	1.2	2.7
$2,000 to $2,999	6.0	3.7	6.4	3.3	1.7	1.8	1.8	4.8
$3,000 to $3,999	6.4	8.9	6.5	3.9	2.2	2.3	2.1	5.1
$4,000 to $4,999	6.0	4.4	6.0	4.0	2.6	2.5	2.4	3.8
$5,000 to $5,999	6.2	4.4	6.1	4.3	3.5	3.4	2.9	5.0
$6,000 to $6,999	6.2	4.6	5.6	4.6	4.6	4.2	3.3	5.2
$7,000 to $7,999	6.3	5.2	5.8	4.9	5.8	5.3	3.8	5.4
$8,000 to $8,999	12.0	11.7	11.6	13.5	14.3	13.2	9.3	11.9
$10,000 to 14,999	22.7	28.0	24.2	29.1	33.3	32.0	25.0	26.0
$15,000 to $24,999	12.4	22.3	16.8	24.2	23.2	24.9	27.6	20.7
$25,000 or more	4.4	7.2	5.1	7.0	5.8	7.6	18.6	6.7
Median income	$11,374	$11,374	$9,352	$11,776	$11,857	$12,274	$14,281	$10,568
Income below poverty	-	5.4	8.1	5.1	4.5	3.8	3.8	6.2
Percent above $10,000	39.5	57.5	46.1	60.3	62.3	64.5	71.2	53.4

Table 23 *(continued)*

	Norwegians	Spanish	Blacks	West Indians	Japanese	Chinese
Total family heads	201,125	375,255	4,729,091	29,968	80,727	27,713
Percent	100.0	100.0	100.0	100.0	100.0	100.0
Under $1,000	1.5	3.3	6.6	2.6	0.8	1.5
$1,000 to $1,999	3.4	4.0	8.1	2.4	0.8	2.0
$2,000 to $2,999	5.5	5.4	9.0	3.0	1.8	2.2
$3,000 to $3,999	6.0	6.8	9.2	3.9	1.4	2.8
$4,000 to $4,999	5.7	7.3	8.5	4.2	1.6	2.8
$5,000 to $5,999	5.3	7.7	8.2	5.1	2.6	4.5
$6,000 to $6,999	5.4	8.5	7.8	6.3	3.0	4.5
$7,000 to $7,999	5.8	8.6	7.1	6.4	4.0	4.6
$8,000 to $8,999	11.9	16.2	11.6	12.1	10.4	10.6
$10,000 to 14,999	25.7	24.0	15.9	28.0	31.4	27.8
$15,000 to $24,999	17.9	9.4	6.6	20.0	32.9	27.8
$25,000 or more	5.2	1.3	0.8	5.1	9.3	8.7
Median income	$9,826	$7,846	$6,005	$10,624	$13,775	$12,606
Income below poverty	7.6	20.6	30.3	5.1	3.2	6.4
Percent above $10,000	48.8	34.7	23.3	53.1	73.6	64.3

Calculated from: U. S. Bureau of the Census, Census of the Population: 1970, Subject Reports, Final Report PC (2)-1A, National Origin and Language (Washington: Government Printing Office, 1973), pp. 23-40, 65-70.

Table 24
Employment Status and Major Occupation of the Male Population
Fourteen Years Old and Over, by Ethnic Origin, 1950[a]

Subject	Total	English	Germans	Origin Irish	Italians	Poles	Russian Jews
Males employed	9,021,899	455,617	1,283,475	556,598	1,075,069	711,598	597,963
Percent	100.0	100.0	100.0	100.0	100.0	100.0	100.0
Prof., techn., & kindred wkrs.	6.2	11.2	7.3	9.7	6.0	6.9	15.3
Farmers & farm managers	9.7	5.7	14.8	2.8	1.1	2.3	4.9
Mgrs., offs., & props., exc., farm	8.9	14.6	12.5	12.4	11.1	-	25.5
Clerical & kindred wkrs.	11.5	17.6	12.9	12.0	15.2	13.8	23.9
Craftsmen, foremen, & kind. wkrs.	15.4	22.0	22.4	19.3	21.3	22.3	10.5
Operatives & kindred workers	20.8	17.0	16.2	16.3	28.4	31.4	12.0
Private household workers	0.5	0.1	0.1	0.1	0.05	0.5	0.02
Service wkrs., exc. priv. household	9.0	5.5	5.2	10.9	6.5	4.6	2.7
Farm laborers & foremen	4.4	0.2	0.7	0.15	0.1	0.37	0.9
Farm Laborers, exc. unpaid & foremen	3.6	1.0	1.8	0.6	0.5	0.8	2.5
Laborers, exc. farm & mine	13.0	4.5	0.7	5.4	8.3	7.3	-

Table 24 *(continued)*

	Swedes	Norwegians	Spanish[c]	Blacks[b]	Puerto Ricans	Japanese	Chinese[b]
Males employed	330,875	241,033	179,220	3,501,481	64,980	42,499	40,131
Percent	100.0	100.0	100.0	100.0	100.0	100.0	100.0
Prof., techn., & kindred wkrs.	10.3	7.5	1.8	2.2	5.1	6.4	6.3
Farmers & farm managers	13.0	22.4	2.7	13.4	0.2	15.3	1.4
Mgrs., offs., & props., exc., farm	13.3	11.4	2.9	2.1	5.3	8.6	22.2
Clerical & kindred wkrs.	14.3	11.9	7.6	4.2	9.4	9.1	11.2
Craftsmen, foremen, & kind. wkrs.	22.7	18.8	13.2	7.7	32.4	7.6	3.3
Operatives & kindred workers	14.1	12.3	23.6	21.0	0.1	9.7	16.3
Private household workers	0.09	0.09	0.1	1.0	24.6	8.7	1.8
Service wkrs., exc. priv. household	3.8	3.9	6.2	13.2	0.05	8.7	32.3
Farm laborers & foremen	0.7	1.4	2.25	10.3	2.5	2.3	0.1
Farm laborer, exc. upaid & foremen	1.7	3.3	17.5	-	7.1	14.4	1.3
Laborers, exc. farm & mine	4.8	5.7	20.7	23.3	1.6	13.5	1.9

[a] U.S. Census of Population:1950, vol. 4, Special Reports, Part 3.

[b] U.S. Census of Population:1950, vol. 4, Special Reports, Part 3, Chapter B.

[c] U.S. Census of Population:1950, Continetal United States.

Table 25
Employment Status and Major Occupation of the Male Population
Fourteen Years Old and Over, by Ethnic Origin, 1960[a]

Subject	Total	English	Germans	Origin Irish	Italians	Poles	Russian Jews
Males employed	8,627,270	599,610	1,002,960	434,682	1,272,754	784.066	652,605
Percent	100.0	100.0	100.0	100.0	100.0	100.0	100.0
Prof., techn., & kindred wkrs.	9.3	15.1	9.8	13.3	9.6	11.4	20.0
Farmers & farm managers	4.5	3.2	11.7	1.5	0.8	1.6	3.5
Mgrs., offs., & props., exc., farm	9.5	15.0	12.7	12.7	11.6	10.5	23.3
Clerical & kindred wkrs.	7.7	9.5	7.3	14.2	8.8	8.1	7.0
Sales workers	5.8	8.5	6.6	7.8	7.0	6.6	16.0
Craftsmen, foremen, & kind. wkrs.	18.0	17.7	23.1	18.6	23.4	24.0	12.0
Operatives & kindred workers	23.1	14.8	16.1	14.6	23.8	25.3	10.0
Private household workers	0.3	–	–	–	–	–	–
Service wkrs., exc. priv. household	10.1	5.8	5.5	10.4	7.3	8.4	3.0
Farm laborers & foremen	3.9	0.6	1.5	0.4	0.2	5.2	0.5
Laborers, exc. farm & mine	12.1	3.7	4.7	4.3	6.2	–	2.1

Table 25 *(continued)*

	Swedes	Norwegians	Spanish[c]	Blacks[b]	Puerto Ricans[d]	Japanese	Chinese[d]
Males employed	299,583	–	276,392	3,336,641	181,991	113,472	66,704
Percent	100.0	–	100.0	100.0	100.0	100.0	100.0
Prof., techn., & kindred wkrs.	13.1	–	4.2	3.0	2.7	12.6	18.3
Farmers & farm managers	9.7	–	1.3	6.2	0.1	12.0	0.7
Mgrs., offs., & props., exc., farm	14.8	–	3.6	0.9	3.1	9.5	15.5
Clerical & kindred wkrs.	7.6	–	5.8	4.9	7.3	7.6	7.6
Sales workers	7.2	–	3.4	1.2	2.7	5.8	6.0
Craftsmen, foremen, & kind. wkrs.	22.9	–	18.0	9.7	10.6	20.1	6.8
Operatives & kindred workers	13.7	–	18.0	24.3	38.8	11.5	12.5
Private household workers	–	–	–	–	–	5.8	0.6
Service wkrs., exc. priv. household	4.3	–	6.6	0.7	0.06	4.7	22.7
Farm laborers & foremen	1.1	–	10.6	13.9	17.1	5.9	0.4
Laborers, exc. farm & mine	6.0	–	15.8	20.4	6.1	6.2	1.7

[a]Calculated from: U.S. Bureau of the Census, U.S. Census of Population: 1960, Subjects, Nativity and Parentage, Final Report PC (2)-1A (Washington: Government Printing Office, 1965, pp. 34-65, 70-80.

[b]U.S. Bureau of the Census, U.S. Census of Population: 1960, Subject Reports, Nonwhite Population by Race, Final Report PC (2)-1c (Washington: Government Printing Office, 1963), pp. 56-87.

[c]U.S. Bureau of the Census, U.S. Census of Population: 1960, Subject Reports, Persons of Spanish surname. Report PC (2)-1B, pp. 13-38.

[d]U.S. Bureau of the Census, U.S. Census of Population: 1960, Puerto Ricans in the United States Final Report PC (2)-1D, pp. 11-34.

Table 26
Employment Status and Major Occupation of the Male Population
Fourteen Years Old and Over, by Ethnic Origin, 1970[a]

Subject	Total	English	Germans	Origin Irish	Italians	Poles	Russian Jews
Males employed	8,734,692	447,424	657,150	329,688	1,231,052	685,002	586,991
Percent	100.0	100.0	100.0	100.0	100.0	100.0	100.0
Prof., techn., & kindred wkrs.	11.2	19.6	14.3	17.6	12.5	15.5	25.4
Mgrs., adm., & exc. farm	9.8	16.0	13.4	15.0	13.7	11.5	23.5
Sales workers	5.5	8.6	7.4	8.4	7.5	7.2	16.0
Clerical & kindred wkrs.	7.1	9.1	7.6	12.3	9.0	8.7	7.5
Craftsmen, & kindred wkrs.	18.3	20.5	22.0	17.5	23.7	23.6	12.0
Operatives & exc. farm	13.8	9.0	10.3	7.0	11.9	16.7	5.2
Transport equip. operatives	7.0	4.2	4.6	4.9	6.2	4.5	3.5
Laborers, exc. farm	6.8	3.6	4.0	3.7	5.3	4.5	1.9
Farmers & farm managers	1.9	2.0	8.0	0.7	0.6	0.9	2.4
Farm laborers & farm foremen	2.1	0.5	1.3	0.3	0.2	0.2	0.4
Service wkrs., exc. priv. household	21.4	7.2	7.6	12.3	9.3	7.1	3.7
Private household workers	00.2	0.03	0.03	0.03	0.02	0.01	0.0

Table 26 *(continued)*

	Swedes	Norwegians	Hispanics	Blacks	West Indians	Japanese	Chinese
Males employed	204,424	151,127	360,098	3,933,984	27,881	84,142	33,606
Percent	100.0	100.0	100.0	100.0	100.0	100.0	100.0
Prof., techn., & kindred wkrs.	16.7	14.4	6.7	5.6	17.3	20.0	27.7
Mgrs., adm., & exc. farm	16.2	14.3	5.1	3.0	8.6	13.8	14.0
Sales workers	8.0	7.3	3.7	2.0	5.3	5.8	6.0
Clerical & kindred wkrs.	7.7	6.6	7.2	7.8	16.0	8.5	14.2
Craftsmen, & kindred wkrs.	22.0	21.5	21.9	15.2	16.7	22.2	10.5
Operatives & exc. farm	8.6	8.0	17.0	19.8	9.3	6.5	7.5
Transport equip. operatives	3.7	4.3	7.7	10.0	7.6	3.6	1.7
Laborers, exc. farm	3.5	4.0	12.0	16.0	6.0	9.0	4.2
Farmers & farm managers	6.7	11.5	0.5	0.9	0.9	4.3	0.7
Farm laborers & farm foremen	1.0	1.5	6.8	3.5	0.3	2.2	0.4
Service wkrs., exc. priv. household	5.9	6.6	9.2	15.6	14.6	5.5	12.9
Private household workers	0.04	0.0	0.07	0.4	0.06	0.09	0.2

[a]U.S Bureau of the Census, Census of the Population: 1970, Subject Reports, Final Report PC (2)-1A.

185

Table 27

Highest Grade of School Completed by Persons Fourteen Years Old and Over, by Ethnic Origin: Male, 1950[a]

| | | | Percent Distribution by Years of School Completed | | | | | | | |
	Total (thousand)	Total Percent	Elementary 0-4 Yrs.	Elementary 5-7 Yrs.	Elementary 8 Yrs.	High School 1-3 Yrs.	High School 4 Yrs.	College 1-3 Yrs.	College 7 Yrs. or more	Median School Yrs. Completed
Total	11,929,853	100.0	13.6	20.1	18.9	19.2	15.3	5.6	5.1	10.7
English	612,515	100.0	3.9	12.2	21.0	20.4	21.8	9.6	9.1	8.7
Germans	1,673,760	100.0	6.5	18.8	32.2	15.5	14.7	5.5	5.5	10.0
Irish	804,425	100.0	3.8	12.4	23.4	20.6	22.5	7.8	7.8	10.4
Italians	1,364,750	100.0	2.9	12.7	20.1	29.6	23.7	5.6	4.2	9.0
Norwegians	297,325	100.0	4.1	14.6	30.8	16.1	18.2	8.4	6.6	10.2
Poles	871,580	100.0	3.6	13.3	21.8	25.4	21.8	7.0	5.9	10.2
Russian Jews[b]	718,720	100.0	2.1	6.2	13.0	18.6	26.8	14.3	17.5	12.3
Spanish[b]	260,140	100.0	21.5	27.1	14.6	22.1	9.5	2.6	0.9	7.6
Swedes[b]	398,590	100.0	2.5	10.1	26.7	19.2	22.9	9.3	8.2	10.6
Blacks[b]	4,717,840	100.0	26.7	29.3	12.0	15.8	7.5	2.8	1.5	6.6
Puerto Ricans[c]	99,185	100.0	15.9	24.3	19.9	17.9	9.5	3.2	2.2	8.2
Japanese[b]	57,645	100.0	4.1	4.2	13.5	13.9	36.2	11.6	7.7	12.2
Chinese[b]	53,480	100.0	15.1	15.8	11.5	14.3	14.6	9.1	9.1	8.4

[a] U.S. Bureau of the Census: 1950, vol. 4, Special Reports, Part 3, Final Report PC (2)-1A.

[b] U.S. Bureau of the Census: 1950, vol. 4, Special Reports, Part 3, Chapter B.

[c] U.S. Census of Population: 1950, Continental United States.

186

Table 28

Highest Grade of School Completed by Persons Fourteen Years Old and Over, by Ethnic Origin: Male, 1960[a]

| | | | Percent Distribution by Years of School Completed | | | | | | | | |
| | Total (thousand) | Total Percent | Elementary | | | High School | | College | | | Median School Yrs. Completed |
			0-4 Yrs.	5-7 Yrs.	8 Yrs.	1-3 Yrs.	4 Yrs.	1-3 Yrs.	7 Yrs. or More	
Total	12,391,165	100.0	11.1	18.8	17.3	24.3	18.9	7.5	7.0	10.0
English	848,367	100.0	2.9	10.9	17.4	22.2	23.3	11.5	11.8	11.5
Germans	1,475,457	100.0	5.8	18.4	28.5	17.4	16.0	7.3	6.7	8.9
Irish	626,142	100.0	10.8	19.3	22.5	23.4	10.7	11.7	11.0	11.3
Italians	1,505,313	100.0	2.6	11.1	17.4	29.1	25.2	7.4	17.2	10.9
Norwegians	287,051	100.0	3.6	13.6	27.6	16.7	20.4	9.4	8.7	9.9
Poles	938,061	100.0	3.2	12.5	18.7	35.1	22.1	8.7	9.8	10.9
Russian Jews	754,926	100.0	1.8	5.6	11.6	19.2	24.0	15.2	22.7	12.5
Spanish	389,074	100.0	21.1	20.7	13.7	23.8	13.6	5.1	2.1	8.6
Swedes[b]	391,736	100.0	2.3	10.4	23.8	19.6	23.6	10.3	10.1	11.1
Blacks	5,427,941	100.0	18.6	24.3	13.6	12.3	12.7	4.2	2.3	8.3
Puerto Ricans[c]	267,303	100.0	16.1	2.4	18.0	24.7	11.6	3.2	1.7	8.2
Japanese[d]	152,747	100.0	3.3	7.0	12.2	19.5	33.4	12.0	12.2	12.2
Chinese	57,815	100.0	6.4	9.4	9.3	16.1	26.9	13.1	13.9	11.7

[a] U.S. Bureau of the Census: 1960 Final Report PC (2)-1A, Final Report PC (2)-1A.

[b] U.S. Census of Population: 1960, Final Report, PC (2)-1B

[c] U.S. Census of Population: 1960, Final Report, PC (2)-1C

[d] U.S. Census of Population: 1960, Final Report, PC (2)-1D

Table 29
Highest Grade of School Completed by Persons Fourteen Years Old
and Over, by Ethnic Origin: Male, 1970

Percent Distribution by Years of School Completed

	Total (thousand)	Total Percent	Elementary			High School		College		Median School Yrs. Completed
			0-4 Yrs.	5-7 Yrs.	8 Yrs.	1-3 Yrs.	4 Yrs.	1-3 Yrs.	7 Yrs. or More	
Total	10,480,741	100.0	2.3	7.6	13.8	20.6	23.9	8.4	9.6	12.4
English	614,245	100.0	0.4	1.4	12.4	18.2	29.5	13.4	17.5	12.2
Germans	1,028,662	100.0	0.6	3.3	25.3	16.8	21.5	8.5	10.0	10.2
Irish	460,629	100.0	0.5	1.4	13.8	19.3	29.7	11.9	16.4	12.3
Italians	1,355,062	100.0	0.7	1.6	14.0	25.4	30.4	8.4	10.1	11.9
Norwegians	221,605	100.0	0.4	2.0	25.2	15.6	24.5	10.2	12.2	11.3
Polish	785,523	100.0	0.5	2.0	16.0	13.8	26.0	9.2	13.3	11.8
Russian Jews	664,142	100.0	0.5	1.0	9.3	14.7	26.3	14.9	28.6	12.8
Spanish	361,908	100.0	6.9	12.8	10.5	19.8	20.8	7.9	4.6	9.4
Swedes	297,561	100.0	0.3	1.2	19.8	17.5	28.3	11.6	13.9	12.1
Blacks	4,582,583	100.0	4.0	14.0	10.2	23.0	19.8	5.6	3.9	9.3
Chinese	31,908	100.0	3.7	3.5	5.4	10.5	26.0	16.0	27.4	12.7
Japanese	86,923	100.0	0.6	1.3	7.5	12.3	40.8	14.5	18.6	12.6
West Indians	29,990	100.0	1.4	1.9	6.0	20.1	34.0	15.0	14.8	12.4

SOURCE: U.S. Bureau of the Census, Census of the Population: 1970, Subject Reports, Final
Report PC (2)-1A.

Table 30

Class of Worker of the Native Population of Native
Parentage by Ethnic Origin, 1970

Subject	Total	English	Germans	Irish	Italians	Norwegians	Poles	Russian Jews
Males employed	8,762,573	477,424	657,150	329,688	1,231,052	151,127	685,002	586,991
Percent	100.0	100.0	100.0	100.0	100.0	100.0	100.0	100.0
Private wage and salary workers	74.0	74.0	70.0	70.0	72.0	62.9	76.5	66.4
Federal government workers	6.3	4.9	3.7	6.6	5.3	4.9	5.0	4.8
State government workers	2.8	3.5	2.6	3.6	2.5	3.2	2.2	2.6
Local government workers	7.3	7.6	6.3	12.6	8.5	7.3	6.4	5.8
Self-employed workers	8.7	9.7	17.0	7.1	11.3	21.5	9.6	20.2
Unpaid family workers	0.2	0.1	0.4	0.1	0.0	0.3	0.1	0.1
Females employed	5,877,737	278,658	359,589	204,156	650,890	85,486	384,400	319,863
Percent	100.0	100.0	100.0	100.0	100.0	100.0	100.0	100.0
Private wage and salary workers	74.8	73.7	75.4	75.5	80.0	70.0	80.0	71.1
Federal government workers	5.3	3.3	3.0	3.5	2.5	3.8	2.5	3.1
State government workers	4.8	4.5	3.9	4.2	3.0	4.7	2.8	3.6
Local government workers	11.6	13.5	10.8	13.8	9.3	14.5	9.5	14.7
Self-employed workers	2.9	4.0	5.3	2.4	3.6	5.4	3.6	5.7
Unpaid family workers	0.7	1.0	1.7	0.7	0.9	1.8	1.1	1.8

189

Table 30 *(continued)*

	Mexicans	Swedes	Blacks	West Indians	Japanese	Chinese
Males employed	360,098	204,428	3,933,984	27,881	84,142	33,606
Percent	100.0	100.0	100.0	100.0	100.0	100.0
Private wage and salary workers	78.8	69.3	77.0	63.6	63.0	62.9
Federal government workers	6.9	4.5	7.5	11.0	9.1	12.4
State government workers	2.4	3.2	3.0	3.9	5.1	6.3
Local government. workers	6.6	6.4	8.0	16.6	5.2	5.9
Self-employed workers	5.2	2.7	4.6	4.7	17.3	11.4
Unpaid family workers	0.2	0.8	0.1	0.0	0.2	0.8
Females employed	184,714	115,806	3,193,920	23,137	56,240	20,870
Percent	100.0	100.0	100.0	100.0	100.0	100.0
Private wage and salary workers	70.0	71.5	73.5	61.8	67.0	65.5
Federal government workers	4.5	3.3	7.0	7.7	6.3	6.5
tate government workers	3.6	4.7	5.6	5.9	11.2	9.1
Local government workers	8.7	14.2	11.9	22.0	7.2	11.1
Self-employed workers	2.5	4.7	1.8	2.3	5.8	4.9
Unpaid family workers	0.5	1.5	0.2	0.3	2.3	2.6

SOURCE: Calculated from: U.S. Bureau of Census, Census of the Population 1970: Subject Report,
Final Report PC (2)-1A, National Origin and Language (Washington: Government Printing Office, 1973).

Selected Bibliography

Abrahams, Israel. *Jewish Life in the Middle Ages.* London: Macmillan, 1897.

Adams, John T. *The Founding of New England.* New York: Atlantic Monthly, 1963.

Andrew, Charles M. *The Colonial Period of American History.* New Haven: Yale University Press, 1938.

Ardener, Shirley. "The Comparative Study of Rotating Credit Associations." *Journal of the Royal Anthropological Institute* 94, part 2 (1964): 201-229.

Arkoff, Abe. "Need Patterns in Two Generations of Japanese Americans in Hawaii." *Journal of Social Psychology* 50 (August 1959): 75-79.

Arsensberg, Conrad. *The Irish Country-Man: An Anthropological Study.* New York: Macmillan, 1937.

Auletta, Ken. *The Underclass.* New York: Random House, 1982.

Bailey, Thomas A. *The American Pageant: A History of the Republic.* Boston: D. C. Heath and Company, 1956.

Balch, Emily Greene. *Our Slavic Fellow Citizens, Charities Publication Committee.* New York: John Wiley and Sons, 1910.

Banks, Charles. *The English Ancestry and Homes of the Pilgrim Fathers.* Baltimore: Genealogical Publishing Co., 1971.

Batten, J. Minton. *Protestant Background in History.* New York and Nashville: Abingdon-Cokesbury Press, 1946.

Bienenfeld, F. R. *The Germans of the Jews.* Chicago: University of Chicago Press, 1960.

Blassingame, John W. *The Slave Community.* New York: Oxford University Press, 1972.

Blumberg, Paul. *Inequality in an Age of Decline.* Oxford University Press, 1980.

Brown, Lawrence Guy. *Immigration.* New York: Longmans, Green and Company, 1933.

Carmichael, Stokely, and Hamilton, Charles. *Black Power.* New York: Vintage Books, 1967.

Cash, Wilbur, J. *The Mind of the South.* New York: Vintage Books, 1960.

Caudill, William. "Japanese-American Personality and Acculturation." *Genetic Psychology Monographs* 45 (February 1942): 3-102.

Chambers, Jonathon D. "Enclosures and the Rural Population: A Revision." In *The Industrial Revolution in Britain,* ed. A. M. Taylor. Boston: D. C. Heath and Company, 1958, pp. 64-73.

Chenault, Lawrence. *The Puerto Rican Migrant in New York City.* New York: Columbia University Press, 1938.

Chitwood, Oliver P. *A History of Colonial America.* New York: Harper and Brothers, 1931.

Claghorn, Kate H. "The Foreign Immigrant in New York City." United States Industrial Commission, *Reports on Immigration.* 42 vols. Washington, D.C.: Government Printing Office, 1901, 15: 442-494.

Clark, Helen F. "The Chinese of New York Contrasted with their Foreign Neighbors." *Century* 53 (November 1898): 110.

Clark, Victor S. *History of Manufacturers in the United States: 1607-1860.* New York: McGraw-Hill Book Co., 1929.

Clarkson, L. A. *The Pre-Industrial Economy in England 1500-1700.* New York: Schocken Books, 1972.

Cobb. Sanford H. *The Rise of Religious Liberty in America.* New York: Research Service, 1970.

Cochran, Thomas. *The Puerto Rican Businessman.* Philadelphia: University of Pennsylvania Press, 1959.

Commons, John R. *Races and Immigrants in America.* New York: Macmillan, 1913.

Crosby, Fay J. *Relative Deprivation and Working Women.* New York: Oxford, 1982.

Cruse, Harold. *The Crisis of the Negro Intellectual.* New York: Morrow, 1961.

Curtis, Edmund. *A History of Ireland.* London: Methuen and Company, 1968.

Dahl, Robert A. *Who Governs?* New Haven: Yale University Press, 1971.

Darling-Hammond, L. *Equality and Excellence: The Educational Status of Black Americans.* Santa Monica, Calif.: Rand, 1985.

Davie, Maurice. *World Immigration.* New York: Macmillan, 1936.

Davies, Margaret G. *The Enforcement of English Apprenticeship.* Cambridge: Harvard University Press, 1956.

Davis, Allison; Gardner, Burleigh B.; and Gardner, Mary R. *The Deep South.* Chicago: University of Chicago Press, 1965.

Deutsch, Martin. "Equity, Equality, and Need: What Determines Which Value Will Be Used as the Basis of Distributive Justice?" *Journal of Social Issues,* 31(2): 137-149.

Dobb, Maurice. *Studies in the Development of Capitalism.* New York: International Publishers, 1963.

Drake, St. Clair, and Clayton, Horce R. *Black Metropolis.* New York: Harper and Row, 1962.

Du Bois, W.E.B. *The Philadelphia Negro.* New York: Benjamin Blom, 1967.

Elazer, Daniel J. *Cities of the Prairie.* New York: Basic Books, 1970.

Embree, John F. *Suye Mura: A Japanese Village.* Chicago: University of Chicago Press, 1939.

Ernst, Robert. *Immigrant Life in New York City: 1825-1863*. New York: King's Crown Press, 1949.

Eulau, Heinz. *The Behavioral Persuasion in Politics*. New York: Random House, 1967.

Evans-Gordon, Major W. *The Alien Immigrant*. London: William Heinemann, 1903.

Fankelsurd, Alfred O. *The Scandinavian-America*. Minneapolis: K. C. Halter Company, 1915.

Feagin, Joe. R. *Subordinating the Poor*. Englewood Cliffs, N.J.: Prentice-Hall, 1975.

Forester, Robert F. *The Italian Emigration of Our Times*. New York: Russell and Russell, 1968.

Franklin, John Hope. *From Slavery to Freedom*. New York: Alfred A. Knopf, 1974.

Frazier, E. Franklin. *The Negro in the United States*. New York: Macmillan, 1965.

Geiser, Karl Frederick. *Redemptioners and Indentured Servants in the Colony and Commonwealth*. New Haven: Tuttle, Marchouse and Company, 1901.

Gilder, George. *Wealth and Poverty*. New York: Basic Books, 1981.

Glazer, Nathan. *Affirmative Discrimination*. New York: Basic books, 1975.

Gosset, Thomas F. *Race: The History of an Idea in America*. Dallas: SMU Press, 1963.

Grant, Madison. *The Conquest of a Continent*. New York: Charles Scribner's Sons, 1933.

Handlin, Oscar. *Boston's Immigrants*. Cambridge: Harvard University Press, 1959.
_____. *The Newcomers*. Cambridge: Harvard University Press, 1959.
_____. *The Uprooted*. Boston: Little, Brown and Company, 1951.

Hansen, Marcus Lee. *The Atlantic Migration 1607-1860*. Cambridge: Harvard University Press, 1940.

Hernton, Calvin. *Sex and Racism in America*. New York: Grove Press, 1965.

Hirsh, Arthur H. *The Huguenots of Colonial South Carolina*. Durham: Duke University Press, 1928.

Huber, Joan, and Form, W. H. *Income and Ideology*. New York: Free Press, 1973.

Hutchinson, Edward P. *Immigrants and Their Children: 1850-1950*. New York: John Wiley and Sons, 1956.

Jasso, G., and Rossi, P. H. "Distributive Justice and Earned Income." *American Sociological Review* 42 (1977): 639-651.

Jencks, Christopher. *Inequality: A Reassessment of the Effect of Family and Schooling in America*. New York: Harper & Row, 1972, chapter 7.

Jernegan, Marcus W. *The American Colonies: 1492-1750*. New York: Longmans, Green and Company, 1956.

Jones, Maldwyn A. *American Immigration*. Chicago: University of Chicago Press, 1960.

Kinder, Dennis R., and Sears, Donald O. "Prejudice and Politics: Symbolic Racism vs. Racial Threats to the Good Life." *Journal of Personality and Social Psychology* 40 (1981): 414-431.

Kitano, Harry H. L. *Japanese Americans: The Evolution of a Subculture*. Englewood Cliffs, N.J.: Prentice-Hall, 1964.

Kluegel, James R., and Smith. E. R. "Affirmative Action Attitudes: Effects of Self-Interest, Racial Affect, and Stratification Beliefs on Whites' Views." *Social Forces* 61 (1982): 797-824.

———. "Whites' Beliefs About Blacks' Opportunity." *American Sociological Review* 47 (1982): 518-532.

Knowles, Louis L., and Prewitt, Kenneth, eds. *Institutional Racism in America.* Englewood Cliffs, N.J.: Prentice-Hall, 1969.

Kulp, Daniel H. *Country Life in South China.* 2 vols. New York: Columbia University Press, 1925.

Levine, Edward M. *The Irish and Irish Politicians.* Notre Dame, Inc.: University of Notre Dame Press, 1966.

Lewis, Michael. *The Culture of Inequality.* Amherst, Mass.: University of Massachusetts Press, 1979.

Lewis, Oscar. *La Vida.* New York: Random House, 1965.

Lieberson, Stanley. "A Societal Theory of Race and Ethnic Relations." *American Sociological Review* 26 (December 1961): 902-910.

Light, Ivan H. *Ethnic Enterprise in America.* Berkeley: University of California Press, 1972.

Litwack, Leon F. *North of Slavery.* Chicago: University of Chicago Press, 1961.

McConahay, John B., and Hough, J. C., Jr. "Symbolic Racism." *Journal of Social Issues,* 32 (1976): 23-45.

Meier, August. *Negro Thought in America: 1880-1915.* Ann Arbor: University of Michigan Press, 1968.

Meyers, Jerome. "Assimilation to the Ecological and Social Systems of a Community." *American Sociological Review* 15 (December 1950): 367-372.

Mills, C. Wright, and Senior, Clarence. *The Puerto Rican Journey.* New York: Harper and Brothers, 1950.

Myrdal, Gunnar. *An American Dilemma.* New York: Harper and Row, 1962.

Osofsky, Gilbert. *Harlem: The Making of a Ghetto.* New York: Harper and Row, 1963.

Ottley, Roi, and Weatherby, William, eds. *The Negro in New York.* New York: Oceana Publications, 1942.

Parkin, Frank. *Class, Inequality and Political Order.* New York: Praeger, 1971.

Pettigrew, Thomas F. "Race and Class in the 1980's: An Interactive View." 110 *Daedalus* (1981): 233-256.

Philpott, Stuart B. *West Indian Migration: The Monserrat Case.* New York: Athlone Press, 1973.

Pomfret, John E. *The Struggle for Land in Ireland: 1800-1923.* Princeton, N.J.: Princeton University Press, 1930.

Rand, Christopher. *The Puerto Ricans.* New York: Oxford University Press, 1958.

Reid, Ira De A. *The Negro Immigrant.* New York: Columbia University Press, 1939.

Rolle, Andrew F. *American Italians: Their History and Culture.* Belmont, Calif.: Wadsworth Publishing Company, 1972.

Runcimand, Walther G. *Relative Deprivation and Social Justice.* Berkeley: University of California Press, 1966.

Schiava, Giovanni. *The Italians in America Before the Civil War.* New York: Alfred A. Knopf. 1943.

Smith, Abbot Emerson. *Colonists in Bondage*. Chapel Hill: University of North Carolina Press, 1947.

Smith, J. Owens. "Affirmative Action, Reverse Discrimination and the Courts: Implications for Blacks." In *Contemporary Public Policy Perspectives and Black Americans*. Westport, Conn.: Greenwood Press, 1984.

_____. "The Bakke Decision: A Flagrant Denial of Human Rights." *Western Journal of Black Studies* 2 (Winter 1979): 244-255.

_____. "The Politics of Income and Education Differences Between Blacks and West Indians." *The Journal of Ethnic Studies* 13 (Fall 1985): 217-30.

Thernstrom, Stephen. *The Other Bostonians*. Cambridge: Harvard University Press, 1973.

Thomas, Brinley. *International Migration and Economic Development*. Paris. UNESCO, 1961.

Veblen, Thorstein. "The Intellectual Pre-Eminence of Jews in Modern Europe." *Essays in Our Changing Order,* ed. Leon Arozrooni. New York: Viking Press, 1934, pp. 219-32.

Waddel, D.A.G. *The West Indies and Guianas*. Englewood Cliffs, N.J.: Prentice-Hall, 1967.

Weber, Max. *The Protestant Ethic and the Rise of the Spirit of Capitalism*. New York: Charles Scribner's Sons, 1958.

White, Trumbull. *Puerto Rico and Its People*. New York: Frederick S. Stokes, 1938.

Wilensky, H. L. *The Welfare State and Social Equality*. Berkeley: University of California Press, 1975.

Willie, Charles V. *The Sociology of Urban Education*. Lexington Books of D. C. Heath, 1978.

_____. *Race, Ethnicity, and Socioeconomic Status: A Theoretical Analysis of Their Interrelations*. Bayside, New York: General Hall, 1983.

Willie, Charles V., ed. *Black/Brown/White Relations*. New Brunswick, N.J.: Transaction Books, 1977.

Williamson, J. B. "Beliefs About Motivation of Poor and Attitudes Toward Poverty Policy" *Social Problems* 21: 634-648.

Wilson, W. J. *The Declining Significance of Race*. Chicago: University of Chicago Press, 1978.

Wirth, Louis, *The Ghetto*. Chicago: University of Chicago Press, 1929.

Wittke, Carl. *We Who Built America*. Cleveland: Case Western University Press, 1964.

Woodson, Carter G. *A Century of Negro Migration*. New York: Russell and Russell, 1969.

Index

About the Author

J. OWENS SMITH is Associate Professor of Political Science at California State University, Fullerton. Professor Smith specializes in the Black politics of public law, and has published articles in the *Western Journal of Black Studies,* the *Journal of Ethnic Studies,* the *Journal of Negro Education,* and *Umoja,* and contributed to *Contemporary Public Policy Perspectives and Black Americans* (Greenwood Press, 1984).